PENGUIN ANANDA

MOVING INTO THE UNKNOWN

Osho defies categorization. His
everything from the individual
social and political issues facin
written but are transcribed fro
extemporaneous talks to inter
remember: whatever I am sayi
also for the future generations.'

Osho has been described by *Sunday Times* in London as one of the '1000 Makers of the 20th Century', and by American author Tom Robbins as 'the most dangerous man since Jesus Christ'. *Sunday Mid-Day* (India) has selected Osho as one of ten people—along with Gandhi, Nehru and Buddha—who have changed the destiny of India.

About his own work Osho has said that he is helping to create the conditions for the birth of a new kind of human being. He often characterizes this new human being as 'Zorba the Buddha'—capable both of enjoying the earthy pleasures of a Zorba the Greek and the silent serenity of a Gautama the Buddha.

Running like a thread through all aspects of Osho's talks and meditations is a vision that encompasses both the timeless wisdom of all ages past and the highest potential of today's (and tomorrow's) science and technology.

Osho is known for his revolutionary contribution to the science of inner transformation, with an approach to meditation that acknowledges the accelerated pace of contemporary life. His unique OSHO Active Meditations™ are designed to first release the accumulated stresses of body and mind, so that it is then easier to take an experience of stillness and thought-free relaxation into daily life.

Two autobiographical works by the author are available: *Autobiography of a Spiritually Incorrect Mystic*, St Martin's Press, New York (book and e-book), and *Glimpses of a Golden Childhood*, OSHO Media International, Pune, India.

[illegible]

[illegible] TO THE UNKNOWN

[illegible] quest for meaning to the most urgent [illegible] and political issues [illegible] audio and video recordings of his [illegible] international audiences. As he puts it, [illegible] is not just for you. [illegible]

[illegible]

[illegible] Sadhguru [illegible]

[illegible]

[illegible]

OSHO

MOVING INTO THE UNKNOWN

THE DISCIPLINE OF TRANSCENDENCE

PENGUIN
ANANDA

PENGUIN ANANDA
Published by the Penguin Group
Penguin Books India Pvt. Ltd, 7th Floor, Infinity Tower C, DLF Cyber City, Gurgaon 122 002, Haryana, India
Penguin Group (USA) Inc., 375 Hudson Street, New York, New York 10014, USA
Penguin Group (Canada), 90 Eglinton Avenue East, Suite 700, Toronto, Ontario, M4P 2Y3, Canada
Penguin Books Ltd, 80 Strand, London WC2R 0RL, England
Penguin Ireland, 25 St Stephen's Green, Dublin 2, Ireland (a division of Penguin Books Ltd)
Penguin Group (Australia), 707 Collins Street, Melbourne, Victoria 3008, Australia
Penguin Group (NZ), 67 Apollo Drive, Rosedale, Auckland 0632, New Zealand
Penguin Books (South Africa) (Pty) Ltd, Block D, Rosebank Office Park, 181 Jan Smuts Avenue, Parktown North, Johannesburg 2193, South Africa

Penguin Books Ltd, Registered Offices: 80 Strand, London WC2R 0RL, England

First published by OSHO Media International 1976
Published in Penguin Ananda by Penguin Books India 2015

10 9 8 7 6 5 4 3 2 1

ISBN 9780143424932

For sale in the Indian Subcontinent only

Printed at Replika Press Pvt. Ltd, India

A PENGUIN RANDOM HOUSE COMPANY

CONTENTS

PREFACE

Awareness and discipline are the most fundamental things for a seeker. If you discipline yourself without awareness, you will become a hypocrite. If you discipline yourself without awareness, you will become a zombie, a robot. You may not do any harm to anybody, you may be known as a good man or even as a saint, but you will not be able to live your real life. You will not be able to celebrate it; there will be no delight in it. You will become too serious; the playfulness will be gone forever. Seriousness is a disease.

If discipline is without awareness, then you will enforce it and it will be violent, a rape of your own being. It will not give you freedom; it will create more and more, bigger and bigger, imprisonments. Discipline is right if it is based on awareness. Discipline goes completely wrong, becomes poisoned, when it is done not with awareness, but by a blind believing mind.

What is the need of discipline? If you are aware, it seems that awareness is enough. Eventually it is enough, but not in the beginning because the mind has deep patterns, and the energy tends to move from the old habits and old patterns. New channels have to be created.

You may have become aware, but that in itself will not be enough in the beginning because the mind, finding any opportunity to move in any old pattern, immediately slips in a split second. It takes no time to become angry. By the time you become aware, anger has already flashed.

Later on, when your awareness has become total, when your awareness has become an absolute for you, awareness is always there before anything happens, as an a priori. If anger comes, awareness is there before anger; if sexuality possesses you, awareness is there before it. When awareness has become a natural, spontaneous thing, like breathing, when it is there even in your sleep, then discipline can be discarded. But in the beginning – no. In the beginning, when awareness is settling, discipline will be helpful.

Discipline is simply an effort to create new pathways for the energy to move on, so that it need not move on the old pathway.

Osho
The Search

1

THE CHALLENGE OF THE BUDDHA

The Buddha said:
There are twenty difficult things to attain or accomplish in this world:
1. It is difficult for the poor to practice charity.
2. It is difficult for the strong and rich to observe the way.
3. It is difficult to disregard life and go to certain death.
4. It is only a favored few that get acquainted with a Buddhist sutra.
5. It is by rare opportunity that a person is born in the age of a buddha.
6. It is difficult to conquer the passions, to suppress selfish desires.
7. It is difficult not to hanker after that which is agreeable.
8. It is difficult not to get into a passion when slighted.
9. It is difficult not to abuse one's authority.
10. It is difficult to be even-minded and simple-hearted in all one's dealings with others.
11. It is difficult to be thorough in learning and exhaustive in investigation.

12. It is difficult to subdue selfish pride.
13. It is difficult not to feel contempt toward the unlearned.
14. It is difficult to be one in knowledge and practice.
15. It is difficult not to express an opinion about others.
16. It is by rare opportunity that one is introduced to a true spiritual teacher.
17. It is difficult to gain an insight into the nature of being, and to practice the way.
18. It is difficult to follow the steps of a savior.
19. It is difficult to be always the master of oneself.
20. It is difficult to understand thoroughly the ways of Buddha.

Life is not a bed of roses. It is difficult, it is complex. It is very rare to be alive in the true sense of the word. To be born is one thing, to be alive quite another. To be born is to be just biologically here, to be alive is a totally different dimension – the dimension of spirituality.

Unless a man is spiritual he is not alive yet. But to move from the biological realm to the spiritual realm is very difficult, arduous. It is the greatest challenge there is. It is the greatest quantum leap: from the body to the soul, from the material to the immaterial, from the visible to the invisible, from time to timelessness, from out to in. It is arduous.

In this sutra Buddha says there are twenty difficult things. These twenty difficult things can become twenty steps of the challenge. Buddha is talking about these twenty difficult things not to make you beware of them, not to avoid them. It is an invitation, it is a challenge.

These twenty Himalayan peaks are just a challenge for you,

a great invitation. Don't remain in the valley. The valley is very secure, convenient, comfortable. You will live comfortably, you will die comfortably. But you will not grow. You will only grow old, but you will not grow.

Growth happens only when you are accepting a challenge. Growth happens only when you start living dangerously. These twenty things are indicative of how one should live.

There is only one way to live and that is to live dangerously, courageously. You rightly become a human being only when you have accepted this challenge of the Buddha.

We will go into these twenty things. They look small on the surface, but Buddha cannot talk about small things. You will have to go into the depth of these small things, and then you will see – they are really difficult.

Before we enter this sutra, I would like to tell you one thing: that the search for truth is the search for the impossible. Religion itself is nothing but a passion for the impossible. But the beauty is – that impossible happens, that impossible also becomes possible. But you have to pay for it, and you have to pay tremendously. You have to sacrifice yourself utterly. You have to stake your whole life.

If you stake your so-called life, you will attain to what Buddha calls to be alive, to what Jesus calls to be reborn, to what Hindus call to be twice born, *dwij*. Then a totally new dimension and a totally new quality of being arise in you, uncorrupted by time and space, uncontaminated by anything, absolutely and eternally virgin.

Long for the impossible. Desire for the impossible.

> *The Buddha said:*
> *There are twenty difficult things to attain or accomplish in this world.*
> *First: It is difficult for the poor to practice charity.*

Because unless you have it, how can you share it? To share something with somebody else you must have it first. In the first place you must have it, only that which you have can be shared, and this is something that we go on forgetting continuously.

I see so many people trying to share their love and they don't have any love. Of course, their sharing brings misery to them and to others because you can share only that which you have. You may think you are sharing your love, but in fact you share only your misery because that is what you have. You go with hope, you move with dreams, but what is the actual result of it? In fantasy love is good; in reality it becomes a misery, a hell.

You don't have love in your being, that energy is not existent there. First you have to become radiant with love, only then can you share it. Before you can become a lover you have to become love. People think that they will become love only by becoming a lover. Stupid is their logic, illogical is their way of thinking. You cannot become a lover unless you have love – and love you don't have.

Everybody goes on believing that one has the capacity to love, one has just to find somebody to receive. One is full of love energy, one needs only just a receiving end. That's how people go on moving, finding. Many times they find beautiful people, but the total result is misery.

They think they are sharing love; they share only their loneliness. They think they are sharing something divine; they share only their ugliness. They think they are sharing their innermost being, but they share only their dirty surface. They themselves are not aware of their innermost core. That is the meaning of a poor man.

When Buddha talks about a poor man, he does not mean a man without money. When Buddha talks about a poor man, he means a man who is not rich inside – a loveless man. How can he share? How can he become a tremendous sharing? No, charity is not possible. Charity is possible only when you are overflowing. Overflowing is charity.

It is difficult for the poor to practice charity. Remember it in the reverse way also. Whenever you are unable to share, whenever you are unable to practice charity, note down – you must be poor. You may have much in the eyes of others, but deep down you must be poor if you cannot share.

You possess only that which you can give. Only by giving do you become the possessor. If you cannot give, then you are not in possession, you are not the master. Then the thing that you think you possess is possessing you. Then you are possessed by your possession.

Charity is a beautiful flowering of one who has, one who is in possession of his being; one who is not poor, one who is rich. This man may be a beggar on the streets. It has nothing to do with your bank balance. The rich man may be a beggar, but if he has his being, authentic being, if he can love, if he can sing, if he can dance, if he can see poetry in the world he is rich. He may not have anything at all. As far as material things go he may not have anything. But he has something of the spiritual, something which cannot be taken away from him.

Observe this fact: that which you really possess cannot be taken away from you. You can only give it, if you want, but nobody can take it away. That which you don't possess, and by which you are possessed, you can never give – it can only be stolen or taken away, robbed.

Your love cannot be robbed. There is no way to rob it. You can give it voluntarily, you can give it freely, but nobody can rob it. You can be killed, but your love cannot be killed. There exists no way to murder love.

Love seems to be more eternal than your so-called life. Your life can be destroyed very easily: just a hit on the head, a bullet through the heart; very simple, but nothing can destroy love. Love seems to be the only eternal thing: something not belonging to the world of time. You can give it, but nobody can take it.

Your money, your respectability, your power, your prestige – they all can be taken away from you. That which can be taken away from you creates a clinging in the mind. You become poorer and poorer because you have to cling more and more, you have to protect more and more, and you are always afraid and trembling.

The so-called rich people are continuously trembling, trembling. Deep down they are always afraid because they know that that which they have can be taken away. They can never be certain about it. The very uncertainty goes on eating their heart like a worm. You possess only that which grows out of you, which belongs to you, which is rooted in you.

A rich man is one who has poetry in life, dance in life, celebration in life, silence in life, centeredness in life, rootedness in life;

who blooms into his inner sky. The rich man is one who is full, like clouds in the rainy season, ready to shower on anybody who becomes available – or like an opening bud, ready to share its fragrance with any wind that passes by, or any traveler that comes by. Sharing is overflowing.

Buddha says one of the most difficult things is to try to share that which you don't have, and that's what people are doing. They go on trying to love without ever considering the fact that love has not yet grown in their heart. In fact, you don't love yourself – how can you love others? The basic is missing, the very basic is missing.

You are not happy alone, how can you be happy together with somebody else? If you are unhappy alone, when you come together with somebody, you will bring your unhappiness to be shared. That's all you have: your poverty, your rottenness, your misery, your depression, your sadness, your angst, anxiety, anguish, your disease.

Try to possess something which cannot be taken away by anybody, not even by death. Difficult, but possible. It looks impossible. How to be loving without finding a lover? Our whole mind has been conditioned in a wrong way. You can dance without the audience – why can't you love without there being somebody? You can sing without a listener – why can't you love without a lover? Your mind has been conditioned wrongly. You think you can love only when there is somebody to love.

Practice love. Sitting alone in your room, be loving, radiate love, fill the whole room with your love energy. Feel vibrating with a new frequency, feel swaying as if you are in the ocean of love. Create vibrations of love energy around you and you will start feeling immediately that something is happening – something in your aura is changing, something around your body is changing; a warmth is arising around your body, a warmth like deep orgasm. You are becoming more alive. Something like sleep is disappearing. Something like awareness is arising. Sway into this ocean. Dance, sing, and let your whole room be filled with love.

In the beginning it feels very weird. When for the first time you can fill your room with love energy, your own energy, which goes on falling and rebounding on you and makes you so happy, one starts feeling, "Am I hypnotizing myself? Am I deluded? What is happening?" This is because you have always thought that love comes from somebody else: a mother is needed to love you, a father, a brother, a husband, a wife, a child – but somebody.

Love that depends on somebody is a poor love. Love that is created within you, love that you create out of your own being, is real energy. Then move anywhere with that ocean surrounding you and you will feel that everybody who comes close to you is suddenly under a different kind of energy.

People will look at you with more open eyes. You will be passing them and they will feel that a breeze of some unknown energy has passed them, they will feel fresher. Hold somebody's hand and his whole body will start throbbing. Just be close to somebody and that man will start feeling very happy for no reason at all. You can watch it. Then you are becoming ready to share. Then find a lover, then find a right receptivity for you.

I have heard a small anecdote...

The greatest surprise of Mary's life was receiving half a dollar on her fourth birthday. She carried the coin about the house and was seen sitting on the steps admiring it.

"What are you going to do with your half dollar?" her mother asked.

"Take it to Sunday school," said Mary promptly.

"To show to your teacher?"

Mary shook her head. "No," she said, "I'm going to give it to God. He will be as surprised as I am to get something besides pennies."

Whatsoever you are giving to people are just pennies, not even that. And then one day when your love fails – in fact it has never been there even to fail; it has been missing from the very beginning. Just your belief that you were a loving man fails one day – then you start thinking of God and prayer.

God and prayer are possible only when your love has succeeded. When you have become a great lover, then only prayer can arise. Out of small pennies of love, something bigger arises – prayer. Then you have something to offer to God.

But it almost always happens that people who have failed in their life, go to the temple and to the church. Of course, they bring their empty hearts – completely dry, not even tears in their hearts. And then they pray. Then nothing happens. They think the world is godless, they think God is absent, or God is deaf, or God has never existed. Or maybe in the past he existed because so many people talk about him, but he must be dead by now, or he is indifferent.

Nothing is like that. In fact you are missing love energy, and without love energy prayer cannot arise. Prayer is a refined phenomenon of the same energy, love. It is out of love that the subtle fragrance of prayer arises.

God is also tired of your pennies. God is also tired of your poorness. God is also tired of your misery. Bring celebration to God, bring something alive. Don't bring deserts, bring gardens to God. Don't bring corpses, bring somebody dancing, alive.

Buddha's first sutra says: Try to become rich so that you can share.

Second:

It is difficult for the strong and rich to observe the way.

Yes, it is very difficult for the strong and the rich to observe the way because ordinarily only weaklings come to the temple, to the church, to the mosque. The strong people don't come. They are too much in their pride, they are too egoistic, they are not ready to surrender.

People surrender only when they have become absolute failures. People surrender only when they have nothing to surrender. When life has completely crushed them, when they are bankrupt, then they surrender. But what is the point of surrendering when you are a bankrupt?

People remember God only when nothing else seems to help. In deep hopelessness they remember God. It is not possible to remember God in deep hopelessness. When you are full of hope, radiant, vibrating, when there is meaning in your life, when you feel the hands of destiny in your life, when you are riding on waves, when you feel at the top of the world – those are the moments to remember truth, to remember God, to move towards the way.

But Buddha says: *It is difficult for the strong and rich to observe the way.* Why is it difficult for the strong? Because the strong thinks, "I am enough unto myself. What is the need to ask for God's help?" The weak thinks, "I am not enough unto myself so I have to need, I have to ask God." But only when you are strong do you have energy to ask. Only when you are strong will your prayer have enough energy to reach God. Only when you are strong is there a possibility that you can touch higher realms. Out of impotence you cannot reach higher realms. You need an inner strength.

It is difficult for the strong to move towards the way. But that is the only possibility. So if you are feeling strong, move towards the way because these are the right positive moments; this is the opportunity. When you are feeling successful, this is the time to remember. When everything is going well, don't miss this opportunity; this is the time to pray. It looks absurd because our logic is this: that when we are happy, we never remember. We become completely oblivious.

I once asked a small boy, "Do you remember God when you go to sleep?"

He said, "Yes, every night."

And I asked him, "And in the morning?"

He said, "What is the point in the morning? In the night I feel afraid, in the morning everything is okay. What is the need? Why bother?"

This childish attitude seems to be the very common attitude. When you are ill, suddenly you start feeling very religious. When death is approaching close by and you are getting older and older and you start stumbling in life and your feet are no longer strong enough to hold you and you are trembling, you start remembering God. People go on postponing God for their old age.

In India they say... If somebody young comes to me and I initiate him into sannyas, sooner or later somebody comes and he says, "This is not good, he's too young to be a sannyasin. Sannyas is for old people." When they are almost dead, when they are ready to be thrown on the junkyard, when one of their feet is already in the grave, then sannyas.

People go on postponing sannyas until the very end. God seems to be the last item on their list. They have a shopping list – God is the last. When they have purchased everything: consistent, inconsistent, relevant, irrelevant; when they have wasted all their energy, when nothing is left, when they are just exhausted – then they remember God. But who is going to remember God then?

Sannyas is for the young. Sannyas is for the strong. Buddha initiated a new trend into sannyas. He dropped the old Hindu concept that one should become a sannyasin in old age.

Hindus have four stages; they are very calculating, very mathematical. Manu seems to be the greatest mathematician of life – very clever. He has divided life: twenty-five years for education, *brahmacharya*; then twenty-five years for living in the world, the life of a householder, *grihastha*; then twenty-five years for getting ready to leave the world. Looking after children who have become grownups now, who are getting married, who are coming from their universities; and then the last – sannyas, the fourth stage of life. That means after seventy-five years. The last – when everything has happened, when there is nothing else, then God.

This seems to be very insulting. This is very insulting to God, that you are fit for him only when you are dead. It seems you somehow relate God with death, not with life. God should be in the very center of life.

Buddha says it is difficult to be religious when young, but that is the challenge. It is difficult to observe the way when you are strong, but that is the challenge. It is difficult to become religious when you are rich, but that is the only way to become religious.

When you are rich and strong and young, when energy is streaming, when you are ready to do something, when you are ready to go into a venture, when you have courage, when you can take risks, when danger has appeal for you, when death has not weakened you, when you are full of zest and life, that is the point – take the challenge and move into the unknown.

The third:

It is difficult to disregard life and go to certain death.

It is difficult to disregard life and go to certain death. It is very difficult to disregard life. Life is very enchanting, very hypnotizing. It is beautiful, it is a miracle, a magic world – but made of the stuff dreams are made of.

It is difficult to awake in this beautiful dream. When you are having a nice dream: maybe you are on a trip with Marilyn Monroe or something like that, or you have become the president of the United States. When you are having a beautiful dream, nice, as you always wanted it and it is happening, and then somebody shakes you, you become aware – but the dream is lost. You feel annoyed. Is this the right moment? Could you not wait a little more? I was having such a beautiful dream. But a dream is a dream, beautiful or not beautiful. A beautiful dream is also a dream – so futile, a wastage.

Buddha says, *It is difficult to disregard life...* Yes, when life has deserted you then it is very simple. When life itself has deserted you, when you are left behind and life has gone out of you or is going out of you, when life has oozed out of you and you are left just like a dead dry thing, then it is very easy to disregard life. Even then it seems difficult. Even in old age, people go on behaving childishly.

I have heard...

An ancient man described his recent visit to a bordello.

"How old are you anyway?" the madam asked him.

"I am ninety-three," he said.

"Well, you have had it, sir," she told him.

"I have? Ah – then how much do I owe you?"

Now his memory is gone, but still he has come in search of a prostitute. He cannot remember, but the passion persists. He must be on his deathbed. He may have been carried by others to the bordello. To the very end.

This is my observation – that out of a hundred persons, almost ninety-nine persons die thinking of sex. In fact when death comes, the idea of sex becomes very strong because death and sex are opposite each other, they are the polar opposites. Sex is birth and death is the end of the same energy that birth released. So while dying, a person becomes obsessively interested in sex, and that becomes the beginning of another birth.

To die without thinking about sex is a great experience. Then something of tremendous import has happened to you. If you can die without thinking of sex at all, no lurking shadows of sex in your mind, of lust for life, you are dying as one should die. Only one percent of people die that way.

These are the people Buddha calls *srotapanna*: those who have entered into the stream, those who have become sannyasins, those who have taken a step towards understanding what is real and what is unreal, those who have become discriminative of what is dream and what is true.

It is difficult to disregard life and go to certain death. Even when death is coming, then too it is difficult to disregard life – even when death has become certainty. In fact, death is the only certainty, everything else is uncertain. Everything else may happen, may not happen, everything else is accidental. Death is absolutely certain. The day you were born, death became certain. With the very birth, only one thing has become absolutely certain – that you will die.

Death is certain. You may know it or you may not know it; you may look at it, you may not look at it – but death is certain. Still, even with so much certainty one is afraid to go into it. One clings with uncertain life, with dreamlike life. Death seems to be more real than whatsoever you call your life.

Buddha says it is difficult to accept death and move into death, and it is difficult to disregard so-called life. But a man of understanding starts disregarding life and regarding death. He respects death more because death is more certain, must be more part of reality than so-called life because the so-called life is just like dreaming.

You have lived for thirty or forty or fifty years. Now look back, think retrospectively. What has happened in these fifty years? Was it real or just a long dream? Can you make any distinction – if it was real or a dream? How will you distinguish? Maybe you have dreamed all. Maybe it was just an idea in your mind. What proof have you got that it was real? What is left in your hand? Nothing, emptiness and you call it life. And only emptiness results out of it.

Buddha says, better call it death. Now look into death, maybe there is real life.

It is difficult, but a person who becomes interested in death, intrigued by death, the phenomenon of death, becomes a different type of person. He is a *srotapanna*.

The people who cling to the bank are the people who think this life is all. The people who try to understand penetrate deeply into life, become aware that this is not the real thing. Then they take a jump into the river which is going somewhere else – towards death.

Meditation is an effort to die voluntarily. And in deep meditation one dies. In deep meditation, the so-called life disappears and for the first time you encounter death. That experience of encountering death makes you deathless. Suddenly you transcend death. Suddenly you know that which is going to die is not you.

All that can die, you are not. You are neither your body, nor your mind, nor your self. You are simply pure space – which is never born and never dies.

People talk about death very rarely. Even if they talk about it, they talk very reluctantly. Even if they are forced to talk about it, they feel embarrassed – even people who believe that the soul never dies, even people who believe that after death a person goes to the eternal God, to the paradise.

In his *Unpopular Essays*, Bertrand Russell has a telling anecdote.

F. W. H. Myers, whom spiritualism had converted to belief in a future life, questioned a woman who had lately lost her daughter as to what she supposed has become of her soul.

The mother replied, "Ah, well, I suppose she is enjoying eternal bliss, but I wish you would not talk about such unpleasant subjects."

Now if really she is enjoying eternal bliss, then why is this subject unpleasant? One should be happy to talk about it. In fact it is unpleasant to talk about it, and just to hide the unpleasantness, one has invented many theories, beliefs, that after death one goes to eternal heaven. Everybody has to somehow convince himself that he will not die.

Buddha's teaching is that you have to accept the fact that you will die. Not only that – that all that you think you are, absolutely in toto, is going to die. Buddha is very stern about it.

If you ask Mahavira, he will say that the body will die, the mind will die, but your soul? – no, your soul will remain. Now there is some protection. We can think, "Okay, the body will die. We would like it not to die, but we can accept. The body is not me."

In India you can find many monks, *sadhus*, just contemplating: "I am not the body, I am not the body, I am the soul eternal." Now, what are they doing? If they really know that they are the soul eternal, then why this constant repetition? Who are they trying to befool? Why this constant repetition that "I am not the body"? If you are not, you are not – finished.

No, they don't believe really; they are trying to hypnotize themselves. "I am not the body." Repeating it continuously for many years, they may come to an auto-suggestion that "I am not the body," but that is not going to be their experience. It will remain just an auto-suggestion. They have befooled themselves, they have fallen into a delusion.

And then they are saying, "I am the eternal soul – infinite, sat-chit-anand – true, always true; existential, always existential; blissful, always blissful." They are fighting with death and they are trying to find some place where they can hide against death.

Buddha's approach is totally different. He says there is no place to hide. You have to go headlong into it. And Buddha says your body will die, your mind will die, your so-called soul will die – everything, in toto. You are going to die. Nothing is going to remain.

This is very, very difficult to even conceive. But Buddha says, if you can conceive this, and if you are ready for this, only then you will be able to know that innermost space, which is beyond time and space.

But remember, you don't know that space at all, so it has nothing to do with you. Whatsoever is your identity is going to die completely, and that which is going to remain has nothing to do with you.

So Buddha says don't ask about that. Because you are such rationalizing animals, such tricky fellows, that if Buddha says, "Yes, there is an inner space which will remain," you say, "Okay, that's what I call my soul." Again you are back in the old trap.

"So, I am going to survive, nothing to be afraid of." You will find some identity with that inner space.

Buddha keeps completely quiet. He must have been tempted many times to talk about it. It is very difficult to keep secrets when you know, but Buddha has kept it.

It is really almost superhuman to keep secrets. You may have observed the fact. Whenever somebody says to you, "Don't tell it to anybody, keep it a secret," then you are in a difficulty. The whole mind tends to tell it to somebody. There seems to be a natural thing in it. It is as if you eat something; then how can you hold it forever and ever inside your stomach? It has to be defecated. It has to be thrown out otherwise you will have permanent constipation and it will be very disturbing.

The same happens with the mind. Somebody says something to you: "Keep it a secret." Your husband comes home and he says, "Listen, keep it a secret." Now the wife is in trouble because something has gone into the mind. It has to come out, otherwise there will be a mental constipation. And she feels very heavy unless she can find somebody. She is going to talk to the servant, and of course she will say, "Don't tell it to anybody." And the servant will rush faster to his home, to his wife because – what to do? And within minutes the whole town will know.

It is very difficult to keep a secret. You can keep a secret only if it has not come from the outside, remember it. If it has come from the outside, it has to go outside, it cannot be kept. If it has arisen in your own being, if it has flowered within you, if it has existential roots in your own being, you can keep it a secret because it has not come from the outside, there is no need for it to go outside.

Buddha could keep this secret because it was his own experience. Nobody had told it to him, he had not found it in the Vedas, he had not heard it from the traditional sources, he had not read about it. It had not entered in his being. It had bloomed into his own being, it was his own flower. When something blooms into you, it is yours. It is for you to keep or to share.

Buddha is continuously tempted. A thousand times, I think almost every day, people are coming to him and asking him, "Yes, we can understand that the soul will die, the body will die, the mind will die – but the soul, the self, the atman?" And Buddha goes on saying flatly, "Everything will die. Everything that you know as your identity will die. You will die completely and that which will be saved you don't know anything about."

When you disappear, then you will know that which remains. That has nothing to do with you. That existed before you existed. That exists just now, just parallel to you. You never meet with it. You are two parallel lines, you never meet. You are hiding it. When you are not, it is revealed.

Buddha says, go into death as deeply as possible. And that is possible only if you start disregarding your so-called life. To disregard it means to know it – it is a dream.

The farmhand and his girl had just encountered a bulldog that looked mean and hungry.

"Why, Percy," she exclaimed as he started a strategic retreat. "You always swore you would face death for me."

"I would," he flung back, "but that damned dog ain't dead yet!"

People say they can face death, but when it comes to facing death suddenly their whole courage disappears. People say that they can surrender their life very easily. It is not so easy.

Lust for life is very deep. You have watered it for many lives, its roots have gone deep into your being. Even if you cut a few branches, it makes no difference; even if you cut the whole tree, it makes no difference – new shoots will be coming out.

> *It is only a favored few that get acquainted with a Buddhist sutra.*

Buddha says it is very few, a very favored few, a fortunate few, a chosen few, a blessed few, who become acquainted with the wisdom of a buddha.

To be in contact with a buddha, you have to pass through a few experiences that life is illusory, that death is certain. Unless your illusion about life is shattered completely, you will not listen to a buddha. He is irrelevant, he does not exist for you.

Buddha exists for you only if you have become alert that this life is fleeting, slipping by; that this life is just a shadow, not a reality – a reflection in the mirror. When all your dreams about life are shattered, then you become interested in a buddha. And when you become interested, only then is there a possibility to understand Buddhist wisdom, the wisdom of an awakened man.

Who is an awakened man? One who has come to know what is dream, one who has come to know what is not dream. When you are asleep, dream looks real. In the morning when you awake, then you know that it was unreal. A buddha is one who has awakened – awakened out of this so-called life and has come to realize that it is a dream.

If you are also feeling the pain, the frustration, the misery of this dream life, this futile life, only then you start moving towards a source of light; otherwise not. Buddha says those are the few favored ones.

Fifth:

> *It is by rare opportunity that a person is born in the age of a buddha.*

It is by rare opportunity... Yes, it is so because a buddha is rarely there. Thousands of years pass, then a person becomes a buddha, and even then it is not necessary that he will start teaching. He may not teach at all. He may simply disappear into the unknown. There is no necessity that he should become a master. So, buddhas are few, and then buddhas who become masters and help people on the way are even fewer.

It is by rare opportunity that a person is born in the age of a buddha. So if you can find a person who is awakened, if you can find a person who is a little different from you, if you can find a person in whose eyes you don't see the clouds of sleep and around whom you can feel the aura of awakening, then don't miss the opportunity because it may not be for many lives that you will come across such a man again.

> *It is difficult to conquer the passions, to suppress selfish desires.*

It is difficult to conquer passions... That's why Buddha says a courageous man will not bother to go to the top of the Himalayas.

Yes, it is difficult, but nothing compared to conquering your own passions. A real man of courage will not try to go to the moon. It is difficult, but nothing compared to conquering your own passions and lust for life.

The greatest adventure in life is to become passionless, to become free of lust. To just be without any hankering to be something else; to just be herenow, with no desire for the future, no desire for any repetition of the past, with no projection.

It is difficult not to hanker after that which is agreeable.

Why do we live in dreams? – because many times dreams are agreeable. That is the trick of the dreams, that's how they persuade you; that is their bait.

I have heard...

Mulla Nasruddin stood quietly at the bedside of his dying father. "Please, my boy," whispered the old man, "always remember that wealth does not bring happiness."

"Yes father," said Nasruddin, "I realize that, but at least it will allow me to choose the kind of misery I find most agreeable."

That's what we are doing – trying to find a misery which appears agreeable. That's your whole search.

Buddha says: *It is difficult not to hanker after that which is agreeable.* Agreeable or disagreeable is not the point because a dream can be agreeable, a lie can be agreeable, sometimes poison can be agreeable, sometimes suicide can be agreeable – that is not the point. The point is what is real.

The real man endeavors to know the real, and the unreal man tries only to find things which are agreeable, comfortable, convenient. Look, watch out. Don't go after the agreeable, otherwise dreams will go on pulling you and pushing you here and there, and you will remain like driftwood.

Let your emphasis be on what is real. Even if it is not agreeable, choose the real. Let me repeat it: even if the real is not agreeable to you, choose the real, become agreeable to it. Then only you can come to truth, there is no other way.

It is difficult not to get into a passion when slighted.

Anger is so easy, so mechanical. You need not have any awareness of it, it is robotlike. Somebody insults you, you become angry. Buddha says try – when somebody insults you remain calm and quiet. Don't miss this opportunity. This is an opportunity to get out of your mechanical world. This is an opportunity to become more conscious. The person is giving you a beautiful chance to grow. Don't miss it.

Whenever you find an opportunity where it is natural to be mechanical, try to be nonmechanical, become more conscious of the situation and that will become your growth ladder. Somebody insults you. It is very easy to be hurt. It is mechanical, you are not needed for it, no intelligence is needed for it. It is very easy to get into a rage, anger, fire. No intelligence is needed for it. Even animals do it, so nothing is special in it.

Do something special. Remain calm and quiet and collected. Relax, watch inside that the mechanical thing does not possess you. Become a little loose from your mechanical habits and your benefit will be tremendous. You will start becoming more and more aware.

It is difficult not to abuse one's authority.

Very difficult because in the first place people seek authority just to abuse it.

You have heard Lord Acton's famous dictum that power corrupts. It is not true. His observation is right in a way, but not true. Power never corrupts anybody, but still Lord Acton is right because we always see people being corrupted by power. How can power corrupt people?

On the other hand, in fact, corrupted people seek power. Of course when they don't have power, they cannot express their corruption. When they have power, then they are free. Then they can move with the power, then they are not worried. Then they come in their true light, then they show their real face.

Power never corrupts anybody, but only corrupted people are attracted towards power. And when they have power, then of course they use it for all their desires and passions.

It happens – a person may be very humble. When he is seeking a political post he may be very humble, and you may know him – you may have known that for his whole life he was a simple and humble person – and you vote for him. The moment he is in power, there is a metamorphosis; he is no longer the same person. People are surprised, how does power corrupt?

In fact that humbleness was false, bogus. He was humble because he was weak. He was humble because he had no power. He was afraid he would have been crushed by other powerful people. His humbleness was his politics, his policy. Now he need not be afraid, now nobody can crush him. Now he can come to his true being, now he can express his own reality. Now he looks corrupted.

Buddha says: *It is difficult not to abuse one's authority.* Difficult because in the first place only people who want to abuse their authority become interested in authority. If you have some authority, watch. Even small authorities corrupt people. You may be just a constable standing on the crossroads, but if you have the opportunity you will abuse it; you will show yourself who you are.

Mulla Nasruddin used to serve as a constable. He caught hold of a woman who was driving a car. Of course, a woman and a car driver never go together, so she was going wrong. Mulla took his notebook and started writing. The woman said, "Wait! I know the chief minister, so don't be worried." But Mulla continued writing, he didn't pay any attention. The woman said, "Do you know, I even know the governor!" But the Mulla continued writing.

The woman said, "Listen, what are you doing? I even know Indira Gandhi!"

Mulla said, "Listen lady, do you know Mulla Nasruddin?"

She said, "No, never heard of him."

He said, "My name is Mulla Nasruddin, and unless you know Mulla Nasruddin, nothing doing."

When you have authority, then one tends... It is so easy, you can watch it all around. You are just standing at the ticket window of a railway station and the booking clerk goes on doing something, and you can see that he has nothing to do. He goes on turning pages here and there. He wants to delay. He wants to show you that now he has the authority. He says, "Wait." He cannot lose this chance to say no to you.

Watch in yourself also. Your son comes and says, "Daddy, can I go out to play?" You say, "No!" And you know well and the son knows well that you will allow him. Then the son starts shrieking and jumping and screaming and he says, "I want to go!" Then you say, "Okay, go." And you know it, it has happened before the same way. And there was nothing wrong in going outside and playing. Why did you say no?

If you have authority, you want to show it. But then the son also has some authority. He starts jumping, he creates a tantrum, and he knows that he will create trouble and the neighbors will listen and people will think wrongly about you, so you say, "Okay, go."

In every human encounter you will see it happening: people are throwing their authority all around; either bullying people or being bullied by others. And if somebody bullies you, you will immediately find some weaker person somewhere to take the revenge.

If your boss bullies you in the office, you will come home and bully your wife. And if she is not a lib movement woman, then she will wait for the child to come home from the school, and she will bully the child. And if the child is old-fashioned, not American, then the child will go to his room and crush his toys because that is the only thing he can bully. He can show his power to the toy. But this goes on and on. This seems to be the whole game. This is what real politics is.

To get out of the political mind is the meaning of this sutra: *It is difficult not to abuse one's authority.* So whenever you have some authority – and everybody has some authority or other. You cannot find a person, you cannot find the last person who has no authority; even he has some authority, even he has a dog he can kick. Everybody has some authority somewhere. So, everybody lives in politics. You may not be a member of any political party, that doesn't mean that you are not political. If you abuse your authority, you are political. If you don't abuse your authority, then you are nonpolitical.

Become more aware not to abuse your authority. It will give you a very new light – how you function – and it will make you so calm and centered. It will give you tranquility and serenity.

> *It is difficult to be even-minded and simple-hearted in all one's dealings with others.*

It is very difficult because people are cunning. If you are simple-hearted, you will be cheated.

Buddha says, be cheated. It is better to be cheated than to cheat. If these are the only alternatives: to be cheated or to cheat; then Buddha says choose the first, be cheated. At least your inner being will remain uncorrupted.

That is the meaning when Jesus says, "If somebody hits, slaps your face, then give him the other side also. If somebody forces you to carry his load for one mile, go two miles. And if somebody tries to steal your coat, give him your shirt also."

The whole meaning is this: that it is better to be cheated, because when somebody is cheating you, he can cheat you only of immaterial things, meaningless things. When you cheat somebody, you are losing something of your inner being, something which is tremendously valuable.

It is very difficult to be even-minded and simple-hearted in one's dealings with others.

It is very simple to be simple-minded when you are alone. That's why many people go to the Himalayas or to the monasteries where they drop out of the world. It is very simple not to cheat when you are alone. It is very simple to be simple when you are alone – but what is the point?

Of course, when you are alone you cannot be dishonest. Of course, when you are alone you cannot lie. Of course, when you are alone you cannot be egoistic, you cannot be competitive, you cannot deceive, you cannot hurt. But that doesn't mean that you have changed and transformed. The real test is in the world.

So, never leave the world – change yourself. It is very easy to change the circumstances, but that is not the real thing – change your consciousness.

> *It is difficult to be thorough in learning and exhaustive in investigation.*

Mind tends to be lazy, all laziness is in the mind. Mind wants to avoid any effort. That's why mind does not want to move in new dimensions. It remains clinging to the old, to the familiar because it knows it is very efficient there. It has a certain proficiency and skill. Now, once you have settled, you don't want to change it.

Many people go on living with a woman or with a man, not because they love the man or the woman, but just because it is familiar. Now it will again be a trouble to move with another woman and start from *ABC*. They are simply lazy.

People go on living the way they are living even if it is miserable, even if nothing exists out of it except anguish. But they continue because at least it is familiar, known. They have become skillful about it and they can go on sleeping. Mind is lazy. This laziness is one of the barriers.

Buddha says: *It is very difficult to be thorough in learning and exhaustive in investigation.* You have not even been thoroughly aware of your life, which is the most important thing here. You have not even investigated it – what it is. You have taken it for granted on the surface. All your knowledge about your life is borrowed. Whatsoever you know is not what you know – it is from somebody else.

I have heard...

A student nurse was faced with the following question on an examination paper: "Name five reasons why mothers' milk is better for babies than cows' milk."

She answered. "First: because it is fresher. Second: because it is cleaner. Third: because the cats can't reach it. Fourth: because it is easier to take with you on journeys."

Try as she would, she could not think of a fifth reason. You try, even these four are not reasons. In desperation, she glanced at the paper of a male student sitting next to her, and then wrote, "Fifth: because it comes in such cute little containers."

This is the way you borrow knowledge, looking here and there. This is all that you know. You have not looked directly. And unless you look direct, you will remain stupid, you will remain mediocre.

It is difficult to subdue selfish pride.

One of the most arduous things in life is not to think of oneself as extraordinary. Of course, this is the most ordinary thing in the world to think because everybody thinks he is extraordinary. Everybody thinks he is extraordinary, so the feeling of being extraordinary is the most ordinary thing. Look around – still you go on thinking that you are extraordinary.

Buddha says it is very difficult, but if you really want to move on the path, start feeling. Just be ordinary. Don't claim any extraordinariness.

And this is the beauty of the whole thing – the moment you become ordinary, you become extraordinary. The moment you don't claim that you are exceptional, you are exceptional because the claim is so ordinary. Everybody is claiming he is unique, exceptional. People may say, may not say, but deep down they know who they are.

Become alert. How can you be extraordinary? Either everybody is extraordinary, then you are also extraordinary – but what is the point? If extraordinariness is just a common quality of everybody, then what is the point of claiming it? Either everybody is extraordinary because everybody comes from the same source of existence, or everybody is ordinary, because everybody comes from the same source of existence.

Whatsoever you think about yourself, think about others also. And whatsoever you think about others, think about yourself also. And then pride will disappear. Pride is always vain. Pride is always for wrong reasons. Pride is like a fever and you can never be healthy with it. It is a temperature.

It is difficult not to feel contempt towards the unlearned.

Buddha specifically mentions it. When you see somebody who is more ignorant than you, you suddenly feel a contempt. It is very difficult not to feel that contempt because when you see somebody more learned than you, you feel jealous. Both these things go together – contempt for those who are behind you and jealousy for those who are ahead of you. Contempt and jealousy simply show that you are continuously comparing yourself with others.

Never compare because all comparison is foolish. Everybody

is just like himself. What is the point of comparing? Who are you to compare, and who are you to fix a criterion to decide who is learned and who is not learned? Who are you to make a criterion who is beautiful and who is not beautiful? Who are you? Why should you judge? Jesus says, "Judge ye not."

It is difficult to be one in knowledge and practice.

Unless the knowledge is your own, there will always be a rift between what you know and what you do. Because whatsoever you do cannot be transformed by knowledge gathered from others. It cannot be changed by borrowed knowledge. It changes only when your insight flowers. It is difficult to have a synthetic, harmonious life between what you know and what you do.

Watch it. Whatsoever you do, in fact, that is indicative that only that is what you know. Whatsoever you know and you don't do, that you don't know at all. Drop it, throw it, it is rubbish! Watch your doing because that is your real knowledge.

You say anger is bad and you don't want to do it, but then somebody insults and you become angry and you say, "What to do? In spite of me I became angry. I know very well that anger is bad, poisonous, destructive; I know it, but what to do? – I became angry."

If you come to me, I will say, "You don't know that anger is poisonous; you have only heard about it. Deep down you know that anger is necessary; deep down you know that without anger you will lose your standing, everybody will be bullying you. Without anger you will not have any spine, your pride will be shattered. Without anger, how can you exist in this world of continuous struggle for survival?" This is what you know, but you say, "I know anger is poisonous."

Buddha knows anger is poisonous. You have heard Buddha, you have listened to Buddha, you have learned something from him – but that is his knowledge.

Whatsoever is your doing, remember, it is your knowing. Go deep into your doing to find out exactly what you know. And if you want to transform your doing, then borrowed knowledge won't do. If you really want to know what anger is, go into it, meditate over it, taste it in many ways, allow it to happen inside you, be surrounded by it, be clouded by it, feel all the pang and the pain and the hurt of it, and the poison, and how it brings you low, how it creates a dark valley for your being, how you fall into hell through it, how it is a downward flow. Feel it, know it and that understanding will start a transformation in you.

To know truth is to be transformed. Truth liberates, but it must be your own.

It is difficult not to express an opinion about others.

Very difficult. We go on unconsciously expressing our opinion about others. Do you know others? You don't even know yourself. How foolish it is to express opinions about others. You may have known somebody for a few days: you know his name, you know how he walks; you have known him in a few situations, how he acts, but do you know him? He is a vast continent. You have known only a fragment of it.

It is as if a page torn from the Bible has come in your hands – winds have brought it to you, torn apart – and you read a few sentences. They are also not complete: somewhere one word is missing, somewhere the ink has been washed by the rain water, somewhere mud has settled, and then you decide about Jesus, or you decide about Christianity. It will be foolish.

It is as if you are brought into a movie which is going on. You enter from one door, you look at the movie, and you go out through the other door; just for a few seconds you are inside and you decide about the whole story. It will be foolish. It will be sheer stupidity on your part. In fact, you will not decide. You will say, "I have not seen the whole movie. I don't know what went before, what was coming afterwards, and I have only been here in the movie hall for a few seconds. Just a few pictures were there, they are almost irrelevant to me, I don't know the context."

That's how we know people. A life is a tremendously rich phenomenon. One never knows because only a part of it comes in the actions, only the tip of the iceberg – the real thing remains inside. What you do is a very small tiny part of what you are. What you do is a very small part of what you think, of what you feel, of what you dream, of what you fantasize, of what goes on inside your being – just fragments.

Buddha says, *It is difficult not to express an opinion about others.* But take the challenge. Resist the temptation. Don't express your opinions about others and you will grow in understanding. Because your opinion becomes a barrier to understanding, it becomes a prejudice.

> *It is by rare opportunity that one is introduced to a true spiritual teacher.*

In fact, to be introduced to a true spiritual teacher is a very unique phenomenon.

First, nobody is searching truth. Even if a master passes you by, you will remain completely oblivious of his existence. That's how it happened when Buddha passed. Millions of people remained oblivious. When Jesus passed, people had not even heard his name. He was an unknown figure. When Mahavira was here, very rare souls came in contact with him. Because you can come in contact with a master only when you are really seeking truth intensely, passionately; when you have *mumuksha*, a fiery desire to know, and you are ready to stake everything for it.

When you are ready to know, when you are ready to become a disciple, only then can you come into the contact of a master, only then can you be introduced to the world of a master. Your readiness to become a disciple will be your introduction.

It is very difficult to become a disciple. It is easy to become a student because a student has no personal relationship. He comes to know things. You go to the university, you are a student. If you come to me as a student, you will miss me because then you hear only what I say, and you will collect it as information; you will become more knowledgeable. But if you really want to come to me, you have to come to me as a disciple.

A disciple is one who says, "I don't know anything. I surrender totally, utterly. I will be just receptive. I trust. I am ready to annihilate myself. If you say, 'Jump into the fire,' I will jump."

A disciple means one who is ready to trust somebody, very difficult; ready to drop himself, ready to go with somebody into the unknown uncharted world. Only a very courageous soul becomes a disciple. To learn, one needs to be humble. To learn, one needs to be totally empty, receptive, sensitive, meditative.

A student needs concentration, a disciple needs meditation. Concentration means he has to listen correctly to what is being said. Meditation means you have to be present rightly; not only listen rightly, that is only a small part of it.

You have to be here with me present rightly: in tune, in harmony, in deep rapport, *en rapport*, so my heart can beat with your heart, so you can breathe with my breathing, so you can vibrate with my frequency.

A moment comes between the master and the disciple when they both start vibrating in the same rhythm. Then something is transferred, then something transpires between them. That which cannot be said can be transferred in those moments. That which cannot be expressed can be handed over in those moments. A transmission beyond scripture – that's how Zen Buddhists express it – a transmission beyond scripture, a transmission immediate, direct.

> *It is difficult to gain an insight into the nature of being,*
> *and to practice the way.*

...difficult to gain an insight into the nature of being... because one has to go inwards. Outwards we go easily. To go outward is to go downward, it is easy. To go inward is to go upward. It is an uphill task, it is difficult.

To go to others is simple – the way of the world. To go to oneself is difficult – it is not the way of the world, not the way of the crowd. Only very few people, rare souls, try to move inwards.

It is difficult to gain an insight into the nature of being and to practice the way. First, it is difficult to have an insight into your own being, and then it is even more difficult to practice it because then you will be practicing nothingness. Then you will be walking as an emptiness. Then you will not be there.

If you go into the deepest core of your being, you will find that man is like an onion – you go on peeling it, layer upon layer, go on peeling it – and in the end only emptiness is left in the hand. Then you have come to the very core of the onion, which is from where it has developed. Out of nothingness it has become something. Out of the immaterial, matter has arisen. Out of no-being, being has gathered.

It is difficult to know it, first because who wants to know that one is not? Who desires to disappear? Who longs for total ultimate death? It is difficult first to know it and then it is even more difficult to practice it because when you are nobody, nothing is left to practice.

To walk like a buddha is really the impossible. It happens, it is incredible, it cannot be believed. How does Buddha walk? Have you ever pondered over it? He has no desire to go anywhere, still he walks. He has no desire to do anything, still he lives. He has no desire to achieve anything, still every morning he gets up, starts helping people. He has nothing to achieve now, nowhere to go – then why does he go on breathing? He is practicing nothingness. It is one of the most incredible phenomena: to come to know that you are not and then still to exist.

Many disappear. Those who disappear, Buddha calls them *arhatas*. When they come to know their inner emptiness, they simply dissolve into it. Then what is the point of even breathing? Why breathe? Why eat? Why drink? Why be? They simply disappear.

Those who try hard, knowing well that they are not, but who still try hard to help others, knowing well that others are just in dream, knowing well that others also don't exist in reality. To have compassion on phantoms, to have compassion on shadows, and still make an effort to help them, is the most impossible thing. But it happens.

You exist because of passion, desire. Buddha has to exist for compassion. He has no desire. There is nothing, no future for him. All that has to happen has happened. Still he practices the way. He moves as alert as he wants you to move. He behaves in the way he wants you to behave.

Jesus was leaving his disciples on the last night and he washed their feet and touched their feet. They were very embarrassed and they said, "What are you doing, master?"

And Jesus said, "There is no need for me to touch your feet, but I am touching so that you will remember: don't become too egoistic. Remember that your master touched your feet, so remember when people come to you as disciples, don't become too egoistic that you know and they don't know, that they are ignorant. Touch their feet." Jesus says that just to help them to remember, he's touching their feet.

Buddha says, "I behave the way you should behave. Not that there is any more any discipline for me, but I go on behaving the way I would like you to behave. For you, still there is much to be done."

A buddha is absolute freedom. He can be in any way, there is no problem. But still he goes on following. Every morning he sits in meditation. What compassion.

Somebody, his great disciple Sariputta, asked Buddha, "Why do you sit in meditation? Because you are twenty-four hours in meditation."

Buddha said, "That's right, but if I don't sit, others will take advantage of it. They will think, 'If Buddha is not meditating, why should we bother?'"

Now he has nothing to meditate, but he sits under the tree every morning so that others can sit under the tree.

> *It is difficult to gain insight into the nature of being, and to practice the way.*
> *It is difficult to follow the steps of a savior.*

Because to follow the steps of a savior is to commit suicide. By and by you have to dissolve yourself. The closer you come to a savior, the more you disappear, the more and more you disappear. When you come the closest, you are not there. One who is ready to dissolve is ready to become a disciple.

> *It is difficult to be always the master of oneself.*

Small things prove that you are a slave. Somebody insults – and anger. You are simply proving that he is the master. He can insult any day and can create anger in you. You are not the master of your anger. Somebody comes and flatters you and you smile. He has brought the smile in you; he is the master. You are not the master.

Buddha says it is very difficult, but try.

I call you swamis. The word *swami* means a master. Try in every way to remain a master. Don't allow anybody to manipulate you. Don't allow anybody to reduce you to just a mechanism. Remain master in every situation. And if you make effort, sooner or later you will start feeling a new power, a new surge of energy in you.

And the last, the twentieth:

> *It is difficult to understand thoroughly the ways of Buddha.*

It is difficult because you are not a buddha yet. Only the similar can understand, only the equal can understand. A Jesus can be understood only by a Jesus. A Buddha can be understood only by a buddha.

How can you understand? If you live in the valley, if you have the language of the valley, and somebody comes from the top of the hill where you have never been, and he talks about the sunlight and the clouds, and the beautiful colors of the clouds, and the flowers that bloom on the top of the hill, how will you understand?

You know only the valley, the darkness, and your crawling life. You will misinterpret, you will translate whatsoever he is saying into the language of your valley. That's why buddhas say, "Come, come with us. Come to the reality we exist at. Come to the top. There only will you be able to understand it." It is not a question of logical discourse, it is a question of changing and transforming your plane of being.

Whatsoever I am saying to you, you can listen to it. In a certain intellectual way you can understand it also, but you will always feel puzzled. You will always feel that this man is talking in contradictions. Sometimes he says this, sometimes he says that. You will always remain in a confusion.

Just the other night a sannyasin came to me and she said, "I was never as confused as I have become listening to you."

I said, "That's right. You were thinking that you know. Now you know that you don't know. You were thinking that everything is okay. Now you know, nothing is okay. You were thinking that this valley is all that exists. Now you know there are unknown peaks. Now the challenge has penetrated your heart. Now the desire has arisen and much has been stirred by the desire. You don't know what those peaks are, but you have started longing for those peaks."

Confusion is bound to happen because the language of the valley and the language of the peak are two different languages. There has been a meeting between the two, chaos has arisen.

"But don't be bothered by it," I told her. "Start moving towards the direction I am indicating, and as you move higher your confusion will start changing into a fusion. Confusion will be left behind in the valley. By the time you reach the peak everything will be crystal clear."

It is difficult to understand thoroughly the ways of Buddha. It is enough if you can even understand a bit of it. Try hard, don't leave any stones unturned. Try hard to understand knowing well it is almost impossible, but try hard. By your very effort you will become integrated. A center will be born in you and that center will become a transforming point.

One day you are all destined to be buddhas. The whole thing will be understood only on that day, not before it. You will have to grope in the dark, but don't be lazy – grope.

The door is there, certainly. If you go on groping, you are bound to find it. The hill exists. If you take courage and start moving beyond the valley, you are bound to reach.

Yes, arduous is the path, dangerous is the path, but that is the only way one matures, grows and attains to life abundant.

Enough for today.

2

HAPPY FOR NO REASON

Osho,
Why am I always daydreaming about the future?

It is not only you who is continuously daydreaming, everybody is doing that. Human mind as such is a daydreaming faculty. Unless you go beyond the mind you will continue to daydream because the mind cannot exist in the present. It can either exist in the past or in the future. There is no way for the mind to exist in the present. To be in the present is to be without mind.

You try it. If there is a silent moment when no thought is crossing your being, your consciousness, when the screen of consciousness is absolutely unclouded, then suddenly you are in the present. That is the moment, the real moment, the moment of reality, the moment of truth. But then there is no past and no future.

Ordinarily, time is divided into these three tenses: past, present, future. The division is basically wrong, unscientific because present is not part of time. Past and future are only parts of time. Present is beyond time, present is eternity.

Past and future are part of time. Past is that which is no more, and future is that which is not yet, both are nonexistential. Present is that which is. The existential cannot be a part of the nonexistential. They never meet, they never cross each other's way. And time is mind; past accumulated is what your mind is.

What is your mind? Analyze it, look into it. What is it? – just past experiences piled up, accumulated. Your mind is just a blanket term, an umbrella term; it simply keeps, holds your whole past. It is nothing else. If by and by you take your past out of the bag, the bag will disappear.

If past is the only reality for the mind, then what can the mind do? One possibility is that it can go on chewing, re-chewing the past again and again. That's what you call memory, remembrance, nostalgia. You go again and again backwards; again and again to the past moments, beautiful moments, happy moments. They are few and far between, but you cling to them. You avoid the ugly moments, the miserable moments.

But you cannot do this continuously because it is futile, the activity seems to be meaningless. The mind creates a meaningful activity; that's what daydreaming about the future is.

The mind says, "Yes, past is good, but past is finished; nothing can be done about it. Something can be done about the future because it is yet to come." So out of your past experiences you choose those which you would like to repeat again, and you drop experiences that were very miserable, painful, that you don't want to repeat in the future.

So your future dreaming is nothing but past modified, better arranged, more decorated, more agreeable, less painful, more pleasant. This your mind goes on doing. And this way you go on missing reality.

Meditation simply means a few moments when you are not in the mind, a few moments when you slip out of the mind. You slip in reality, in that which is. These existential moments are so tremendously ecstatic that once you taste them, you will stop day-dreaming.

Daydreaming will continue unless you start tasting meditation. Unless you are nourished on meditation, you will go on starving and hankering for some food in the future. And you know the future is not going to bring it because today was future just one day before. Yesterday it was future, and you were daydreaming about it. Now it is there. What is happening? Are you happy? Yesterday was also one day in the future. The past was all part of future one day, and it has slipped, and the future will also slip. You are befooling yourself in daydreaming.

Become a little more aware and try to bring your consciousness more and more to the facticity of existence. See *this* flower, don't think about *that* flower. Listen to *this* word I am uttering, not to *that* word that I am going to utter. Look at me right now. If you postpone even for a single split moment, you miss me.

Then it becomes a habit, a very ingrained habit. Tomorrow you will also miss, and the day after tomorrow also because you will remain the same. Not only that, your habit of daydreaming will have become stronger.

The other night I was reading a beautiful Japanese story. Such stories exist in all the folktales of the world, on similar patterns. It is a beautiful story. Listen to it.

There was once a man who hewed stones from the rock. His labor was very hard and he labored much, but his wages were slight and he was not content.

Who is content? Not even emperors are content, so what to say about a stonecutter? His work was certainly hard and the payoff was almost nothing.

He sighed because his labor was hard, and he cried, "Oh, I wish I was rich so I could rest on a couch with a cover of silk." And an angel came from heaven, saying, "You are what you have said."

And this really happens – not only in parables and stories, it happens in real life. Whatsoever you think about yourself, starts happening. You create your world by your thought, you create your world by your desire. Whatsoever you insist on, starts happening. Reality goes on cooperating with you. It waits for the moment, for the day, when you will cooperate with it. Until then, it goes on cooperating with you.

The angel said, "You are what you have said." And he was rich, and he did rest on a couch, and the cover was of silk.

But then the king of the land went by with horsemen in front of his carriage and behind the carriage there were also horsemen, and a golden parasol was held over the head of the king.

When the rich man saw this, he was vexed that no golden parasol was held over his own head and he was not content. He sighed and cried, "I wish to be a king." And the angel came again and he said, "You are what you have said."

And he was king and many horsemen rode in front of his carriage, and there were also horsemen behind his carriage and a golden parasol was held over his head, and the sun shone hot rays and scorched the earth so that the grass shoots withered. And the king complained that the sun burned his face and that it excelled him in power and he was not content. He sighed and cried, "I wish to be the sun." And the angel came and he said, "You are what you have said."

And he was the sun and he directed his rays upward and down, to the right and to the left – everywhere – and he scorched the grass shoots on earth, and the countenances of kings who were on earth.

And a cloud placed itself between him and the earth, and the rays of the sun bounced back from it and he grew wrathful that his power was resisted. He complained that the cloud excelled him in power and he was not content. He wished to be the cloud, which was so powerful, and the angel came and he said, "You are what you have said."

And he became a cloud and placed himself between the sun and the earth and caught the rays so that the grass grew green. The cloud rained large drops on the earth causing the rivers to swell and floods to carry the houses away, and he destroyed the fields with much water. He fell upon a rock which did not yield, and he splashed in great streams, but the rock did not yield, and he grew wrathful because the rock was not yielding to his power, and the power of his streams was in vain and he was not content.

He cried, "That rock has been given power which excels mine. I wish to be the rock." And the angel came and he was the rock, he did become the rock, and did not move when the sun shone nor when it rained.

And then there was a man with a pick and with a chisel and with a heavy hammer, and he hewed stones out of the rock and the rock said, "How can it be that this man has power that excels mine and hews stones out of my lap?" and he was not content.

He cried, "I am weaker than he. I wish to be that man." And the angel came from heaven, saying, "You are what you have said."

And he was a stonecutter again. And he hewed stones from the rock with hard labor, and he labored very hard for small wages and he was content.

I don't agree with the conclusion. That is the only disagreement with the story, otherwise the story is beautiful. I don't agree with the conclusion because I know people, they cannot be so easily content. The wheel is complete. The story in a way has come to a natural end, but the real stories in life don't come to any natural end. The wheel again starts moving.

That's why in India we call life the wheel. It goes on moving, goes on repeating itself. As far as I can see, unless the stonecutter became a buddha, the story must have been repeated again. Again he will become discontent. Again he will long for a beautiful couch and a cover of silk, and again the same thing will start. But if this stonecutter was really content, then he has jumped out of the wheel of life and death. He has become a buddha.

This is what goes on happening to each mind: you long for something, it happens, but by the time it happens you see that you are still discontent. Something else is creating the misery now.

This is something to be understood: that if your desire is not fulfilled you are frustrated; if it is fulfilled, then too you are not fulfilled. That is the misery of desire. Fulfilled, you are not fulfilled. Suddenly many new things arise.

You had never thought that when you will be a king, and horsemen will be in front of you and at the back of you, and a golden parasol will be over your head, the sun can be so hot that it can scorch your face. You had never thought about it. Then you dreamed of becoming a sun, and you become a sun, and you had never thought about the cloud. Now the cloud is there and proving you impotent.

And this goes on and on and on, like waves in the ocean – nonending, unless you understand and simply jump out of the wheel.

Life is here, life is now. God is here and God is now. If you are searching for him in your daydreams, your search is in vain because God is nothing but deep contentment.

The mind goes on telling you: "Do this, be that. Possess this, possess that – otherwise how can you be happy if you don't have this? You have to have a palace, then you can be happy." If your happiness has a condition to it, you will remain unhappy. If you cannot be happy just as you are, a stonecutter – I know the labor is hard, wages are poor, life is a struggle, I know – but if you cannot be happy as you are, in spite of it all, you are not going to be happy ever.

Unless a man is happy, simply happy, for no reason at all, unless a man is mad enough to be happy without any reason, a man is not going to be happy ever. You will always find something destroying your happiness. You will always find something missing, something absent. And that missing will become your daydream again.

And you cannot achieve a state where everything, everything is available. Even if it is possible, then too you will not be happy. Just watch the mechanism of the mind: if everything is available as you want it, suddenly you will feel bored. Now what to do?

I have heard this, and I think it is reliable, that people who have reached heaven are bored. It is from very reliable sources, you can depend on it. They are sitting under their *kalpatarus*, the wish fulfilling trees, and they are bored because the moment they say something the angel appears and immediately he fulfills their desire. There is no gap between their desire and their fulfillment. They want a beautiful woman, a Cleopatra, and she is there.

Now what to do with such a Cleopatra? It is pointless, and they get bored.

In Indian Puranas there are many stories of *devas* who became so bored in heaven that they started longing for the earth. They have everything there. When they were on the earth, they were hankering for heaven. They may have been great ascetics, they may have renounced the world, women, everything, to attain to heaven. Now they have reached heaven they are hankering for the world.

I have heard...

The pilot of a new jet plane was winging over the Catskills and pointed out a pleasant valley to his second-in-command.

"See that spot?" he demanded. "When I was a barefoot kid, I used to sit in a flat bottomed rowboat down there fishing. Every time a plane flew by, I would look up and dream I was piloting it. Now I look down and dream I am fishing."

Now he has become a pilot. First he was a poor boy, fishing, and jet planes would roar above and he would look up and he would dream that "one day God willing, I will become a pilot." The thrill of the open sky, the winds, the vastness... He must have been dreaming, and he must have been feeling very miserable – just a poor boy, fishing in an ordinary rowboat.

Now he says to his second-in-command, "Now I am the pilot. Now I look down and dream I am fishing." Now the small beautiful lake deep down in the valley with beautiful trees, and birds singing, and the meditative relaxation of fishing; now he must be dreaming about retirement, how to get rid of this piloting.

That's how it goes on and on. When you are not famous you want to be famous. You feel very hurt that people don't know you. You pass through the streets, nobody looks at you, nobody recognizes you. You feel like a nonentity.

You do hard work to become famous. One day you become famous. Now you cannot move in the street. Now the crowd stares at you. You don't have any freedom. Now you have to remain closed in your chamber. You cannot get out, you are imprisoned. Now you start thinking about those beautiful days when you used to walk on the streets and you were so free, as if you were alone. Now you hanker for those days. Ask the famous people.

Voltaire writes in his memoirs that once he was not famous – as everybody was one day not famous – and he desired and desired and he worked hard, and he became one of the most famous men in France. His fame increased so much that it became almost dangerous for him to go out of his room because in those superstitious days people used to think that if you can get a piece of the clothes of a very great man it becomes a protection; it has tremendous value, protective value. It protects you against ghosts, against bad accidents and things like that.

So if he had to go to the station to catch a train, he would go under police escort, otherwise people would tear his clothes. Not only that his skin would be torn and he would come home with blood flowing.

He became so fed up with this fame that he could not even go out of his house, people were always there like wolves to jump upon him. He started praying to God, "Finished! I have known this. I don't want it. I have become almost a dead person." And then it happened. The angel came, must have come, and he said, "Okay." By and by his fame disappeared.

People's opinions change very easily, they don't have any integrity. Just like fashion, things change. You can be famous one day, the next day you can become the most notorious man. One day you are at the top of your fame, the next day people completely forget about you. One day you are the president, the next day you are just citizen Richard Nixon. Nobody bothers.

It happened that people's minds changed, the opinion, the climate changed, and people completely forgot about Voltaire. He would come to the station and he would long that at least someone, at least one person must be waiting there to receive him. And nobody would come to receive him, only his dog.

When he died there were only four persons giving him the last good-bye; three were men and the fourth was his dog. He must have died in misery, again hankering for fame. What to do? This is how things go on.

Mind will never allow you to be happy. Whatsoever the condition, the mind will always find something to be unhappy about. Let me say it in this way: mind is a mechanism to create unhappiness. Its whole function is to create unhappiness.

If you drop the mind, suddenly you become happy for no reason at all. Then happiness is just natural, like breathing. For breathing, you need not be even aware. You simply go on breathing. Conscious, unconscious, awake, asleep, you go on breathing. Happiness is exactly like that.

That's why in the East we say that happiness is your innermost nature. It needs no outside condition; it is simply there, it is you. Bliss is your natural state, it is not an achievement. If you simply get out of the mechanism of the mind, you start feeling blissful.

That's why you will see that mad people are happier than so-called sane people. What happens to mad people? They also get out of the mind – of course in a wrong way, but they get out of the mind. A madman is one who has fallen below the mind. He's out of the mind. That's why you can see that mad people are so happy. You can feel jealous. You can even daydream, "When will this blessing happen to us?" He is condemned, but he is happy.

What has happened to a madman? He is no longer thinking of the past and no longer thinking of the future. He has dropped out of time. He has started living in eternity.

It also happens the same way to the mystic because he goes above mind. I am not telling you to become mad, but I am telling you that there is a similarity between the madman and the mystic. That's why all great mystics look a little mad and all great mad people look a little like mystics.

Watch a madman's eyes and you will find his eyes very mystic: a glow, some otherworldly glow, as if he has some inner door from where he reaches to the very core of life. He is relaxed. He may have nothing, but he is simply happy. He has no desires, no ambitions. He is not going anywhere. He is simply sitting there; enjoying, delighting.

Yes, madmen and mystics have something similar. That similarity is because both are out of the mind. The madman has fallen below it, the mystic has gone beyond it. But the mystic is mad with a method, his madness has a method in it. The madman has simply fallen below.

I am not saying become mad. I am saying become mystics. The mystic is as happy as the madman and as sane as the sane man. The mystic is as reasonable, even more reasonable than so-called rationalist people, and yet so happy, just like mad people. The mystic has the most beautiful synthesis. He is in a harmony. He has all that a madman has and he also has all that a reasonable man has. He has both. He is complete. He is whole.

You ask, "Why am I always daydreaming about the future?" You are daydreaming about the future because you have not tasted the present. Start tasting the present. Find out a few moments where you are simply delighting.

Looking at the trees, just *be* the look. Listening to the birds, just be a listening ear. Let them reach to your deepest core. Let their song spread all over your being. Sitting by the side of the beach, just listen to the wild roar of the waves, become one with it because that wild roar of the waves has no past, no future. If you can tune yourself with it, you will also become a wild roar. Hug a tree and relax into it. Feel its green shape rushing into your being. Lie down on the sand, forget the world, commune with the sand, the coolness of it; feel the coolness saturating you. Go to the river, swim, and let the river swim within you. Splash around and become the splashing.

Do whatsoever you feel you enjoy, and enjoy it totally. In those few moments, the past and future will disappear and you will be herenow. And those moments will bring the first good news, the first gospel of God.

The gospel is not in the Bible. The gospel is in the rivers and in the wild roar of the ocean and in the silence of the stars. The good news is written all over. The whole universe is a message. Decode it. Learn its language. Its language is that of herenow.

Your language is that of past and future. So if you go on speaking the language of the mind, you will never be in tune, in harmony with existence. And if that harmony is not tasted, how can you stop daydreaming? – because that is what your life is.

It is as if a poor man is carrying a bag of ordinary stones, thinking that they are great diamonds, rubies, emeralds, and if you say to him, "Drop these. You are a fool. These are just ordinary stones," he cannot believe you. He will think you are tricking him. He will cling to it because that's all he has.

I will not say to that man to renounce his bag. I will try to show him real rubies, emeralds, diamonds. Just a glimpse of them and he will throw the bag. Not even that he will renounce it because there is nothing to renounce, they are just ordinary stones. You don't renounce ordinary stones.

He will simply become aware that he was living under an illusion. Now there are real diamonds. Suddenly his own stones fade, they disappear. And he will simply empty his bag immediately without your telling him because now he has something else to put in the bag. He will need the bag, the space.

So I don't say to you drop going into the future, drop going into the past; rather, I would like to say to you make more contacts with the present. When present arises with its grandeur, its beauty, everything else pales, renunciation follows awareness like a shadow.

Osho,
It seems to me that you are nothing but a trickster. It also seems to me that I have to cooperate with your tricks for my own good. Is this possible? Is not this all a bit crazy?

You call it a bit crazy! It is absolutely crazy! And I have to be a trickster with you. Try to understand. If somebody is in an illusion, you cannot bring him out by talking about the truth. An illusion can be destroyed only by another illusion. Poison is to be destroyed by other poison. If you have a thorn in your foot, another thorn will be needed to take it out.

All buddhas are tricksters. You don't need reality, reality is already there. You just need a shock so that you can open your eyes, so that your eyes pop open and you can see. You just need a trick.

Somebody is fast asleep. What do you do? You shake him, you put an alarm and when the bell starts ringing, what are you doing? You are simply creating a disturbance. That's what all devices are. You are fast asleep. Not that reality is not there, reality surrounds you, but you are fast asleep.

I am not here to give you the truth. Nobody can give you the truth. Truth you already have, but somehow you have tricked yourself into lies. Now you will need bigger, stronger lies to crush your lies. All philosophies are lies, devices, to help you to come out of your lies.

A man was brought to me. He was very much afraid of ghosts. They were just in his imagination – they are always in your imagination – but just to say to him, "This is your imagination," was not going to help. Everybody was saying that to him. "You are just imagining. Where are the ghosts? We don't see them."

He was seeing them continuously, they were surrounding him. Somebody was standing on the right, somebody was standing on the left, somebody was standing at the back – they were following him everywhere. It was impossible for him to sleep, it was impossible to be alone because they were torturing him. Now what to do?

Everybody had been saying to him that this was imagination. The doctor had said to him that this was imagination, the psychiatrist had said that nothing could be done, he was simply imagining, he had no real problem. But whether he had a real problem or not, you cannot deny his problem. He had a problem: real, unreal is immaterial. For him it was real. He was suffering, his suffering was real.

When he came to me, I looked to his right and I said, "Perfectly right, the man is there." He smiled at me, I was the first man who understood him. And I said, "By your left side also I can see people, and they are following you. How do you survive with so many ghosts?"

He said, "Nobody listens to me," but he relaxed. He touched my feet. He said, "You are the only person, otherwise I go on proving and nobody listens. They say, 'It is all imagination, you are in a sort of delusion. Drop imagination, there are nothing like ghosts.'"

But I said, "I can see. Who are these people?" His father was with him, his wife was with him, and they became afraid when I said, "Yes, they are there." And he said to his father, "Now, listen to what Osho is saying. And you were thinking I am a fool." Now he gained his confidence.

What I was saying was a lie; there were no ghosts, but that is not the point. The man was suffering from lack of confidence, the man was suffering from fear. Now, just by accepting his lie I am also a liar. I am saying, "Yes, they are there." I helped him to regain his confidence. He looked better, he looked stronger. Maybe the ghosts are there, but he is not wrong. Maybe the ghosts are still there, but he is not a fool, not an idiot. And I told him, "Nothing to be worried about. There are methods, we will deal with them."

He said, "That's what I am asking people. Help me! Give me something to deal with them."

I said, "Don't be worried. And as I can see, they are not stronger than you." Immediately his height was greater than before. He took a deep inhalation, his spine became erect. I gave him just an ordinary locket, nothing in it, empty, and I told him, "You just keep it with you and whenever you feel they are there, you just hold it in your hand, and they will start becoming afraid; they will be frightened and they will start rushing. Don't be worried, just hold it in your hand."

He tried and he laughed. He said, "They are doing that. They are running away from me. Now I'm not afraid."

In just two weeks time he was a normal man. When he was normal and the ghosts had disappeared and he had regained his normality, I told him, "Now, give me that locket because it has nothing in it."

He said, "What do you mean?"

I said, "There were no ghosts. The medicine was as false as the disease." But then he could understand. He laughed, he said, "But you tricked me out of it. If you had said the same thing to me fifteen days ago, I would have never listened to you, but now I know, and if you say, I believe."

I opened the locket, it was empty. I said, "You can see, it is just empty. Just the idea that you have the power has helped. Now I would not like you to carry this locket forever because now this will become a disease. If someday it is lost, you will start trembling, and those ghosts which have gone will come back because the locket is lost."

All your illusions are just illusions. They are illusions. You are not really ill, you have imagined illness. You have not really fallen away from God, you have only dreamed about it. You have never been expelled from the Garden of Eden, you have only thought it that way. You are still in the Garden of Eden. You still exist in the very heart of God. There is no way to get out of it. It is just your dream.

How to destroy a dream? One has to be very, very skillful about it. You cannot just say to people, "This is your dream." They won't listen. Their eyes are so full of dream they won't be able to see. You have to accept their reality, only then can you help.

I have heard...

Once upon a time a young woman dreamed that a handsome prince rode up to her, scooped her up in his arms, kissed her and rode off into the night with her.

"Goodness!" she cried in a frightened voice. "Where are you taking me?"

"You tell me," answered the prince sharply. "It is your dream."

It is your illusion that you have gone astray, now I have to bring you home. It is your dream that you have forgotten God, and I have to remind you. It is your dream that you think that you are miserable, and I have to remind you that you are not.

But just by saying that this is all maya, illusion, you will not be helped. I have to be very skillful about it. I have to persuade you. I have to really be a salesman. I have to persuade you by and by. Hurry will not help. Impatience will not help. If I say too much to you, you will not be able to absorb it.

One man asked me once, "Osho, you go on talking every day, morning and evening. How is it possible?"

I said, "All lies! So what is the difficulty in it? If I am talking only truth, then there is not that much truth to talk every morning, every evening. That much truth does not exist."

You have some lie in your life; I create another lie, an antidote. Once both the lies come in contact, they cross each other, they cancel each other. You are left with the truth. I am not saying the truth. If you listen to me, my lie will kill your lie and the truth will be left behind.

Truth is there. I cannot give it to you. Nobody can give it to you. You are truth, so all that I can do is to create antidote lies for you – that's what all religions are. The day you will understand, you will laugh.

When Bodhidharma attained to his enlightenment, it is said he started laughing. The laughter was mad, he could not contain, he was rolling on the ground. Other bodhisattvas gathered, other seekers gathered and said, "What is happening to you?"

He said, "It is absolutely ridiculous. I cannot believe that truth was never lost, that we had only imagined that we had lost. And then comes this Buddha, this trickster, and he says, 'Come here! Behold, this is the truth!' and he hands you another lie. But it helped tremendously. Both the lies canceled each other."

Of course when you come against the lie created by a buddha you cannot win. Your lie is very amateurish. When a buddha lies, it is perfect and professional. He lies very knowingly and deliberately.

A magician performed brilliantly in the salon of an ocean liner. On this ship was a parrot who hated the magician. Every time the magician did a trick, the parrot would scream, "Phony! Phony! Take him away!"

In the course of the voyage the ship sank. The parrot and the magician ended up on a long plank. One day passed, they said nothing, they were enemies. Two days passed, still they said nothing. Finally the parrot could down his suspicions no longer. He glared at the magician and squeaked, "All right, wise guy. You and your damn tricks! What did you do with the ship?"

One day it is going to happen between you and me – the whole ship, the whole ship you call samsara, the world. What I am doing is just sabotaging.

"It seems to me that you are nothing but a trickster." Perfectly true. "It also seems to me that I have to cooperate with your tricks for my own good." Perfectly true. There is no way to escape. "Is this possible?" It is already happening. "Is not this all a bit crazy?" It is absolutely crazy. But you are crazy and only a crazy master can help you.

One day you will realize the tremendous compassion of all those who have become awakened to the truth. It is their compassion that they go on devising methods for you, knowing well that in fact no method is needed. But, looking at you, it seems almost impossible that you will be able to come out of your dreams and illusions without methods. You have gone too far.

If you are left alone, you will go on farther and farther away because one thing leads to another; it is a chain thing. If you understand, then there is no need for any device. If you understand, in that very moment you have already arrived because you had never departed.

Higgins lived in Staten Island, New York and worked in Manhattan. He had to take the ferryboat home every night. One evening he got down to the ferry and found there was a wait for the next boat, so he decided to stop at a nearby bar. Before long, Higgins was feeling no pain.

When he got back to the ferry slip, the ferryboat was just eight feet from the dock. Higgins, afraid of missing this one and being late for dinner, took a running leap and landed right on the deck of the boat.

"How did you like that jump buddy?" said Higgins to a deckhand.

"It was great," said the sailor. "But why didn't you wait. We were just pulling in."

That's what one day you are going to realize. That in fact there was no need to jump. But right now it is difficult and that's why I go on telling you, "Jump! Take a quantum leap!" Knowing well the boat is just coming in. But you are drunk, you are almost unconscious. You don't know what is going and what is coming. You don't know what is in and what is out. Everything is mixed, is in a chaos and a confusion in you. Hence religions are needed.

If some day man becomes healthy, silent, aware, religions will disappear from the world, they will not be needed. Religions don't show that the world is in a good shape, they simply show that the world is in a very bad shape. If in your house a doctor is needed every day, then things are not going well. When for years the doctor is not needed, then things are going well.

A Hindu monk came to see me once, and he said that this

country – as Hindus always go on claiming that this country is the most religious country in the world. I asked him, "Why? What is the evidence for it?"

He said, "Evidence, you ask me? It is so clear cut. All the twenty-four *tirthankaras* of the Jainas were born here, twenty-four buddhas were born here, all the avatars of Hindus were born here. God has come to this earth so many times. Is it not a proof that this country is religious?"

I said, "This is simply a proof that this country must be very anti-God. Otherwise what is the need of God coming here so many times? Krishna himself in the Gita says, I told him that whenever there will be darkness, and whenever there will be evil in the world, he will come. What does it show? – that whenever he comes, things are wrong. And he has been coming to India so many times. That simply shows that India must be in a very irreligious state, very ill. The doctor has to come again and again."

In a healthy world religion will disappear. Just as in a healthy world psychoanalysis will disappear. If people are really happy, then all methods to make them happy will be irrelevant. Then priests and temples and churches will not be needed. Then by and by people will start forgetting about Jesus, Buddha, Christ, Krishna. There will be no need.

That's what Lao Tzu says: "When in the ancient days people were really religious, nobody had ever heard of religion." True. Says Lao Tzu, "In the ancient days, when people were simple, nobody had ever heard about saints because everybody was a saint, a saintly soul. When people became ill, evil, then saints became important in contrast."

Maybe it was so in the beginning, or maybe it was not so. At least this much we can hope – that in the end this must be so. A day must come when all devices are useless. For humanity maybe it will take a long time to come, but for you, individually it can come any moment. This moment is as much open for its coming as any other moment.

Just look at the fact that you go on creating illusions around you. Don't create those illusions and then no devices are needed, no yoga is needed, no discipline is needed, no character is needed. Just don't create your illusions. Then all medicinal arrangements become futile. You can go and throw all of them on the junkyard. Then you are simply a being, in tune with the whole.

> *Osho,*
> *Before taking sannyas, I was on the verge of committing suicide. Now I am too happy to say, but still I am searching for something I don't know. Osho, after all, what do I want? Please say something.*

Sannyas is a real suicide. You say, "Before taking sannyas, I was on the verge of committing suicide." You have committed it, and you have committed it on a deeper plane. Destroying the body would not have helped much. You would have been born again in a similar pattern of body because your mind would have remained the same.

By committing suicide, by jumping into a river, or in the ocean, or from a hilltop, you can destroy the physical part of you. But your physical part is not basic; your mental part is the base. Your mental part carries the blueprint for the physical. Your mind will jump into another womb and will start gathering another physical part. It will be born again. Suicide is useless. I am not against suicide because it is a crime, I am against suicide because it is futile, it is foolish, it is stupid.

If you really want to commit suicide, then become a sannyasin. Then you will be destroying the mind, the deep blueprint for your future lives. That's what Buddha said, "become a *srotapanna*, enter the stream." Rather than jumping from the cliff, rather than jumping into the ocean and dying a physical death, jump into a buddha and die a spiritual death. That's what sannyas is all about: dying in me. It is carrying your own cross.

If you are really fed up with your life, then destroy the very possibility of its being repeated again and again. Become a *srotapanna*. Then you will become a *skridagamin*; once more you will come. Then you will become an *anagamin*; no more you will come.

The *anagamin* is the one who has committed real suicide. He never comes back. He is really finished with the world, he has closed his accounts with the world. He has now far better ways of being. He does not come into this mess, he does not descend into this darkness, this ugly hell. He goes on soaring higher and higher towards the very source of light.

You say, "Before taking sannyas, I was on the verge of committing suicide." In fact only a person who is on the verge of suicide can be a real sannyasin. When you are really fed up with life, bored with it, looking at its ridiculous absurdity, the vicious circle moving round and round and leading nowhere. When you understand that nothing is happening in it and you are unnecessarily suffering – you are becoming more and more dark, heavy, weighty, you are losing wings; you are becoming more and more like a dead thing. When you see this – that life is killing you, not making you really alive – then two doors open: suicide or sannyas.

Let me tell you, in the East few people commit suicide. In the West, many more people commit suicide. The eastern people think that they are less suicidal, that's why it is so. Western psychologists think that the western mind is more suicidal, that's why it is so. Neither what the eastern people say, nor what western psychoanalysts say is the truth.

The truth is that in the West, sannyas has disappeared, so whenever one is fed up with life only one alternative is available – suicide. In the East sannyas is as much an alternative as suicide. If you count sannyasins and the persons who commit suicide in the East, then the number will be exactly the same. There will be no difference.

Sannyas is a transformation of life. Suicide is an escape from life. In both the ways you go beyond. In both the ways you get rid of this so-called life. But by suicide it is only a temporary thing: again you will be back, again and again you will be back.

With sannyas the door opens. You may not come back, or even if you come, you will come in a better way, more aware. Even if you come, you will come to learn something, to mature. In the East, the whole concept of growth is to grow out of life, to grow beyond life.

Sannyas is creative, suicide is destructive. In suicide, you are simply doing something desperate. In sannyas, you are doing something very deliberate to transform your ways, your very style of life. In fact it is not with life that you are fed up, it is with your way of life. It is not really with life that you are fed up because in fact you don't know what life is, but with your pattern of life: the narrowing that you have made your life, the tunnel-like phenomenon that you have created out of your life, the imprisonment that you created out of your life.

You don't know what life is, you know only a tunnel thing: dark, dirty, confining, crushing, crippling, paralyzing, and in the end you see there is nothing but death. So what is the point of being tortured? Why not commit it today? If it is going to happen tomorrow, then why wait for tomorrow? That is the logic of the suicide.

In fact people who commit suicide are more intelligent than those who never think about it. Only idiots never commit suicide, only idiots are never bored, only idiots never become aware of the futility of their life.

Intelligent people are bound to think sometimes, "What is the point of it all? Why am I going, for what? Nothing has happened, nothing seems to happen, nothing can be hoped out of it – the whole thing seems to be hopeless. Then why go on?" The suicidal idea arises because of intelligence. So I say, idiots never think about suicide; intelligent people think about suicide.

But those who are really intelligent, not moderately intelligent but at the very peak of their intelligence, they think of sannyas. Because they think, "This whole exists. If I am not able to find the meaning of it, maybe it is my style that is not allowing me to find the meaning of it. If I am not capable of being happy, maybe somewhere I have put conditions which don't allow me to be happy. Maybe there is another way to live." That "another way to live," that alternative way to live, is what sannyas is.

"Can't I live non-ambitiously? Ambitiously I have lived and found misery comes, grows more, becomes intense – suffering and suffering and suffering. I have tried ambition, now let me try non-ambition. Let me have a one-hundred-and-eighty-degree turn. Let me be converted." Conversion means a one-hundred-and-eighty-degree turn, about turn.

"Greed I have tried, now I will try no-greed. Possessiveness I have tried, now I will try sharing. Mind I have tried, now I will try no-mind, meditation. Sex I have tried, now I will try love, compassion. I have lived in an unnatural way, the way the society has forced on me; now let me try the natural way – the way of Tao, the way of *dhamma*, the way of *rit*. I have lived in conflict, struggle, fighting; now let me try surrender, now let me try let-go. I have been trying to go upstream, now let me try going downstream, with the stream, wherever it leads." This is what sannyas is.

So, let me repeat. The most stupid person never thinks about suicide. Of course, he cannot even dream about sannyas. He has not that much intelligence to look into the futility of so-called life. In the middle are those intelligent people who become aware that life is futile, but who are not intelligent enough to become aware that maybe it is just my style, not life itself. They think of suicide and they sometimes commit suicide.

Then there are the pinnacles of intelligence: a Buddha, a Christ, a Lao Tzu, a Zarathustra; who immediately see the point, "I am missing because my ways are wrong." And they change their ways, they change their life pattern radically. That radical transformation is sannyas.

I would like to say to you that you have really committed suicide, and in a better way, in a very intelligent way, the way it should be committed. You have become a sannyasin.

"Now I am too happy to say, but still I am searching for something I don't know." It happens. When you are a worldly man, you know what you are searching for: you are searching money, better sex objects, power, prestige – things are clear. You have been trained for them, you have been educated for them, you have been conditioned for them. Your mind knows what you are seeking. Your mind computer has been fed goals.

When you become a sannyasin, you are really in a chaos for a few days because the old goals become meaningless and the new goal is not clear. In fact, sannyas is not going to give you a new goal. Once all the old goals disappear, suddenly you will see there is no goal.

One has to live life without any goal; then one lives tremendously beautifully because to live life with a goal means to live in the future. Then the stonecutter wants to become the rich man, the rich man wants to become the emperor, the emperor wants to become the sun, and the sun wants to become the cloud, and the cloud wants to become the rock, and the rock again wants to become the stonecutter. Then it is a wheel.

When you don't want to become anybody – when you simply accept whosoever you are, when you drop all goals, all future orientations, all ends; you drop time, you drop desire, you drop mind – then suddenly you are here and the whole universe is available, this great energy surrounding you, dancing around you, inviting you to participate with it.

Sannyas is not a goal. Sannyas is an understanding that goals don't exist.

The universe is always fulfilled. Not that the fulfillment has to happen somewhere else, it is already happening. That's why you will feel for a few days, "After all, what do I want?" Old wants have disappeared and you have not yet become grounded into a no-wanting attitude.

There is a Zen story...

There was once a red-haired man who had no eyes and no ears. He also had no hair, so he was called red-haired only in a manner of speaking. One has to call him something.

He was not able to talk because he did not have a mouth. He had no nose either. He did not even have any arms or legs. He also did not have a stomach, and he did not have a back. And he did not have a spine, and he also did not have any other insides. He did not have anything in fact, so it is hard to understand who we are talking about. So we had better not talk about him any more.

By and by... First you call him the red-haired man because one has to call him something.

When you are moving in a worldly wheel, I invite you, I say, "What are you doing there, are you not going to try God?" You become greedy about God. You say, "Okay. Here I am getting nothing, maybe there is something in God." You jump out of the wheel, then you ask me, "What about God?"

I say, "In fact nobody knows anything about him, whether he existed or not. It is just a manner of saying." We call him the red-haired man because one has to call him something, mm?

Then by and by you go along with me, and by and by the story is revealed to you: "There was once a red-haired man who had no eyes and no ears. He also had no hair, so he was called red-haired only in a manner of speaking. He was not able to talk because he did not have a mouth. He had no nose either. He did not even have any arms or legs..."

By and by, the more you try to understand me, I become more and more truthful. The more I see that now you are getting in tune with me, there is no need to lie too much. "He did not even have any arms or legs. He also did not have a stomach, and he did not have a back..."

And when I see that you are not disturbed, you are listening to the story well up to now, then I say, "...and he didn't have a spine." I have to move very cautiously because you can become afraid and go back to your wheel. "And he also did not have any insides..."

When I see that up to now you have come, and of course you feel a little puzzled, but now the truth can be said: "He didn't have anything. So it is hard to understand who we are talking about. So we had better not talk about him any more." About whom? – about the red-haired man.

Hinduism, Christianity, Judaism, they start the story – they talk about the red-haired man – and Buddha ends it: there is nobody, not even you. He says, first drop ambition, drop desires. Don't think you are the body, don't think you are the mind; then don't think you are the self. Then in fact we should not talk about you because you are not.

By and by we go on eliminating. First we say, drop worldly goals because it will be too much to tell you to drop all goals, you will not understand. You can understand that worldly goals should be dropped because you have suffered much and nothing has come out of it, you are frustrated. You say, "Okay. I was also thinking to drop it." And you say, "Good, so I will change. I will drop the worldly goals. Now I will look for God, heaven and paradise." And I go on laughing inside me. I say, "Okay, first drop these, then we will see."

Once you have dropped those, then by and by I will persuade you to drop God, self, nirvana, *moksha* – because when every goal is dropped, only then you are in tune. The goal is a jarring note. The goal simply says you are missing. The goal says there is some condition which has to be fulfilled, only then can you become happy.

When all goals disappear and life is not looked on as a desire project, when life is not thought of as a work and becomes play, *leela*, then – then you are at home, then you have arrived.

Osho,
If you take gossiping out of social interaction, it seems little is left except uncomfortable silences. So what is socializing about?

Of course the question is from a woman. The woman exists with gossip. Man has many more things to do, gossiping is not all. Woman has nothing else to do, she has only gossiping.

It is really difficult to think, conceive of what is left if all gossiping is dropped. The questioner is right. She says "then only uncomfortable silences are left."

Why do you feel uncomfortable about silence? Why is it so embarrassing? It is true, her insight is right. You have always felt it, everybody knows it. If you sit with somebody and you don't have anything to say, then one starts feeling embarrassed. One finds something to talk about. So people talk about weather, climate – useless. They both know that it is raining outside, so what is the point? Or it is a beautiful morning, so what is the point?

I have heard…

Mulla Nasruddin was traveling together with a friend for two days in a train without even a word passing between them. On the third day the friend at length ventured to remark that it was a fine morning.

"And who said it was not?" replied the Mulla. "And who said it was not?"

Silence is embarrassing because we have completely forgotten the dimension of silence. Whenever we are silent it seems empty. It is not full of radiance, presence. When we are talking there is something. When we are not talking, it is only absence of talk. Our silence is just absence of talk, that's why it is embarrassing, empty, not even a word to fill it. One feels very poor, stuck. But if you really know how to be silent, then it will not be embarrassing or uncomfortable.

Sometimes it happens in your life also. Those moments are rare and one tends to forget them because they don't fit with your main pattern. Sometimes sitting with a friend there is no talk, you just enjoy each other's presence. It is not embarrassing, it is very fulfilling. It is not uncomfortable, in fact to talk in those moments will be uncomfortable. It will disturb the music that is flowing between the two. It will be an interference, a distraction if you talk. You love a woman and you are sitting holding each other's hands on the beach or on the river or looking at the stars...

Everybody must have come to a few moments when silence is communicative, when it is expressive of your heart – more than any word. When something transpires between two hearts, when some energy is transferred from one polarity to the other: from yin to yang, from yang to yin; when suddenly you feel a link which is not verbal, a link which is existential; when suddenly you feel that you have become one energy throbbing with one rhythm breathing together, being together, merging and melting into each other – then silence is not uncomfortable. It is tremendously warm, it is not cold. You don't miss talk; in fact, if somebody starts talking you will feel offended, it will be sacrilege.

But we have lost that dimension. We don't know how to be silent, we only know how to talk. We have been trained for talking: parents, schools, colleges, universities – they all train you for talking. And people who can talk skillfully become very important. In fact, talking seems to be the greatest art.

If you cannot talk you will never become a part of the society. If you cannot talk well you will never become famous in any way. Poets, priests, politicians, all people who become important, significant, are really good talkers. The society knows only one way to communicate and that is talk. And the other way is completely lost.

I am not against talking. How can I be? That would be against myself. I am not against talking, but if you don't know the dimension of silence then your talk will be empty, then your talk will be just dead words. Then your words will be just like a freight train carrying dead wood.

If you know the dimension of silence, then your words become alive because something of your silence can be carried by the words. When your words carry something of your innermost silence, are soaked in it, when some fragrance of that silence goes with the words towards you, only then words are meaningful, significant. Otherwise they are meaningless, otherwise they are just gibberish.

I am in favor of both. I am not telling you to become dumb and not talk to anybody. I am telling you, sometimes be so silent that you have something to say. Be so silent that you experience something which can be conveyed. Otherwise what will you convey? Be silent, enjoy silence, and feel silence as presence, not as absence.

Silence is presence of your awareness, your being. Fill your silence with your own presence, radiance, and feel it as a positive phenomenon; don't look at it just as absence of words. It is not absence. If you can be positively silent, if you can enjoy it, if you can rejoice it, you will be tremendously benefited. And not only you, others who come in contact with you, they will also be tremendously benefited. Then sometimes be silent with them, when it is the season to be silent.

There are moments when talking is dangerous, when silence is golden. There are moments when talking is beautiful: it is poetry, it is expression. But remember always, first you must have something to express, and to have that you will need silence. Silence gives you the poetry; words can relate it to others.

In your ordinary life find a few extraordinary moments of silence. Sitting under the tree on the bank of the river, or just sitting in your room doing nothing – just sitting, feeling silence, cherishing it, tasting it, being nourished by it, being so overflowingly silent that if somebody passes by with his head full of words, even he will have a breeze of silence – that's what happens when you sit near a master. His silence starts being infectious. It comes like a breeze, dances around you, soothes you, cools you, warms you, makes you more alive, makes you feel loved, cared for as if a mother is just singing a lullaby.

In the close affinity of a master, in *satsang*, that is the real thing – that something starts happening between two energies. The master starts falling into you like a waterfall, tremendously silent. And his silence makes you silent. For the first time you have a few glimpses of what silence is. Then you have something to say, something to sing about, something to dance about.

I am not against talking, but your talking should not be empty. I am not even against gossiping. I myself gossip so much. But let your gossiping also be creative, not destructive. Let your gossiping also have a quality of poetry and creativity in it. Gossip about God – what are gospels? Gossip about God, gossip about truth, gossip about beauty, gossip about grace, grandeur. Gossip about this wonder that surrounds you. Gossip about the unknown.

What do you do with your gossiping? You are very destructive. People gossip only as a means to destroy others, to hurt others. Don't be aggressive, then nothing is wrong in gossiping.

All the parables of Jesus are gossips, and all the stories of Mahavira and Buddha are gossips. All the Puranas of the Hindus are tremendously beautiful gossips. It is impossible to improve upon them, they have done the last, the ultimate thing in gossiping.

The West cannot understand it. They think these are just myths, stories, they are not true. That is not the point. Who said they are true? They are truer than truth. They are not just true. They are truth told in beautiful language so that people who cannot understand truth, even they can understand it. They are cosmic gossips. They are indicators of something beyond the known, beyond the word, beyond the expressed. They are fingers raised towards the ineffable.

"If you take gossiping out of social interaction, it seems little is left except uncomfortable silences." Right now it will be so because your social interacting is nothing but gossiping, criticizing, slandering. Your social interaction is nothing but subtle violence. If it is left, you don't know how to be silent. It will be uncomfortable, it will be embarrassing.

First learn how to be silent. Learn it with trees and rocks, they are silent and they are not uncomfortable at all. Learn it from the stars, they are silent, not embarrassed at all. Learn what positive silence is. Be meditative, it will come to you.

And then by and by stop destructive gossiping. Gossip about something beautiful. Gossip something about the really significant. Let your gossiping also be a sort of communication for that which cannot be communicated. And of course you will never feel embarrassed, and your social interaction will not be just an impotent gesture; it will be real communication.

I have heard...

Mulla Nasruddin's wife told him that he must stop exaggerating about "the one that got away," and said that next time he did it in company she would cough to remind him.

Some friends called on them shortly afterwards and Nasruddin, after behaving himself for a while, suddenly said, "I had this fish on my line last week. It must have been six feet long." Just here his wife coughed loudly. "And," continued Nasruddin, "half an inch wide."

I'm not saying to change it so abruptly. Go slowly. I'm not saying to be so abruptly dramatic. First learn silence, then learn what beautiful gossiping is. Then start practicing it. Not only you will be benefited by it, others will also be benefited by it.

All beautiful poetry is gossiping. All beautiful story telling is gossiping. Tell beautiful stories, invent beautiful stories, be a little creative. And that very thing will change your relationship with others. Your relationship will not just be a formality, it will become really intimate.

Osho,
What did we do to deserve you as our guru, our master?

I don't know anything about you, but I must have done terrible karma to deserve you!

Enough for today.

3

IN ACCORD WITH THE WAY

A monk asked the Buddha:
Under what conditions is it possible to come to the knowledge of the past and to understand the most supreme way?
The Buddha said:
Those who are pure in heart and single in purpose are able to understand the most supreme way. It is like polishing a mirror which becomes bright when the dust is removed. Remove your passions and have no hankering and the past will be revealed unto you.
A monk asked the Buddha:
What is good and what is great?
The Buddha answered:
Good is to practice the way and to follow the truth. Great is the heart that is in accord with the way.

Life in itself is not the goal. The goal surpasses life. The life is just an opportunity to realize the goal. The goal is hidden deep in life, you cannot find it on the surface. You will have to penetrate to the very center. Life is like a seed, in itself it is not enough. You will have to work hard so the seed sprouts, becomes a tree and comes to bloom.

This is one of the most fundamental things to remember: that man has to surpass himself, that life has to transcend itself. If you don't understand this then you will be lost in the means and you will forget the end. That's what happens ordinarily: we become too attached with life and we forget that life was just an opportunity to understand something which is deeper than life, higher than life; superior, far superior than life.

If you get too obsessed with life itself, it is as if somebody was sent to the university and he became too attached with the university and he could not leave it, and he could not even conceive of leaving it. The university is there just to educate you for something greater. The university is to prepare you for the universe, that's why we call it the university. It itself is not the universe, just a preparation.

In the East, life is just like a university, a discipline, a training for something far beyond it. If you become too attached to life, then you will be coming back again and again every year to the university. Then it is futile, pointless. A university is to get ready, a university has to be renounced one day. It is just a preparation and if the preparation becomes endless, then it becomes a burden.

That is what has happened to many people. They take life as the goal; then they go on preparing, they go on preparing endlessly. They never go on the journey, they simply prepare for the journey. And if their life becomes an impotent gesture, no wonder; it is natural, it has to be so.

Just think about yourself always consulting timetables, always getting ready to leave, always inquiring from the tourist office, and never leaving, never going anywhere. You will go mad.

Nothing is wrong with life itself, but if your attitude is this – that life is an end unto itself – then you will be in trouble. Then your whole life will become meaningless. The meaning is there, but the meaning is transcendental to it. The meaning is there, but you will have to penetrate to that core where it is revealed.

To think of life as the goal is to remain on the periphery. That periphery Buddha calls the wheel. The symbol of the wheel is very significant and has to be understood. The periphery, Buddha calls the wheel; it goes on moving. You can watch a bullock cart moving, the wheels move. They move on some-thing which is unmoving: the center remains unmoving, the hub remains unmoving. On an unmoving hub, the wheel goes on moving.

If you only look at the wheel, you will be looking at the temporal. If you become capable of looking at the hub, you will be able to penetrate the eternal. If you only look at the periphery, you will be watching the accidental. If you become capable of reaching to the center, to the hub, you will be able to know the essential. And unless you come to know the essential, you will be repeating the same thing again and again and again.

The world is called the wheel because things go on repeating themselves again and again, and you by and by become repetitive. And the more you repeat yourself, the more you are bored. The more you are bored, the more dull and stupid you become. You lose intelligence, you lose freshness, you lose awareness. You become a robot, a mechanical thing.

Watch people around you. They have become robots. They just go on doing the same thing again and again. Every morning, every evening, they go on moving in the same rut, and of course they look dead. There is no spark in their eyes, you cannot find any ray of light.

Buddha calls this continuous repetition of the wheel, samsara. To get out of it, to get out of this rut, is nirvana.

Before we enter the sutra, a few things have to be understood. Life is the game of the games, the ultimate game. It has tremendous meaning in it if you take it as a game and you don't become serious about it. If you remain simple, innocent, the game is going to impart many things to you. Sometimes you were a tiger, and sometimes you were a rock, and sometimes you became a tree, and sometimes you become a man; sometimes you were an ant, and sometimes an elephant: Buddha says all these are games. You have been playing a thousand and one games, to know life in every possible way. By playing game after game, the player may experience all the permutations of matter in evolution. That is the goal of life.

When you exist like a tree, you know life in one way. Nobody else can know it except the tree. The tree has its own vision. When clouds come in the sky and the sun shines and there is a rainbow, only the tree knows how to feel it. It has a perceptivity of its own. When the breeze passes by, the tree knows how to be showered in it. When a bird starts singing, only the tree knows, only the tree has ears for it – for its music, its melody. The tree has a way to know life its own way. Only a tree knows that way.

A tiger has another way of knowing life. He is playing another game. An ant is playing a totally different game. Millions of games. All these games are like classes in a university. You pass through each class, you learn something, then you move into another class. Man is the last point.

If you have learned all the lessons of life and the lesson of being a human being, then only will you become capable of moving into the very center of life. Then you will be able to know what God is, or what nirvana is.

All through these games you have been trying to approach God through many directions, in many ways, in many perceptivities. But the goal is the same: that everybody is trying to know what the truth is. What is the mystery of this life? Why are we here and who am I? And what is this that goes on existing?

There is only one way to learn it, and that is the way of existence. But if you just move from one class to another like a sleepwalker, a somnambulist, unconscious, dragged from one class to another, not moving deliberately and consciously, you will miss.

That's how many people arrive at the point of being human beings and they cannot see any God. That simply shows they have missed the lessons, they avoided the lessons. They were in the classes but they have not got the point. Otherwise every person who has arrived at the stage of being human must be religious.

Being human and being religious must become synonymous. They are not synonymous. Very rarely a few people are religious. By religious I don't mean a person who goes to the church every Sunday. By religious I don't mean a person who is Christian, Mohammedan, Hindu, Jaina, Buddhist. By religious I don't mean that you belong to a religious organization. When I say religious I mean a person who is aware that life is so full of transcendence that from everywhere life is overflowing into something bigger than life, that every step is leading you towards God, truth, nirvana, freedom; that whether you know it or not, you are moving towards the ultimate temple.

When a person starts feeling it in his very guts, then a person is religious. He may go to the church, he may not go to the church; that is irrelevant. He may call himself a Christian or a Mohammedan or a Hindu, that is irrelevant. He may not call. He may belong to any organization, he may not belong – but he belongs to God.

And when I say God, remember that by God I mean that which transcends. That is always ahead of you. You are always coming closer to it, approaching closer and closer and closer, but it always remains ahead of you.

God is that omega point which always remains the goal. You come close to it but you can never possess it. It cannot ever be in your hands. You can drop yourself completely in it, you can merge yourself in it, but still you will know that much remains to be known. In fact the more you know, the more you feel that much remains to be known. The more you know, the more you become humble. The mystery: infinite, ineffable, cannot be exhausted. That inexhaustible source, that transcendental source, is what I mean by God. And by calling a person religious, I mean one who has become alert about the transcendental.

When you are alert about the transcendental, your life has a beautiful charm, a grace – then your life has energy, intelligence; then your life has a sharpness, a creativity; then your life has a holy aura to it. By becoming aware of the transcendental you become part of the transcendental. It has penetrated in your awareness. A ray of light has entered into the dark night of your soul. You are no longer alone, and you are no longer a stranger in existence. You are deeply rooted in it. This is your home.

A religious person is one who feels existence as his home. A religious person is one who feels existence constantly evolving and evolving, going higher and higher, towards that ultimate omega point where you disappear, where all limitations disappear and only infinity is left, only eternity is left.

So this game of life has to be played very skillfully. Buddha calls skill, *upaya*. It is one of his most beautiful words. He says, "be skillful." If you are not skillful you will miss much that is valuable. "Be skillful" means be aware. Just don't go on dragging yourself half asleep, half awake. Shake yourself into awareness. Bring more awareness into each act of your life, into each step of your being. Then only, with open eyes, you start seeing something which cannot ordinarily be seen when you are asleep, when you are unconscious. Shake all the dust from the eyes.

Be skillful and live life consciously. Otherwise life becomes boring. You feel it. You know how it feels. Sooner or later everything feels boring, one is bored to death. One goes on living because one is not courageous enough to commit suicide. One goes on living just in the hope that sooner or later one will die – the death is coming.

Mulla Nasruddin was going on a world tour and he was traveling in a ship for the first time. He was very seasick. The captain came to him and said, "Don't be worried, Nasruddin, I have been working as a captain for twenty years and I have never seen any man die from seasickness. Don't be worried."

Mulla said, "My god! That was my only hope, that I will die. You have taken even that hope!"

People are living just in the hope that some day or other they are going to die. So they go on saying to themselves, "Don't lose heart, death is coming."

If you are waiting for death, if you are so bored, then there is no possibility for any encounter with God. The encounter can only happen in radiance, in sharpness, in awareness.

Why do we get bored? The Buddhist explanation is of tremendous import. Buddha says you have done the same things not only in this life, you have been doing them for millions of lives, hence boredom. You may not remember them, but deep down the memory is there. Nothing is lost as far as memory is concerned.

There is a reservoir of memory. Buddha calls it *alaya vigyan*, reservoir of memory. It is exactly what Jung calls the collective unconscious. You carry it. The body changes, the identity changes, but the bundle of memories goes on jumping from one life to another. And it goes on accumulating, gathering. It goes on becoming bigger and bigger.

Nothing is lost as far as memory record is concerned. If you look into yourself, you have the whole record of existence in you because you have been here from the very beginning, if there was any beginning. You have always been here. You are an intrinsic part of this existence. All that has happened to existence has happened to you also, and you carry the record.

You may not know it, but you have loved millions of times. Again falling in love – it is nothing new, it is a very old story. You have done all the things that you are doing: you have been ambitious, you have been greedy, you accumulated wealth, you became very famous, you had prestige and power. This has happened many, many times, millions of times. And you carry deep down in the unconscious the reservoir of memories, and whatsoever you are doing looks futile, pointless, meaningless.

I have heard...

A newspaper reporter was interviewing Mulla Nasruddin on his hundredth birthday. "If you had your life to live over," he asked, "do you think you would make the same mistakes over again?"

"Certainly," said the old Mulla, "but I would start a lot sooner. I would start a lot sooner..."

This is what is happening out of mistakes. You only learn how to start them sooner, you don't learn how to drop them. You only learn how to start them sooner and how to do them more efficiently next time.

Buddha says if you can penetrate this reservoir of memories then you will be really fed up. Then you will see "I have been doing the same thing again and again." And then in that state of awareness, you will start doing something new for the first time.

And that will bring a thrill, a fresh air into your being.

There are two time concepts in the world. In the West the linear time concept has been prevalent. Christians, Jews, Mohammedans; they are all offshoots of one Judaic concept of life. They have believed in the linear concept of time; that time is moving in a line. The Eastern concept – the Hindu, the Buddhist, the Jaina concept – is different. It is circular, time is moving in a circle.

If time is moving in a line, then things are not repeated again. The line goes on moving, it never comes back to meet and move on the same old track again. If time is thought to be circular, then everything is being repeated. And the eastern time concept seems to be truer because every movement is circular.

Just watch all the movements. The seasons moving around the year are circular: again comes the summer, again, again; in the same way it moves. The earth moves in a circle, the sun moves in a circle, the stars move in a circle. And now Albert Einstein has suggested that the whole universe is also moving in a circle. Not only that, Einstein introduced a very strange concept to the physics, and that is the concept of circular space. The whole space is circular.

The East has always thought that the circle is the natural way of things. Things move in a circle and by and by they become circular. All movement is circular. Then time also has to be circular because time is nothing but pure movement. If you think about time as circular then the whole world view changes. Your whole life is also circular according to the eastern way of seeing.

A child is born: birth is the beginning of a circle, death is the end of the circle. The old man in his last moments again becomes as helpless as a child. And if things have gone rightly, he will become as innocent as a child. Then the circle is complete. Then his life was a round-shaped life. Then his life will have a grace. If the circle is not complete, then the life will have something missing in it. Then there will be holes in his life, and his life will be tense. It will not be round, graceful.

Buddha says that in each life the wheel moves once. The circle becomes complete. Another life, the wheel moves again. The spokes are the same: again childhood, again youth, again old age; the same desires, the same passions, the same lust, the same rushing, the same ambition, the same struggle, conflict, the same aggression, the same ego, and again the same frustration, the same misery. This goes on and on and on.

If you can penetrate into your deepest memories, then you will be able to see that you are not doing anything new here. That's why in the East they say there is nothing new under the sun. Everything has been done millions of times.

So it became a very methodological thing in Buddhism and Jainism for every seeker to penetrate into his past memories. It became a necessary thing because Buddha says unless you can see the whole nonsense of repetition, you will continue to repeat.

Just think about it. If you come across the whole record and you see that for millions of times you have been falling in love, and every time you were miserable – now it is time enough to understand, now don't be foolish again. If you see that for millions of times you were born and you died again, and every birth brings death, then now what is the point in clinging to life. Then renounce it. If you see that every time you expected, you were frustrated, your expectations were never fulfilled, then what is the point now? Now drop expecting.

This became a basic meditation, to go into one's past memories. If you look in even one life, you will see constant repetition. Even in very old age, you go on being the same way. It simply shows that you have not learned anything in life. Everybody passes through experiences, but that is not necessarily learning.

There is a difference between passing through life and learning. Learning means you go on looking at your experiences. You keep a record of the experiences, you observe your experiences, and you gather certain wisdom through them. You were angry and you did something foolish. Again you are angry and you do something foolish. Again you are angry, but you never take account of all your angers, and you never look at the mechanicalness of it, and you don't learn a lesson out of it. Then you experienced, but you have not learned anything. If you simply experience, you become old. If you learn, you become wise.

All old people are not wise. Wisdom has nothing to do with old age. A real man of understanding can become wise at any time – can even become wise as a child. If you have a penetrating understanding, even a single experience of anger and you will be finished with it. It is so ugly. A single experience of greed and you will be finished with it. It is so poisonous.

I have heard...

"I am leaving home!" shouted Mahamud to his father, Mulla Nasruddin. "I want wine, women, adventures!" His old man got up out of his chair.

"Don't try to stop me!" shouted Mahamud at him.

"Who is trying to stop you?" exclaimed old Mulla. "I am coming with you."

The same foolishness continues: young and old, educated, uneducated, poor, rich – all seem to be in the same boat. They don't seem to learn. If you learn, a totally different vision arises in your life.

I have heard...

It was in the early barnstorming days of aviation, and the old fellow had finally worked up enough nerve to take a flight on a plane. When the rickety plane landed, the old fellow crawled out and said "Sir, I want to thank you for both of those rides."

"What are you talking about?" asked the pilot. "You only had one ride."

"No," replied the passenger, "I had two rides – my first and my last."

If you understand a thing, then it is your first and last. Then you have had enough of it. Then it is not one ride, it is two rides.

This sutra today consists of a question from a monk.

> *A monk asked the Buddha:*
> *Under what conditions is it possible to come to the knowledge of the past and to understand the most supreme way?*

Under what conditions is it possible to come to the knowledge of the past... Buddha insisted very much, he said, first move towards the past, first go backwards because that is where you have lived for millennia. Just look what you have been doing there, what has been your experience up to now? Go into it, gather some lessons out of it. Otherwise you will tend to commit the same mistakes again and again.

Ordinarily, there is a natural mechanism which does not allow you to remember it. When a person dies and is reborn again, there comes a gap between his past life and the new life, a layer of oblivion, forgetfulness. It is natural because it will be very difficult for you to live if you continuously remember all that has happened before – not only at the end of life, but every day it is happening.

Millions of things happen in the day. You don't remember all. Not that they are not recorded, they are all recorded. It is unbelievable how the mind goes on recording minute, small things. Whatsoever happens around you – you may not be even aware that it is happening, but the mind goes on recording.

For example, you are listening to me, you are focused towards me, you are deep in concentration – but the train is passing by. You may not have heard it at all as far as your consciousness is concerned. If somebody asks you later on, "Was there a train going by, did you hear the noise?" You may say, "I don't remember because I was so concentrated." But your mind has recorded it. Even without your knowing it, mind goes on recording. If you are hypnotized and then asked, the mind will say everything.

If I ask you suddenly, "What happened on the first of January, 1970? What happened, can you remember?" You will simply be blank. That does not mean that nothing happened on that day. Something must have happened: a quarrel with your wife, or a headache. Twenty-four hours, the first of January, 1970 – something must have happened. Twenty-four hours cannot be vacant, otherwise you would have become a buddha. If you had remained empty for twenty-four hours, nothing happening, then nirvana would have happened. But you don't remember at all. You will shrug your shoulders that you don't remember.

Unless something very special happened on that day, that there was a car accident and you were almost killed, maybe you will remember it. Or some other type of accident – you got married –

you will remember it because there is no way to forget it now. You cannot forget and you cannot forgive yourself for it. It remains like a wound. But otherwise you are completely forgetful.

If you are hypnotized and you go in a deep trance and the hypnotist asks you, "Now go backwards, remember the first of January, 1970, and start relating what happened from the morning." You will relate such minute things: that the tea was cold and you didn't like it at all, that the night was not good and you had a nightmare. Things like this you will remember, minute details: that a dog was barking when you were taking your morning tea, that the cup had fallen from your hand and broken. Small things: that you were passing by the side of a tree and the tree had bloomed, and you will remember the smell; or that it had rained and there was a beautiful smell coming out of the earth. You may not only remember, you will relive it. It will be so clear.

Everything is recorded, but you have to forget it. Otherwise your mind will be so cluttered with unnecessary information that you will not be able to manage your life. So there is a natural mechanism which goes on sorting out inside you. Much work continues for twenty-four hours; a great sorting out goes on.

Whatsoever is unessential is thrown into the basement. You may never need it. Then the secondary things which are not so absolutely irrelevant, which you may need sometime but for which there is no urgency, they are put into the subconscious, within reach. If sometimes you need them, you can bring them back to consciousness. And very few things, which you will need every day, are left in the conscious.

For example, two plus two is four. This remains in the conscious. You will need it every day, every moment. That this is your wife and this is your husband remains in the conscious. If you go on forgetting every day, your name and your address and your phone number, it will create difficulties in life.

So everything, almost ninety-nine point nine percent falls into the basement and disappears forever. But it remains there underground. It can be recalled by specific methods. That's what they are doing in primal therapy: they are trying to recall all that has disappeared into the tunnels of the unconscious, to relive it. Once it is relived, you are freed from it.

What primal therapists are doing now, Buddha did twenty-five centuries ago, in a greater way, in a deeper way. Not only with this life, he has done it with the whole past.

You have to pass through the womb again in your memory. Then you have to go back to the death that happened in the last life. Then go on moving to the birth in the last life. And this way one goes on moving back and back and back. And the more you practice it, the more you become efficient in revealing all the mysteries that you have been carrying.

You are carrying a great record, and if you can relive it, you will be able to find out a few lessons from it. Those lessons will be of tremendous value. They will be liberating. They will liberate you from your past.

Once you are liberated from the past, you are liberated from the future also because then there is nothing left to project. Once you are liberated from your past lives, you are liberated from life itself. Then all desires to cling to life disappear. Then you don't want to be born again. Then you don't want to cling. Then you are not afraid of death. Then you don't want to be confined in any womb, in any body. You don't want to be embodied again. You would like absolute freedom.

This learning can be done in two ways – either while you are living, learn it. If you do that you will become a buddha, slowly. If you have not done that, then go backwards and relive your past experiences, your past lives.

The monk asked Buddha: *Under what conditions is it possible to come to the knowledge of the past and to understand the most supreme way?* First you have to understand your past lives, then only can you ask in a meaningful way how to get out of it: where is the exit, the way? When Buddha talks about the way, he means the way out. You have entered into life, now where is the way out?

I have heard...

Mike was going to Dublin for the first time and his friend Pat was giving him a few hints on what to do and where to go in the big city.

"What do I do when I go to the zoo?" asked Mike.

"Be careful about the zoo," advised Pat. "You will see fine animals if you follow the words 'To the Lions,' or 'To the Elephants,' but take no notice of 'To the Exit.' It is a fraud. It is outside I found myself when I went to look at it."

We have been doing that, we have been avoiding the door that takes us out of life. We have avoided it for so long that it has almost become invisible to us. We have ignored it so long that it almost does not exist for us. Even if we come across it, we will not be able to recognize it.

"To the Exit." These words have become very faint, they have almost disappeared. We know only the entrance into life, we don't know the exit.

Entrance of course we know because we have entered many times. Again and again we enter in the womb. Here you die and there you enter – almost within minutes, at the most within days. Here you die – even while dying, your mind starts planning where to enter. You have not yet died and you are planning already for the future: where to enter, how to enter. The fantasy has started working again.

Remember, it is your decision to enter in the womb, that's why you enter. You are not thrown in it, you choose it. As the entrance exists, so exists the exit.

The monk is asking:

> *Under what conditions is it possible to come to the knowledge of the past and to understand the most supreme way?*
> *The Buddha said:*
> *Those who are pure in heart and single in purpose are able to understand the most supreme way.*

Those who are pure in heart and single in purpose... People who live in their heads will find it very difficult to move into the past because the head is always in the future. Head is really a mechanism to plan for the future. It always moves ahead of you, it is like a radar.

You must have seen a radar in a plane. The radar moves ahead of the plane, that is its whole meaning: two hundred miles ahead, four hundred miles ahead. On the radar, the clouds that are four hundred miles ahead start appearing because within seconds the plane will be reaching there. So the pilot has to know beforehand because if he comes to know only when he has reached then it will be too late, the speed is so much.

Mind is a radar, your head is a radar system. It goes on groping in the future, it goes on planning for the future. It is never here in the present. And it has nothing to do with the past: it has already disappeared.

The whole interest of the head is in the future. Even if sometimes it looks at the past, it looks only to find few clues for the future. Even if it wants to look into the past, it is just as a help to prepare for the future. But the interest, the center of interest is the future.

Buddha says *...pure in heart and single in purpose...* People who are not in the head but in their heart, only they can enter into the past lives. Heart is very close to the unconscious basement, head is farthest away. Heart is closer to your navel center. Just somewhere near the navel is the corresponding point in the body with your unconscious. You have to come to the heart. Heart is midway between the head and the navel.

If you become more and more full of feeling, full of heart, you will become capable of knowing, of entering into that great story of your past lives. It is not only your biography, it is the biography of the whole universe. Because sometimes you were a tree, and still in your mind, deep down in the unconscious, you are carrying all those memories of being a tree. Someday you were a tiger, and someday you were a cat, and someday you were an elephant, and someday you were a woman, and someday you were a man, and millions of memories are there. The whole drama of life is there, in a very condensed form. If you go into it, it starts playing. You can again listen to those sounds.

That's why in hypnosis it is possible that if you hypnotize a person and tell him that now he has become a tiger, he becomes a tiger. You may have seen hypnotists doing it on the stage. They tell a man, "You have become a woman. Now walk!" And the man walks like a woman.

It is very difficult, but he manages. He may have never walked like a woman. Now, how does he suddenly start walking like a woman? It is very difficult because the woman has a totally different structure of the body. Because of the womb existing in her body, she has a different type of skeleton, she moves in a different way. Her movement is more round and more shapely. She cannot run fast. A man moves differently.

But under hypnotic influence, the man can walk like a woman, the woman can walk like a man. Not only that, a person who has never heard a single word of Arabic or Latin or Chinese, can be provoked under hypnosis to speak Chinese. And if the hypnosis is really deep, he may start speaking Chinese. It is a miracle, and the hypnotist has not been yet able to explain it. How to explain it? What happens?

The explanation is simple if you understand Buddha's hypothesis. Buddha says – and it is agreed with by all the eastern masters – that a man has been everything in his past life. You have been Chinese, you have been Japanese, you have been a German, you have been a Tibetan. So if somewhere deep in your memories the life that you lived as a Chinese person is still there, it can be provoked under hypnosis. It can be revealed. You can start speaking Chinese. You have never heard a single word of it, you don't know anything about it.

A human being is vast. It is not so confined as you think. You think you are a Hindu, or a Mohammedan, or a Christian, or an Indian, or Japanese, or Chinese. These are just boundaries on your conscious mind. On the unconscious you are infinite territory. You are all. Not only Hindu and Mohammedan and Christian, but even a tiger, a cat, a mouse, a lion, a tree, a rock, a cloud. You are vast. You are as vast as this universe.

Once you start entering, you will become tremendously aware that no limitation exists. All limitations are a sort of belief. You believe, that's why they are there. If you drop them they start disappearing.

Those who are pure in heart and single in purpose... People who are more heart oriented are single of purpose. They are not crooked, they are not cunning. The head is very cunning. The head is like a fox – very calculating and very subtle in its ways. If it wants something, it will never go direct. If it wants something, it will go zigzag. It will say something else, it will do something else. It would like to get something else. The head is very political, diplomatic.

You can watch it in yourself, how the head goes on deceiving, how the head goes on being political. It is never authentic. It cannot be. The heart is authentic. It knows no deception. It goes direct. The heart moves in straight lines, the head goes very zigzag.

Buddha says a person who wants to move into his past lives will need singleness of purpose. Crookedness won't do. One will have to follow straight, simple, direct ...*are able to understand the most supreme way*. These people who are simple, heart oriented, single, straight, direct, immediate – these people enter easily.

It has become more and more difficult since the days of Buddha to enter into past lives. It was so simple in Buddha's time. People were simple. Almost every sannyasin that was initiated by Buddha had to pass through past experiences, and the same was true with Mahavira.

There is a famous story. A prince took sannyas, was initiated by Mahavira. But he had lived almost always in comfort, in richness and now life was very hard with Mahavira. He had to move naked, to sleep on hard floors with no clothes. It was difficult.

The first night he started thinking of dropping out, this was not for him. There were so many mosquitoes – as there have always been in India, they seem to be the constant enemies of meditators. He could not meditate: so many mosquitoes; and he was naked and it was cold, and the place where he was sleeping was just in the middle, and hundreds of sannyasins were staying there. The whole night he could not sleep, people were coming and going. It was very crowded and he had never lived that way, that was not his way of life.

So in the night he started feeling that the next morning he would leave. It is said that in the middle of the night Mahavira came to him. He was surprised. He said, "Why have you come?"

Mahavira told him, "I have been watching you. I know your difficulty. But this has happened before. This is in fact the third time. You have been initiated twice before in your other lives and every time you have left."

He said, "What do you mean?" And Mahavira told him to do a certain technique of meditation that he calls *jati smaran* – the method to remember the past life. And he told him, "You just do this the whole night: sit in meditation and by the morning, whatsoever you decide..."

He went into his past life. It seems very simple, it must have been. People must have been simple. He went into his past life so easily. And by the morning he came, he was full of new light. He touched Mahavira's feet and he said, "I have decided to stay. Enough is enough. I looked into... Yes, you were right. How long can I go on repeating it again and again? It is insulting to take sannyas and leave it; it is below dignity. No, it is not good for a warrior like me to be afraid of mosquitoes, to be afraid of small inconveniences. But you were right. It had also happened twice before the same way. I was initiated and the first night I became disturbed, and the next morning I left. And I was going to do it again. I am so grateful to you that you reminded me. Otherwise I would have committed the same thing again, thinking that I am doing this for the first time."

All the sannyasins of Buddha and Mahavira had to pass through *jati smaran*, through the memory of all the past lives. Today it has become very difficult. Difficult because the head has become very heavy. Head is so heavy and energy is so much monopolized by the head, that it is not flowing in the heart at all. And the path towards past lives goes through the heart.

So if you want to remember past lives – and it is a great experience, very revealing and very liberating – you will have to live for a few months and years a very simple-hearted life, the life of feelings. Don't allow your thinking to dominate you, let feeling balance it. Don't allow logic to be dictatorial, let love decide. And by and by you will see the ways of the heart are very simple. And they are always single in purpose.

When the heart falls in love with somebody, then there is no problem, then your love object is the only love object for you. The moment the heart has fallen in love with a woman, then that is the only woman in the world. Then all the women have disappeared for you. Heart is single in purpose. But if the head had fallen in love – in fact it has not fallen in love, it simply pretends – then it is difficult. Then any woman that passes on the street attracts you, provokes you. Then any passing influence distracts you. Love knows single purpose because love is really of the heart.

If you are here with me through the heart, then it is a totally different relationship. Then it is going to be eternal. Then I can die, you can die, but the relationship cannot die.

But if it is only of the head, if you are simply convinced by what I am saying, not convinced by what I am – if you are only convinced by what I am saying, my logic, my argument – then this relationship is very temporary. Tomorrow you will be convinced by somebody else. Tomorrow somebody else can give you a better argument. Then it disappears.

Just two nights ago a young man from the West came, the husband of a sannyasin. I asked him, "Have you something to say to me? Why have you come to me?"

He said, "My wife told me to come to you."

I said, "Then it is not worth – because your wife told you to come to me so you have come. Your coming is very accidental. You have not come to me. You are simply obliging your wife. Then don't waste my time. You can oblige your wife in many other ways. This is no way."

Then he listened to me, I talked to his wife, and then in the end he said, "I am thinking to take sannyas."

I asked him, "Thinking? Then it will be difficult. Even if you are convinced by thinking, you may become a sannyasin outwardly; inwardly you will never be a sannyasin because it will be a head thing. Sannyas is not a logical conviction, it is a conversion in love."

But he couldn't understand. He said, "I will think about it."

If he comes, then too he will not be coming because he will come only because he is convinced, his head is convinced. He will not be convinced by me, he will be convinced only by his head, or maybe by his wife. The wife may persuade him. She persuaded him to come from Europe to here, so she can persuade him to change the clothes also. He may find some rationalizations, but the whole thing is pointless.

Unless you come through the heart, you don't come. Unless you reach me through the heart, you don't reach at all. Remember it: religion is something that happens in your source of feelings. It has nothing to do with your thinking.

...pure in heart and single in purpose are able to understand

the most supreme way. And once you have seen your past lives, suddenly you see the way out because so many times you have come in, again and again. The way to come in is really the way to come out also. You just have to move in the opposite direction.

The way is the same. The entrance and the exit are not two. The direction is different. When you enter into the house, you enter from the same door. You go out of the house, you get out of the same door. Just your direction is different.

So Buddha says, if you look into your past lives and you see again and again you are clinging with life, clinging with lust, ambition, ego, greed, jealousy, possessiveness – those are the ways you have been coming in again and again. Those are the ways to go out.

If greed is the way to come in, no-greed is the way to go out. If ego is the way to come in, no-ego is the way to go out. If lust, desire, passion, is the way to come in, then no-passion, no-desire, or desirelessness is the way to go out.

> *It is like polishing a mirror, which becomes bright when the dust is removed. Remove your passions and have no hankering and the past will be revealed unto you.*

So Buddha says three things. First, pure in heart, single of purpose. Third, he says that your consciousness is so cluttered that your mirror is not reflecting. Otherwise you have such a beautiful mirror with such a penetrating clarity that wherever you move your mirror of consciousness, you will be able to see everything that exists in that dimension.

If you move your mirror towards the past, the whole past in toto will be revealed to you. If you move your mirror towards the future, the whole future will be revealed to you. If you move your mirror to the present, the whole present will be revealed to you. Your consciousness is your key.

It is like polishing a mirror which becomes bright when the dust is removed. Too much dust from thinking, too much dust from impressions is covering your mirror. You have completely forgotten, the mirror looks like a brick. Clean it, wash it – that's what we are doing in meditations. It is just an effort to clean the mirror so it mirrors whatsoever is.

Remove your passions and have no hankering and the past will be revealed unto you.
A monk asked the Buddha:
What is good and what is great?
The Buddha answered:
Good is to practice the Way and to follow the truth. Great is the heart that is in accord with the Way.

Tremendously beautiful is his definition of the great. Understand it as deeply as possible. *Good is to practice the way*… First one has to know the way: no greed, no violence, no desire. In a way, all are negatives because whatsoever you know as positive has been the door to come in. Eliminate the positive and you will find the door to go out.

Good is to practice the way. Buddha says, knowing the way, recognizing the way in a clear, mirrorlike consciousness, the first thing that one has to do is to practice it. Just by recognizing, it won't help. Just by recognizing, it is not going to transform you. You have to walk, you have to discipline.

Good is to practice the way and to follow the truth. You have had a vision of truth. It is very far away like a distant star. Clear vision, but the distance is great. You have to follow, you have to move towards it slowly, gradually. You have to prepare for the journey. This Buddha calls good. This is what virtue is.

Great is the heart that is in accord with the way. When you are practicing, there is bound to be a little struggle. When you are disciplining yourself, there is bound to be a little conflict because the old habits will come in the way. You have always been greedy, now suddenly you decide not to be greedy. The whole past will come in the way, will distract you. Old habits will again and again possess you; again and again you will forget and waver. There is bound to be struggle.

So Buddha says it is good but not great. Great is the man whose struggle is gone, whose discipline also is gone; who is simply spontaneously in accord with the way is the great man. That's what Buddha calls great – in accord – he is so surrendered that it is now natural for him.

Not to desire has become as natural to him as it is natural

ordinarily to desire. Not to be ambitious has become as natural as it is natural for people to be ambitious. People are habitually in discord with the way, and he becomes naturally in accord.

Pythagoras calls this state *harmonia*. That is the right word – in accord, *harmonia*, in harmony. Lao Tzu calls this Tao. Buddha calls it *dhamma*.

To be in accord – as if you are not swimming, not struggling; you are completely relaxed and floating with the river. You are so one with the river that there is not even a slight distance between you and the river. You don't have any of your desires, you don't have any private goals. You go with the river to the ocean. A man of *harmonia*, accord, Tao, *dhamma*, is the most beautiful flowering in this world. He is the lotus flower of consciousness.

Great is the heart that is in accord with the way. But it cannot happen immediately. First you will have to discipline, and then you will have to drop discipline also. First you will have to make it a point to relax, and then you will have to forget relaxation also. First you will have to fight with your old ingrained habits, and once you have got over them, you have to drop new habits that you must have created in fighting with the old. First you have to meditate, then one day you have to drop meditation also.

Meditation is good, dropping meditation is great. Being a saint is good, being holy is great. Being a good person is good, but not great because a good person still carries a subtle fight with the bad. He is constantly conflicting with the devil, with the evil inside himself. He is not at ease, he cannot relax. He knows that if he relaxes, the old, the past, is big and powerful and he will be possessed, and he will be thrown off balance. He has to continuously balance himself. A good man, a saint, is still not in absolute accord. He is trying hard, he is trying his best, and it should be appreciated that he is trying, that's why Buddha calls him good.

So never be satisfied by good. Remember, to be great is the goal: to be so deeply in accord that you simply disappear and only the *dhamma* remains, only the Tao remains, only the nature remains. You are just a wave in the ocean and you don't exist separately. Your separate existence, your self, has to be dropped.

The bad man has a self. The self is created by fighting against the law, against nature. The bad man has a self. He creates the self by fighting against *dhamma*. Whatsoever is good, he fights against it and creates a self. The good man also has a self. He fights against his bad habits that he has created in the past. Because of fight, he also has a self.

The bad man has an ego, the good man has an ego. The bad man's ego is based on his mischief. The good man's ego is based on his virtue. But both have egos.

The great is one whose ego has disappeared, who is completely immersed, merged into the whole. To be so merged into the whole, to be in such a harmony is to be great. That is what is required. That is what has to be remembered continuously. Never lose sight of it.

Life is just a training. One has to become so transcendental that not even good satisfies. One has to be continuously in a divine discontent to attain to this excellent transcendence where you are lost and only the whole is. When you have completely surrendered, when you have given way to the whole, you have become just a space.

If you want to use non-Buddhist terms, you can call it surrender to God. You are so empty that God can descend in you. If you want to use Buddhist terms, then he says, you are not there – now only the law functions, now only the *dhamma*, the Tao goes on functioning. To function in such accord is bliss, *sat-chit-anand*.

Enough for today.

4

THE BLESSED ONE

Osho,
Why do you call yourself Bhagwan? Why do you call yourself God?

Because I am, and because you are, and because only God is. There is no other way, there is no other way to be. You may know it, you may not know it. The only choice is between ignorance and knowledge. The choice is not between whether to be a god or not to be a god, the choice is whether to recognize it or not. You can choose not to call, but you cannot choose not to be. But it has to be understood because it is one of the most radical standpoints about life.

Life is made of one thing: call it God, call it matter, call it electricity; one thing is certain, that life consists of only one thing. At the deepest, life is one unity. You can call it whatsoever you like. Scientists used to call it matter, now they have decided to call it electricity. Religious people decided to call it god, non-religious people decided to call it the world. But one thing is certain: that there exists only one thing.

Now, calling it *ABC* does not matter. Whatsoever you call it, it does not change the reality but it can change you. It will show your attitude. A person who calls the world matter cannot grow: he has dropped all future possibilities, he has closed his door, he has denied his destiny. Now he has no opening; he is a windowless atom, a monad, closed – going nowhere because matter cannot have any destiny, matter cannot have any growth, matter cannot have any potentiality, matter cannot have any experiencing.

The moment you say that life is nothing but matter, it does not change life. Because you call it matter it does not become matter, but by calling life matter you become a closed thing. By calling life matter you become a thing. You lose your personality, you lose that throb of aliveness. Something inside you suddenly goes dead. Then you are a grave, you will drag. The dance will be lost. Your life will become more like prose, it will not have any poetry.

When you call this life God, you bring poetry to it, you bring a vision, you open doors. You say, "More is possible." You say, "We are not the end." Higher peaks of possibilities arise in your vision. You start dreaming. The moment you say this existence is divine, dreams become possible. Then you can live a life of adventure: God is the greatest venture, it is the greatest pilgrimage.

Calling existence divine, you bring something new to your vision: then you are not finished, then you are not a full stop; then you are a rushing river moving towards the ocean. By calling existence divine, you bring dynamism to your life. Then you are not stale, stagnant. Then fantastic possibilities are there, just courage is needed, and you can go on and on and there is no end to it.

There are only two ways to give a label to life. One is the way of the realist: he calls it matter. The other is the way of the poet, the dreamer: he calls it God.

I am an unashamed poet. I'm not a realist. I call myself God, I call you God, I call rocks God, I call trees God, and the clouds God. The whole consists of only one thing and I have chosen to call it God because with God you can grow, with God you can ride on great tidal waves, you can go to the other shore. God is just a glimpse of your destiny. You give personality to existence. Then between you and the tree it is not emptiness. Then between you and your beloved it is not emptiness, God is bridging everything. He surrounds you, he is your surround. He is within and he is without.

When I call myself God, I mean to provoke you, to challenge you. I am simply calling myself God so that you can also gather courage to recognize it. If you can recognize it in me, you have taken the first step to recognizing it in yourself.

It will be very difficult for you to recognize it in yourself because you have always been taught to condemn yourself. You have always been taught that you are a sinner. Here I am to take all that nonsense away. My insistence is that it is only one thing that is missing in you – the courage to recognize who you are.

I call myself God to help you, to give you courage. If this man can be a God, why not you? I'm just like you. By calling myself God I am not bringing God down, I am bringing you up. I am taking you for a high journey. I'm simply opening a door towards the Himalayan peaks.

Once you start recognizing that you are also divine, you become unburdened. Then there may be errors but there are no sins any more. You are not a sinner. You may be mistaken, you may be wandering on a stray paths, but you are not a sinner. Whatsoever you do, you cannot lose your godhood, that is your nature.

You can be a sinner, but still you cannot lose your godhood. Then, by becoming a sinner your God becomes a sinner, that's all. You can be a fool, but that simply shows that God within you has chosen to play the game of being a fool, that's all. Millions of forms, but all forms divine. Millions of forms, all complementing each other and making this whole world a great cosmos.

Calling myself God, I am just hinting something to you. I'm not interested in what you call me, that is pointless. It is just indicative, a gesture. I'm saying to you, "Look at me, I'm just like you." If I can recognize the divinity within me, if I can respect my own being, why not you? Be respectful towards your own being.

It is not going to help that you go and worship a stone in the temple unless you start worshipping yourself, unless you start being respectful to your own being, unless you feel reverence for your own existence – that's what I mean when I call myself God.

I respect my being. I don't feel any condemnation about me. I am happy as I am. I am tremendously happy as I am. I am tremendously grateful as I am.

The Indian term for God, *bhagwan*, is even better than God. That word is tremendously meaningful. It simply means the blessed one, nothing else. *Bhagwan* means the blessed one, one who is fortunate enough to recognize his own being.

It has no Christian associations. When you say "God," it seems as if I have created the world. I deny all responsibility, I have not created this world. I am not that much of a fool. The Christian idea of God is one who has created the world. *Bhagwan* is totally different. It has nothing to do with creating the world. It simply says one who has recognized himself as divine. In that recognition is benediction. In that recognition is blessing. He has become the blessed one.

You can also become; if I can become, why not you? Nothing is lacking, just the courage to penetrate your own soul, just the courage to encounter yourself. You have been taught to be sinners: condemned, crushed, crawling on the earth. Your wings have been cut and destroyed.

Calling myself Bhagwan, I would like simply to say to you to gather courage, reclaim your wings – the whole sky is yours. But without wings it is not yours. Reclaim your wings and don't allow anybody to condemn you. Respect yourself. If you cannot respect yourself, you cannot respect anybody else.

When you respect yourself, a great respect arises. Then you respect the tree, the rock, the man, the woman, the sky, the sun, the moon, the stars. But those ripples of respect arise only when you have started respecting yourself.

I call myself Bhagwan because I respect myself. I am tremendously fulfilled as I am. I am the blessed one. I have no discontentment. That is the meaning of *bhagwan*: when you have no discontentment, when each moment of your life is a fulfillment, when you don't desire anything in the future; your present is so full, overflowing – when there is no hankering.

That's why we call Buddha, Bhagwan. He has denied God in his cosmology. He says there is no God, no creator. Christians become very puzzled when Buddha says there is no God, no creator. Then why do Buddhists call him Bhagwan?

Our meaning of "Bhagwan" is totally different. We call him Buddha, Bhagwan, because he has now no more desires. He is contented. He is happy and at home. He has come home, that is his blessedness. Now there is no conflict between him and existence. He has fallen in accord, in harmony. Now he and the whole are not two separate things, they vibrate in the same way. He has become part of the orchestra of the whole, and by becoming a part of this great orchestra of stars and trees and flowers and winds and clouds and seas and sands, he has become blessed – we call him Bhagwan.

Go on this adventure. Once you use a certain word, that word creates many things; words are very creative. If you call the world just matter, that very word pulls you down. So there is nothing else, just matter? Then all else that looks superior to matter must be illusory.

That's why a materialist goes on saying that the *samadhi* of Patanjali is illusion, the nirvana of Buddha is imaginary, the satori of Zen masters is just a game of the mind. Why does the materialist go on denying these things? Once you have this concept of matter, that everything has to be reduced to matter, then there are many things that cannot be reduced to matter. How to reduce the experience of satori into matter? The only possible way is to deny it, say it is not.

Nietzsche says, "God is dead, God is not," because if God is, then you have to accept Jesus, you have to accept Buddha, you have to accept Patanjali, Lao Tzu, Zarathustra. They are like rainbows, bridges between the known and the unknown. But you have to raise your eyes towards the sky.

If you look down into the earth and you go on digging there, you cannot look at the rainbows. If you deny the existence of sky itself and somebody says, "Look up!" You will say, "Where? There is no up." And if somebody says, "I am seeing a beautiful rainbow in the sky." You will say, "You must be hallucinating, you must be in a delusion. What are you talking about? There is no sky, so there is no possibility for any rainbow."

By denying God, we deny all possibilities of all rainbows. But then man becomes stuck. Then you are not going anywhere, then you are a stagnant pool just waiting to die. For a materialist there is nothing else – just waiting to die. His life becomes a tremendous burden, anguish.

Jean-Paul Sartre calls man a useless passion. If there is no God, he is right. If there is no God, then why are you existing, for what? If you cannot become God, then what is the point of it all? Why go on existing and why go on carrying this anguish, angst, this anxiety, this tense life? Why? Why continue this nightmare? Why not drop out of it?

In one of Dostoevsky's great novels, *Brothers Karamazov*, one character says to God, "If I ever meet you, I want to give back this ticket that you gave me to enter into the world. Take it back. I don't want to be here, it is so pointless."

Jean-Paul Sartre is right. If there is no God then existence is meaningless. Then it is just a tale told by an idiot, full of fury and noise, signifying nothing. Then it is a madhouse.

With God, with the very concept of God, things start falling in line. Then it is not just a tale told by an idiot, then life has meaning. The meaning comes from the beyond. The meaning always comes from the transcendental. The meaning is always surpassing that which is. If you deny all future possibilities, then meaning disappears, then life is futile.

I call myself God because I would like to introduce you to a life of passionate meaning, full of meaning: a life of significance, grandeur, beauty, truth. With God everything becomes possible. Without God everything becomes impossible.

A man without God is not a man at all. He resembles man, but he is not a man because he has no transcending meaning in him. He is like a tree without flowers. The tree exists, no fulfillment.

Unless flowers bloom and the fragrance is released to the winds, the tree exists in vain. You can go and listen deeply, you will find it crying and weeping, deep in its heart you will find pain. When flowers come to a tree, poetry has started happening – something transcendental.

Can you ever imagine flowers by looking at the roots? If you have never seen any flowers and I bring the roots of a beautiful flowering bush and show you the roots, can you imagine that flowers are possible from looking at ugly roots? You will simply deny. But hidden in these roots are flowers.

Somebody is needed to nourish these roots, to protect these roots, to water these roots, to give them light and shade and sun and wind and rains, and one needs to be tremendously trusting that something is going to happen because long will be the waiting. Then, one day a miracle happens – the tree is blooming. You cannot believe your eyes. How did those ugly roots get so transfigured, so transformed? How have those ugly roots become such beautiful roses? Impossible. Illogical. It should not really happen. It goes against all reasoning, but it is so. If you exist without a God, you are a tree without flowers, a rosebush without roses. And what is a rosebush without roses? – just thorns.

When I call myself Bhagwan, I am simply saying to you, "Look at me, the roses have bloomed." And what has happened to me can happen to you. So don't feel desperate and don't feel depressed. Look at me and your hope will come back, and you will not feel hopeless.

Allow me to enter you. At least allow my fragrance to enter your nostrils. Let me get to your heart. Let me stir your heart a little so that your own flowers start growing, your own buds start opening their petals.

Calling myself Bhagwan is just a device. I can drop it any day. The moment I see it has started working, the chain has started; the moment I see that now it is no longer needed, a few people have become aflame, now they will be enough proof – there will be no need to call myself Bhagwan. They will be enough proof. If a few of my sannyasins start blooming, I will drop calling myself Bhagwan. The device will have worked.

One day a few years back, I called Yoga Chinmaya and told

him to find a new word for me because I was going to function in a new way. I was known all over the country as the *Acharya*. The *acharya* means a master, a teacher. I was a teacher, and I was teaching and traveling. That was just the introductory part of my work, that was to invite people.

Once the invitation reached, I stopped traveling. Now those who want, they should come to me. I have gone to their home, knocked on their doors. I have told them that I am here and any day the desire arises in them, they can come. I will wait. I have shown them the path towards me. Then one day I called Yoga Chinmaya and I told him, "Now find a new word for me because the word *teacher* will not be enough."

He brought many names for the new function that I was going to take. He said, "Maharishi, great seer." I said, "That is comparative – seer and great seer, *rishi* and maharishi. No, that is not good. And everybody cannot be a seer. It is a talent. A few people can become seers, everybody cannot become a seer."

Then he said, "*Paramahansa*, the great swan?" Again it is comparative. And it is a symbol of hierarchy. In certain old sannyasin orders, *paramahansa* is the last stage. Just as in Buddhist terminology, *arhat* is the peak, one has arrived. In Hindu terminology, *paramahansa* is the peak – but it shows graduation, step by step. It is mathematical, calculative.

He said, "Then what about *Avadhuta*?" That too is another comparative term, belonging to another sect of sannyasins. It is again parallel to arhat and *paramahansa*, belonging to the Tantrikas. *Avadhuta* is their last stage. But it shows achievement.

I said, "Find something which is universal. Find something which is not relative." And then he found *bhagwan*. It is a non-comparative term. You cannot be godlier than God. Godder than God you cannot be. It is a non-comparative term. And it does not show any achievement, it simply shows your nature. Not that one has to become God; one is God, one has simply to recognize it.

It does not show any talent. There is somebody who is a great poet, somebody who is a great seer, a great visionary; somebody a great painter, somebody a great musician, somebody a great dancer – these are all talents. All cannot be great dancers, you cannot all be Nijinskys. And all cannot be great painters, you cannot all be van Goghs. And you all cannot be great poets, you cannot all be Tagores and Pablo Nerudas. But *bhagwan* you all are. It does not show an achievement; it simply shows your universality, your very nature. Already you are God.

I loved the term. I said, "That will do. At least for a few years it will do, then we can drop it."

I have chosen it for a specific purpose and it has been serving well because people who used to come to me to gather knowledge, they stopped. The day I called myself Bhagwan, they stopped. It was too much for them, it was too much for their egos. Somebody calling himself Bhagwan? – it hurts the ego. They stopped. They were coming to me to gather knowledge. Now I've changed my function absolutely. I started working on a different level, in a different dimension. Now I give you being, not knowledge. I was an *acharya* and they were students; they were learning. Now I am no longer a teacher and you are not here as students.

If you are here as students, sooner or later you will have to leave because you will find yourself in the wrong place, you will not fit here. Only if you are a disciple, then you can fit with me because now I am to give something more. If you are here for knowledge, then sooner or later you will see you have to go somewhere else.

I am here to impart *being*. I am here to make you awake. I am not going to give you knowledge, I am going to give you knowing and that is a totally different dimension.

Calling myself Bhagwan was simply symbolic – that now I have taken a different dimension to work. And it has been tremendously useful. All wrong people automatically disappeared and a totally different quality of people started arriving.

It worked well, Chinmaya's choice was good. It sorted out well. Only those who are ready to dissolve with me remained, all others escaped. They created space around me. Otherwise they were crowding too much, and it was very difficult for the real seekers to come closer to me. The crowds disappeared. The word *bhagwan* functioned like an atomic explosion. It did well. I am happy that I chose it.

Now people who come to me are no longer argumentative. Now people who come to me come to drink me, to eat me, to digest me. Now people who come to me are great adventurers of the soul. And they are ready to risk – to risk all and everything.

Calling myself Bhagwan is a device. Sooner or later, when you have grown up and you have understood the point, and when your presence here has created a different quality of vibrations, I will stop calling myself Bhagwan. Then there will be no need, then the whole atmosphere will be throbbing with godliness. Then people who will come, it will shower on them, it will penetrate into their hearts. There will be no need to call me anything, you will know. But in the beginning it was needed, and it has been of tremendous help.

The last thing about it – I am not a philosopher. Always remember me as a poet: my approach towards life is that of poetry, is that of romance. It is romantic, it is imaginative. I would like you all to be gods and goddesses. I would like you to reveal your true being.

Calling myself God is a challenge. It is a subtle challenge. There are only two ways to settle with it. One is you say, "This man is not God," and go away, because then what are you doing here? If this man is not God then why waste your time? You go away. Or, you accept that this man is God, and then you start being with me, and your own godliness starts flowering.

One day you will also be a god, a goddess. Accepting me as God is in fact deep down accepting the possibility that you can also be God, that's all. The very acceptance that this man can be God stirs something that has been fast asleep within you. Then you cannot remain as you are, something has to be done. Something has to be transformed, something has to be known. You cannot live at rest any more. A dream has taken possession of you.

I was reading an anecdote…

The cute and efficient young maid seemed to enjoy her work until one day without warning she gave notice.

"Why do you wish to leave?" the lady of the house asked. "Is there anything wrong?"

"I just can't stand the suspense in this house a minute more," the maid replied.

"Suspense?" said the confused mistress. "What do you mean?"

"It is the sign over my door," the girl explained. "You know, the one that says: 'Watch ye, for ye know not when the master cometh. Watch ye, for ye know not when the master cometh.'"

She misunderstood it, but it created a continuous suspense, uneasiness. "Watch ye, ye know not when the master cometh."

If you decide to go with me, you will become more and more watchful. And the more watchful you will become, the more you will be able to understand me, the more you will be able to understand what has happened, what has transpired within my soul. You will become more and more a participant in this happening, in this dance, in this singing.

And by and by you will see, the master is coming. And it is not coming from the outside, it is coming from your innermost core, it is arising from your depths.

The master cometh, the God comes, but not from the outside. He comes from your very center. He has been there waiting for you to call him. He has been there since eternity waiting that some day you will look in.

I looked in and I found him there. My message is simple: that I have found the god within me. My whole effort is to persuade you: look within, the master cometh. Yes, it is possible. Yes, he comes. And he does not come from the outside, he explodes from the inside. He arises in you. He is your future, he is your destiny.

You may know it, you may not know it. You are already in him and he is already in you. The only question is how to become aware. "Watch ye, for ye know not when the master cometh."

The only question is of becoming a watcher on the hills. Become a witness – alert, observing – and you will be fulfilled.

Osho,
What does it mean to live dangerously?

To live dangerously means to live. If you don't live dangerously, you don't live. Living flowers only in danger, living never flowers in security; it flowers only in insecurity.

If you start getting secure, you become a stagnant pool. Then your energy is no longer moving. Then you are afraid because one never knows how to go into the unknown. And why take the risk? The known is more secure. Then you get obsessed with the familiar. You go on getting fed up with it, you are bored with it, you feel miserable in it, but still it seems familiar and comfortable. At least it is known. Unknown creates a trembling in you. The very idea of the unknown and you start feeling unsafe.

There are only two types of people in the world: people who want to live comfortably – they are seeking death, they want a comfortable grave; and people who want to live – they choose to live dangerously because life thrives only when there is risk.

Have you ever gone climbing the mountains? The higher the climb the fresher you feel, the younger you feel. The greater the danger of falling, the bigger the abyss by the side, the more alive you are when you are just hanging between life and death. Then there is no boredom, then there is no dust of the past, no desire for the future. Then the present moment is very sharp like a flame. It is enough. You live in the here and now.

Or surfing, or skiing, or gliding. Wherever there is a risk of losing life, there is tremendous joy. Because the risk of losing life makes you tremendously alive. Hence people are attracted to dangerous sports.

People go climbing the mountains. Somebody asked Hillary, "Why did you try to climb Everest, why?" And Hillary said, "Because it is there – a constant challenge." It was risky, many people had died before. For almost sixty, seventy years, groups had been going, and it was almost a certain death. But still people were going. What was the attraction?

Reaching higher, going farther away from the settled, the routine life, you again become wild, you again become part of the animal world. You again live like a tiger or a lion or like a river. You again soar like a bird into the skies, farther and farther away. And each moment the security, the bank balance, the wife, the husband, the family, the society, the church, the respectability are all falling away and away, distant and distant. You become alone.

This is why people are so interested in sports. But that too is not real danger because you can become very, very skilled. You can learn it, you can be trained for it. It is a very calculated risk – if you allow me the expression, calculated risk. You can train for mountaineering and you can take all precautions.

Or like driving, speed-driving. You can go a hundred miles per hour. It is dangerous, it is thrilling. But you can become really skillful about it, and the danger is only for outsiders; for you it is not. And even if it is there, it is very marginal. And then, these risks are only physical risks, only the body is involved.

When I say to you, live dangerously, I mean not only bodily risk, but psychological risk, and finally spiritual risk. Religion is spiritual risk. It is going to such heights from where, maybe, there is no return. That is the meaning of Buddha's term, *anagamin*: one who never returns. It is going to such a height, a point of no return; then one is simply lost. One never comes back.

When I say live dangerously, I mean don't live the life of ordinary respectability: that you are a mayor in a town, or a member of the corporation – this is not life – or you are a minister, or you have a good profession and are earning well and money goes on accumulating in the bank and everything is going perfectly well. When everything is going perfectly well, simply see it – you are dying and nothing is happening. People may respect you, and when you die a great procession will follow you. Good, that's all. And in the newspapers your pictures will be published and there will be editorials, and then people will forget about you. And you lived your whole life only for these things.

Watch – one can miss one's whole life for ordinary, mundane things. To be spiritual means to understand that these small things should not be given too much importance. I am not saying that they are meaningless. I am saying that they are meaningful, but not as meaningful as you think.

Money is needed. It is a need. But money is not the goal and cannot be the goal. A house is needed, certainly. It is a need. I am not an ascetic and I don't want you to destroy your houses and escape to the Himalayas. The house is needed, but the house is needed for you. Don't misunderstand it.

As I see people, the whole thing has gone topsy-turvy. They exist as if they are needed for the house. They go on working for the house. As if they are needed for the bank balance – they simply go on collecting money and then they die. And they had never lived. They never had a single moment of throbbing, streaming life. They were just imprisoned in security, familiarity, respectability.

Then if you feel bored, it is natural. People come to me and they say they feel very bored. They feel fed up, stuck. What to do? They think that just by repeating a mantra they will become alive again. It is not so easy. They will have to change their whole life pattern.

Love, but don't think that tomorrow the woman will be available to you. Don't expect, don't reduce the woman into a wife. Then you are living dangerously. Don't reduce the man into a husband because a husband is an ugly thing. Let your man be your man, and your woman your woman. And don't make your tomorrow predictable. Expect nothing and be ready for everything. That's what I mean when I say live dangerously.

What do we do? We fall in love with a woman and immediately we start going to the court, or to the registry office, or to the church to get married. I'm not saying don't get married. It is a formality. Good, satisfy the society. But deep in your mind never possess the woman. Never for a single moment say that you belong to me. Because how can a person belong to you? And when you start possessing the woman she will start possessing you. Then you both are no longer in love. You are just crushing and killing each other, paralyzing each other.

Love, but don't let your love degrade into marriage. Work, work is needed, but don't let work become your only life. Play should remain your life, your center of life. Work should be as a means towards play. Work in the office and work in the factory and work in the shop, but just to have time, opportunity, to play. Don't let your life be reduced into just a working routine because the goal of life is play. Play means doing something for its own sake.

You even come to me to meditate, and you take meditation also as work. You think something has to be done to achieve godliness. It is nonsense. Meditation cannot be done that way. You have to play, you have to take it as fun. You have not to be serious about it. You have to enjoy it.

When you enjoy it, it develops. When you start taking it as work, as a duty to be done – because you have to do, you have to achieve *moksha*, nirvana, liberation – then again you have brought your foolish categories into the world of play. Meditation is play, it is a *leela*. You enjoy it for its own sake.

If you enjoy many more things for their own sake, you will be more alive. Of course, your life will always be in a risk, danger. But that's how life has to be. Risk is part of it. In fact the better part of it is risk, the best part of it is risk. The most beautiful part of it is risk. It is every moment a risk. You may not be aware. You breathe in, you breathe out. There is risk. Even breathing out, who knows whether the breath will come back or not? It is not certain, there is no guarantee.

But there are a few people whose whole religion is security. Even if they talk about God, they talk about God as the supreme security. If they think about God, they think only because they are afraid. If they go to pray and meditate, they are going just in order that they remain in the good books – in God's good books: "If there is a God, he will know that I was a regular churchgoer, a regular worshipper. I can claim." Even their prayer is just a means.

To live dangerously means to live life as if each moment is its own end. Each moment has its own intrinsic value. And you are not afraid. And you know death is there and you accept the fact that death is there, and you are not hiding from death. In fact, you go and encounter death. You enjoy those moments of encountering death – physically, psychologically, spiritually.

Enjoying those moments where you come directly in contact with death, where death becomes almost a reality, is what I mean when I say live dangerously.

Love brings you face to face with death. Meditation brings you face to face with death. Coming to a master is coming to your own death. Facing somebody who has disappeared, is entering an abyss in which you can be lost, and you can become an *anagamin*.

Those who are courageous, they go headlong. They search all opportunities of danger. Their life philosophy is not that of insurance companies. Their life philosophy is that of a mountain climber, a glider, a surfer. And not only in the outside seas they surf, they surf in their innermost seas. And not only on the outside they climb Alps and Himalayas; they seek inner peaks.

But remember one thing: never forget the art of risking, never, never. Always remain capable of risking. And wherever you can find an opportunity to risk, never miss it, and you will never be a loser. Risk is the only guarantee to be truly alive.

Osho,
I feel stuck. I feel I have an essential being inside which wants to get out. It feels a lot more alive and dangerous than the one I drag around with me. It wants to grab girls and sexually enjoy.
But you have said that for lifetimes the energy has gone down; time for a change. It wants to fume and rage at getting a half-cup instead of a full cup of milk.

The half-cup will always remain half because it is in the very nature of desires that they cannot be completed. It is the very nature of desire to remain half, to remain discontent. It is the very nature of desire to remain desiring.

You desire one thing. When you get it, by the time you get it, your desire has increased. You were desiring ten thousand rupees. By the time you get ten thousand rupees, your desire has gone farther ahead. Now it is asking for twenty thousand rupees.

In fact nothing has changed. You had five thousand rupees with you and you were desiring ten thousand rupees. Now you have ten thousand rupees, you are desiring twenty thousand rupees. The proportion is the same. The distance between you and your goal is the same. It remains the same. The cup remains half. There is no way through desire to come to fulfillment. Buddha has said it is not the nature of desire to be fulfilled. Fulfillment comes only by desirelessness.

Now, this is one of the most important paradoxes: if you drop desiring you will be fulfilled. The more you desire, the more you are getting into desire, the farther and farther away you go from your possibility of fulfillment. One desire creates many more desires; then many more desires, millions more. It is like a tree. First it is one, then many branches, then many small offshoots, and on and on it goes.

The person has asked, "I feel stuck..." Everybody who has been living in desire feels stuck. The problem is that if you don't try to fulfill your desire, you remain unfulfilled. If you try, even if you get the goal of your desire, then you remain unfulfilled – then too, nothing changes. This is the nightmare of life.

I have heard about a madhouse. A visitor had come, and the doctor, the superintendent, was taking him round. They came to a cage. A man was beating his head, pulling his hair, crying, and holding a small picture near his chest. Pathetic, the scene was very tragic.

The visitor asked, "What happened to this unfortunate man?"

The doctor said, "He used to love a woman and he could not get her. She decided to marry somebody else. Since then he has been mad. He is carrying that picture continuously – day, night, awake, asleep – and he goes on in deep anguish. His misery is immense."

Then they reached another cage, just in front of the first one. Another person was raving mad, hitting against the walls, fighting with some shadows. He was almost violent, aggressive; he looked like a murderer. And the visitor asked, "What happened to this man?"

The doctor started laughing. He said, "The woman married this man! And this is what has happened by marrying the woman."

One is suffering because he could not get, another is suffering because he could get.

There are poor people who are suffering because they don't have riches. And there are rich people who are suffering because now they have riches and yet they have nothing. There are unsuccessful people who are in tremendous pain because they failed and life failed them. And there are successful people who are simply empty, all life gone out of them. They put everything at stake and they succeeded and now what to do?

Nothing fails like success. When it comes, you cannot believe what you were desiring. You can have a big house, and you can have respect and money, and suddenly you see, you are just empty and your whole life has been a wastage. Things have accumulated and you have disappeared. Things are there, possessions are there, but the master is missing. This is the nature of desire. Everybody feels stuck.

"I feel stuck. I feel I have an essential being inside which wants to get out." That is not your essential being because the essential being is that which has no desire. The being that desires is the accidental being. Be careful what words you use.

The essential is one which has no desire. It is already fulfilled. That which desires is the accidental. It is continuously unhappy, continuously in discontentment, continuously frustrated and goes on desiring. And the problem is the more you desire, the more you get frustrated. The more you get frustrated, the more you desire. A vicious circle, and one goes on moving in it and is crushed by the wheel.

"I feel I have an essential being inside which wants to get out." The essential being never wants to get out. The essential being is your innermost core, it is your innerness. It never wants to get out. There is nothing for it to go anywhere. It is already where it should be. The essential is one which is already where it should be, which is already that which it should be. The essential is the ideal, the essential is the natural, the spontaneous.

"I feel I have an essential being inside which wants to get out." This is not your essential being that wants to get out. This is your accidental being. Maybe it arises because you are identified with the body, or it arises because you are identified with the mind. "It feels a lot more alive and dangerous than the one I drag around with me." Yes, it is. It at least appears to be more alive. It at least deceives you to be more alive. Follow it and you will find that it tricked you.

That's what people find by the time death is approaching. Their sex tricked them, their lust tricked them, their greed tricked them, their ambition tricked them. And now everything is gone, all energy lost, and they are going empty-handed. They have not matured. They have not got anything that they can carry beyond death.

Life is that which cannot be destroyed by death; remember, that is the definition. And anything alive, if it is truly alive, is beyond death. It cannot be taken away by death. Nothing can destroy it. Aliveness is eternity.

"It feels a lot more alive..." It simply deceives you. It is very tricky, it is very persuasive. It is a great salesman "...and dangerous than the one I drag around with me." Yes, and it is dangerous; not for you – it is dangerous for others. For you, it is just an illusion.

Of course it is dangerous, but not in the sense that I was talking about danger. That's what everybody is doing. That is nothing new. Everybody is greedy and everybody is full of lust. That is nothing new, that is nothing risky. That is the way of the world. Even animals are doing that, trees are doing that. Everybody is doing that. It is dangerous in a different way. It is dangerous in the sense that it is destructive. It will destroy you, and it will destroy others. It is not creative.

Love is creative. Sex is destructive. And there is a lot of difference between the two. Sometimes you start thinking that your sexuality is your love. Then you are deceived. Sexuality can play the game of love, but it is a counterfeit game. I am not against sex, but I am certainly against sexuality. And the difference is that sex is a natural thing and sexuality is a mind thing.

To love a woman is natural, to love a man is natural. To reproduce children is natural, nothing wrong in it. But to think about women, to carry pornographic pictures, to fall asleep every night thinking about women – women and women and women – that is sexuality.

Mulla Nasruddin went to his psychiatrist. And the psychiatrist said, just as a test, "Look at the clock on the wall. What does it remind you of?"

He looked at the wall and said, "Of women."

The clock? The psychiatrist said, "Okay, what does this chair remind you of?"

"Of course," Mulla Nasruddin said, "of women." Even the psychiatrist was shocked – the chair? And then a camel was passing, so he said, "And what does this camel remind you of?" Now, this is the farthest thing from a woman – a camel.

And he said, "Of women of course."

The psychiatrist said, "This is too much. How can the camel remind you of women?"

Mulla Nasruddin said, "It is not a question of the camel or anything else. I never think about anything else. Everything reminds me of women. Even nothing reminds me of women. I simply think about women and nothing else."

Now this is sexuality. And the same is trying to erupt in the questioner. "It wants to grab girls and sexually enjoy." Now nothing is wrong in falling in love with a woman, but to grab a girl is ugly. Be a little more artful and a little more gentlemanly. Grabbing? The very word is aggressive, the very word is violent – as if you don't have any respect for the woman you love. Grabbing? Is she a thing? Do you want to rape?

This is what goes on happening in the ordinary mind. It has fallen from sex, it has become sexual. Sex is natural, normal. You love a woman, you love a man – good. But then you are finished. If you love a woman, you are finished with being concerned with other women. Then that one woman represents all women, then that one man becomes all the men in one. Then the whole mankind is there. When you love a woman, you have found the essential woman that you were looking for. Now you are not looking at every passerby, and your mind is not grabbing. "It wants to grab girls and sexually enjoy."

First thing to remember: if you grab a woman you will never enjoy because enjoyment cannot be forced. It is a subtle rhythm. When a woman also loves you, only then this music arises between the two which gives joy, delight.

You can grab a woman, and that's what people are doing. Somebody is doing just by physical force, somebody is doing by money-force – because he has money so he can purchase any woman – somebody is doing by some other means. As I see, out of a hundred, ninety-nine people have grabbed women and men. Rarely it happens that a person is in love.

When you are in love, you don't grab the woman and the woman does not grab you. When you are in love, love possesses you both. When you are in love, you don't possess each other. You possess not – not at all. And when you are in love, you don't think about enjoyment; it is there. All thinking about enjoyment exists because it is not there, it is missing.

Joy is something which happens as a consequence; it is not a result. You cannot make any effort to be joyful. You can move into some activity so deeply that you forget yourself and joy arises. Joy arises only when you are not. This is what Buddha says: "When the self disappears then joy arises."

The self can disappear in meditation. The self can disappear in love. The self can disappear in prayer. The self can disappear in dance, in singing and painting. The self can disappear anywhere if you are completely lost in any activity, and the activity is so deep that you are no longer a doer there; you have become one with it. It happens sometimes.

Once a young man came to me. He was a good runner, a champion runner, and he asked me how to meditate. He was so bubbling with energy, he was a great runner. He said, "When I sit, and you tell me to sit silently, I cannot sit; the energy is so much. Is there any possibility for me to ever become meditative?"

I said, "You forget about meditation. You run, and you drop yourself in running. One day meditation will happen."

He said, "What are you saying? Just by running? Has anybody ever become a buddha just running?"

I said, "Yes, there is a possibility because a person can become a buddha in any activity."

He said, "I will try."

After a week he came and he said, "It is unbelievable. I cannot even believe that it has happened. Something tremendously beautiful happened. I was running, I was going as fast as I could. And as you had said, I forgot myself completely. I was not performing, it was not a competition. I was simply in it: the sun falling on my being, showering me, the morning breeze, the birds singing, and the empty bank of the river. And I was running and running.

"And by and by I started falling into a rhythm with the river, with the breeze, with the trees. And suddenly, yes, it was there. I was so full of joy. I have never been so joyful. Tell me, has it really happened? Because I cannot believe that just by running – and I have been running for many years and it has never happened." He was not losing himself, running was a performance.

Now, one of the most miserable things is happening in the West, people are even making love a performance. They read Masters and Johnson, and they read Kinsey and his reports, and they read other so-called great sex researchers, and now they are trying to perform.

They go on looking whether the woman is having the orgasm or not, whether she is thinking that the man is the greatest man in the world or not. And the woman is also thinking in the same way – seeing whether she is fulfilling the man and giving him great ecstasy or not. Now both are performing and the whole thing is destroyed. Now they are simply acting, they are no longer in it.

In the West, this century is proving the worst century for love. They talk too much about love, so many books are there but something is missing. Love is becoming a performance.

I am saying to you that even a thing like running – if it is no longer a performance – will give you the same orgasm that love can give, and the same ecstasy that meditation can give. Even cleansing the floor, you can attain to *samadhi*.

Sarita goes on cleaning. I hope one day she achieves her *samadhi* through cleaning. She is moving by and by towards it. Sometimes she even misses my talks because she has to clean, and she enjoys cleaning so much that I say, "Okay, you miss the talk. You will not be missing me."

Even an ordinary activity, very ordinary activity, can have tremendous import once you are completely lost in it. Don't be a performer.

"It wants to grab girls and sexually enjoy." If you grab a girl you will have a corpse in your hands, not a human body. You can make love to a corpse; there have been people. It is said that when Cleopatra died some foolish people dug her out of her grave and raped her – with a dead body. But this is not so strange. As I see, many people are doing it. It is not very strange. Cleopatra was tremendously beautiful, and men are foolish.

H. G. Wells has written that if Cleopatra had had a little smaller nose the whole history of humanity would have been different. Men are such fools that their whole history can be different if Cleopatra had had a little smaller nose. It must have been; H. G. Wells is right. The whole history would have been different. And some fools raped the dead body.

But this is happening on a very large scale. If your woman is not ready to love you in that moment – maybe she is your wife; that does not make it certain – if she is not ready out of her own heart, if she is not flowing in it, you are making love to a dead body. If your man is not ready, drawn into it, losing himself into it, you are making love to a dead body.

You can grab, but you will never reach the woman. The woman or the man can never be grabbed. And you can try to enjoy and you will be only frustrated because nobody has ever attained any enjoyment by trying it. Enjoyment comes like a shadow. The whole effort is ridiculous.

Let me tell you an anecdote...

Mulla Nasruddin and his wife were at the ballet. He suddenly started laughing. The wife asked, "Why?"

"I was just wondering what the audience would do if I suddenly jumped on the stage, grabbed one of the girls, threw her down and made violent love to her," he said.

The wife thought a little and began to laugh. He asked, "Why?"

"I was just thinking," she said, "what would you do if the audience gave you a standing ovation and screamed for an encore. If the audience screamed, 'Once more!' what would you do?"

It will be really ridiculous. Performance is ridiculous. Don't be a performer.

Never think of grabbing a woman or a man. Love – love is beautiful, but loving needs a tremendous transformation in you because it is a surrender. You have to surrender, you have to be respectful. You have to revere the other person, his being. Love is prayer. And if sex happens as part of love – sex is spiritual – then sex is no longer sexual, then it is a spiritual ecstasy. It is meditative and prayerful.

"But you have said that for lifetimes the energy has gone down; time for a change. It wants to fume and rage at getting a half-cup instead of a full cup of milk." The very nature of desire is such, and you are tackling it in a very foolish way. Try to understand the nature of desire. I am not saying repress it. I am saying understand it because repression will not help. In fact, repression has brought you to this stage.

The questioner must have been repressing. See, he has repressed his natural desires so much that they have become corrupted. Now he thinks that is his essential being. It is nothing but his repressed being. Then you can go on and on in your head, playing again and again the same repressed desires. And it is not going to fulfill you.

I am not saying be repressive. I am saying be skillful, be aware.

It happened...

When Syble got to be twenty-eight without any prospects of getting married, her mother nagged her into inserting an ad in the matrimonial column. The ad read: Beautiful exotic young heiress seeks correspondence with devil-may-care gentleman who wants to go places fast.

After the ad appeared, the mother asked anxiously, "Well, any answers?"

"Just one," sighed the daughter.

"Who wrote it?" demanded mama.

"I should not tell you," said the daughter.

"But it was my idea," shouted mama, "and I insist on knowing."

"All right," said the daughter, "you asked for it. It is from papa!"

If you go on repressing, then it will become uglier and uglier. And in old age all your repressions become very strong because you become weak and your repressions take revenge.

I am not saying to repress. I am saying understand. Only if understanding can help, then it is good. And understanding helps.

Meditate on your sexuality. See it through and through. Let it become transparent. And the first thing needed is at least make your sexuality normal, let it be sex. Don't think in terms of grabbing, be a little more romantic. Don't be so aggressive and violent, be a little more poetic about life, and a little more graceful.

First let your sexuality come to a normal point of sex, and then let your sex follow your love. Never put your sex before love. Love should be the driving force and sex should follow it.

Once you have done this much, you are on the right track. Soon you will realize that whatsoever you have been calling your essential self was your repressed self. And once that repressed self is dispersed, eliminated, and you have become natural, healthy, whole, then your essential self will come into your vision for the first time.

The essential self is your innermost god. The essential self is what truth is. The essential self is no-self.

Enough for today.

5

BE A LIGHT UNTO YOURSELF

A monk asked the Buddha:
What is most powerful and what is most illuminating?
The Buddha said:
Meekness is most powerful for it harbors no evil thoughts, and moreover it is restful and full of strength. As it is free from evils it is sure to be honored by all.
The most illuminating is a mind which is thoroughly cleansed of dirt, and which, remaining pure, retains no blemishes. From the time when there was yet no heaven and earth till the present day there is nothing in the ten quarters which is not seen, or known, or heard by such a mind. For it has gained all knowledge and for that reason it is called "illuminating."

Life can be lived in two ways. One is that of the soldier, and the other, that of the sannyasin. Either you can fight with life or you can relax with life. Either you can try to conquer life or you can live in a deep let-go. The path of the soldier is the wrong path because it is impossible to conquer life. The part cannot conquer the whole, frustration and failure is absolutely certain. You can play around with the idea, but it is not going to succeed, it is doomed to failure. The soldier tries to conquer life and in the end finds he has been crushed by life, defeated by life, destroyed by life.

Life destroys nobody, but if you fight with it you will be destroyed by your own violence. Life is not against you, how can it be? Life is your mother, it is life that has brought you here. You are born out of it. You are a ray of its light, a wave of its ocean. You are intrinsic and organic to it, you are not separate. But if you start fighting your own source of energy, you will be destroyed. Your very concept of fight will poison you. And of course, the more you feel that you are losing the battle, the harder you will fight. The harder you fight the more frustrated you become.

The soldier's way is the ordinary way. Almost ninety-nine point nine percent of people follow it; hence there is so much misery, hence there is so much hell. It is created by you, by your wrong approach towards life. Once you understand it, you start getting in tune with the whole, you start getting into a dance with the whole. You lose fighting, you start cooperating. The moment you decide to cooperate, you have become a sannyasin.

The religious person is one who has no idea of separation from the whole: who never thinks, never dreams that he is separate; who has no private goal of his own, who simply moves with life in total trust. If you cannot trust life, who are you going to trust? If you cannot allow life to flow through you, you will be missing – you will be missing this tremendous opportunity to be alive. Then you will get worried, then you will be caught in your own mind, and then misery is the natural outcome.

To understand that conflict is not the way to be happy is the greatest understanding. To understand that cooperation is the way to be blissful – and your dark night of the soul is over and the morning has come, and the sun is rising on the horizon – you will be transformed.

This very understanding is a transforming force: that cooperation is the key, not conflict. Trust is the key, not doubt. Violence is not the way – love. This is the basic framework.

Now the sutra:

> *A monk asked the Buddha:*
> *What is most powerful and what is most illuminating?*

We are all asking only these two questions. First, what is most powerful? Because we are all on a power trip. We want to be powerful because we feel we are impotent, we feel we are weaklings, we feel we are limited. A thousand and one limitations surround you. Everywhere you come against a wall and you feel powerless. Each moment of life brings you the feeling of helplessness.

So, the question is very pertinent, a very human question. What is the most powerful thing in the world? The monk must have been a seeker of power. Now, you have to understand it; the very effort, the very desire to be powerful is one of the obstacles in attaining to power. People who try to become powerful never become powerful. They are destroyed by their own search because the effort to become powerful means you are in conflict. You want to fight, that's why you want to be powerful. Otherwise, why do you need power in the first place? You must have some aggression, some violence, some grudge. You want to prove and perform. You want to prove to others that you are powerful and they are not. Deep down somewhere, like a shadow in the unconscious, an Adolf Hitler is seeking its way towards your conscious mind, or a Nadir Shah, or a Napoleon, or an Alexander. Everybody is carrying an Alexander within himself.

This desire for power has created many things in the world. Science has come as a desire for power, and it has created power. But that power is destroying humanity. It has come to such a state that people like Albert Einstein feel that they have committed a crime against humanity. In the last days of his life, somebody asked Albert Einstein, "If you were born again, what would you like to become?"

He said, "Never a physicist again, never a scientist. Rather, I would like to become a plumber."

He was a very sensitive man, very understanding. And only in the end could he understand that he has released so much energy, and he has made humanity aware of such a destructive force – atomic energy – that if humanity destroys itself, he is bound to be one of the most responsible persons.

The very framework of science is to conquer nature. That is the very terminology of science – conquest of nature. We have to overpower nature and we have to destroy all mysteries of nature, and we have to find all the keys of power, wherever it is. But the very idea takes you away from nature, makes you antagonistic to it and becomes destructive. The ecology of the earth has been destroyed by this power seeking. In the outside, in the inside, both, the natural rhythm of life is disturbed.

I have heard...

A very unusual idea occurred one day to Frederick of Prussia. He was in the country when he saw some sparrows eating some grains of wheat. He started to think and reached the conclusion that these small birds consumed a million pecks of wheat a year in his kingdom. This cannot be allowed. They have to be either conquered or destroyed.

Since it was difficult to exterminate them, he promised a price for each dead sparrow. All Prussians became hunters and soon there were no more sparrows in the country. What a great victory.

Frederick of Prussia was very happy. He celebrated the event as a great conquest over nature. The king was very happy until the following year when he was told that caterpillars and locusts had eaten the crops because without sparrows the whole rhythm of life was destroyed. Sparrows go on eating caterpillars and locusts. There being no sparrows, the whole crop was destroyed by caterpillars. Then it was necessary to bring in sparrows from abroad. And the king said, "I certainly have made a mistake. God knows what he is doing."

The great scientific minds of this century are coming, by and by, slowly, reluctantly to recognize that a great mistake has been made.

The very desire to be powerful is against nature because the very desire to be powerful is antagonistic. Why do you need to be powerful? You must be thinking in terms of somebody is to be destroyed: power is needed to destroy, power is needed to dominate, power is needed to conquer.

The monk must have asked, "What is the most powerful thing in the world?" In fact the actual word must have been *siddhi*. The monk must have asked, "What is *siddhi*, what is power?"

Science tries to penetrate nature to get more power, and there are many systems which penetrate your innermost being, but again the goal is to get more power. Whether you become powerful in a scientific way, or you become powerful in a psychic way, it makes no difference. Now the West is becoming interested in psychic sciences, but the urge is the same – to be more powerful.

So first try to understand why man seeks power in the first place. The very desire is that of a soldier. You want power because without power you cannot be a great ego. For ego, power functions as food, nourishment. You seek power because only with power will you be able to say "I am." The more money you have, the more power you have, the more you can feel at ease with your "I am," the more you can destroy people, the more you can feel that nobody can destroy you.

Now psychologists say that people are interested in murdering, killing in war because when they kill others they feel very powerful. They feel power against death. They think they can create death, they can kill others. Now, they feel in a deep way that they have become immortal. Even death is under their control. It is foolish, but the idea arises. People who love killing are people who are afraid of death.

Adolf Hitler was very much afraid of death, so much so that he never allowed anybody to stay with him in his room in the night. Not even a girlfriend was ever allowed, he was so afraid of death. Who knows, the girlfriend may turn out to be a spy, may be an agent in the hands of the enemy. Who knows? He never even trusted love.

He was one of the most lonely men who has ever existed on

earth; and so afraid, continuously trembling. But he continued killing people, that was just to balance the fear. The more he killed, the more he felt that he had power. The more he felt that he had power, the more he felt that death could not destroy him. He started feeling as if he was immortal.

Have you watched, in wartime people look very radiant, in wartime people look very fresh? Ordinarily they look very bored. When war starts, you can see: their step has changed, their eyes have now a glimmer, a radiance; their face looks more alive, as if the dust of the boredom is gone. Something sensational is happening. It should not be so, but whenever there is war people feel a power over death – they can kill. Immediately, in the shadow of their unconscious they feel, "Even death is within our boundary. We can bring it or we can stop it." People love destruction just as a measure of providing security against death.

The search for power is the search not to surrender, not to feel helpless, not to be in a state where you are not in control. And the religious man is doing just the opposite. He is seeking a state where he is not in control but the whole is in control – call it god, call it the supreme, or whatsoever you like to call it.

The religious person is one who wants to be in such a deep harmony that there is no question of conflict. He is seeking love. He is seeking a love affair with the universe. He never asks about power. He asks how to lose separation, how to merge. He asks, "How to be in such a total surrender that I don't move in any way against the whole or separate from the whole, so that I can move with the river of life. And wherever the river of life goes, I can go with it."

What is most powerful...? asked the monk.

> *The Buddha said:*
> *Meekness is most powerful...*

Jesus says, "Blessed are the meek, for they shall inherit the earth." The statement looks absurd because the meek, they have never been powerful enough to inherit the earth. And we cannot conceive that they will ever be able to inherit the earth. But Jesus is saying something very true: "Blessed are the meek." And when he says they shall inherit the earth, he is saying this same message that Buddha is saying: "Meekness is most powerful," that is his meaning when he says they shall inherit the earth.

Meekness is powerful, but the power has a totally different connotation now. Meekness is powerful because now there is nobody against you. Meekness is powerful because you are no longer separate from the whole, and the whole is powerful. Meekness is powerful because you are no longer fighting, and there is no way of your being defeated. Meekness is powerful because with the whole you have already conquered. All victory is with the whole. Meekness is powerful because you are riding on the wave of the whole. Now there is no possibility of your ever being defeated.

It looks paradoxical because the meek person is one who does not want to conquer. The meek person is one who is ready to be defeated. Lao Tzu says, "Nobody can defeat me because I have accepted defeat already." Now how can you defeat a defeated person? Lao Tzu says, "Nobody can defeat me because I am standing as the last person in the world. You cannot push me any further back – there is no 'further back.' I am the last person."

Jesus also says, "Those who are last in this world will be first in my kingdom of God." Those who are the last will be the first? It does not seem possible in this world. In this world, aggressive people, violent people tend to become powerful, tend to be victorious. You will find the most mad people in the most powerful places because to reach to that point one has almost to be crazy for power, the competition is such. The competition is so violent that how can a meek person reach to a state of power? No, but that is not the meaning.

When Buddha says, *Meekness is most powerful...* he is saying you cannot defeat a meek person because he has no desire to conquer. You cannot force a meek person to be a failure because he never wanted to succeed. You cannot force a meek person to be poor because he has no desire for riches. Poverty is his richness. Not to be anybody in particular is his way of life. To be a nobody is his very style.

What can you take away from him? He has nothing. He cannot be cheated, he cannot be robbed. In fact, he cannot be destroyed because he has already surrendered that which can be destroyed. He has no self, no ego of his own.

It happened...

When Alexander was going back from India, he wanted to take a sannyasin with him. When he was coming to conquer India, his teacher, the great philosopher Aristotle, had told him, "When you are coming back, bring a gift to me. I would like to see a sannyasin from India." That is something very original to the East. That contribution belongs to the East. The West has given great warriors, the East has given great sannyasins. Aristotle was intrigued with the very idea of sannyas, what it is.

Alexander, going back, remembered. He inquired. The people of that village where he was staying told him, "Yes, there is a sannyasin, but we don't think you will be able to take him back." He laughed at the foolishness of the villagers because who can prevent Alexander? He said, "If I want to take the Himalayas, even they will follow me. So you don't be worried, just tell me where he is." They told him.

He was a naked fakir, a naked man standing just by the side of the river outside the village – a beautiful person. Dandamis was his name, that's how Alexander's historians have remembered him. Two soldiers were sent. They told the sannyasin, "Alexander the Great wants you to follow him. You will be a royal guest. Whatsoever you need will be provided, every comfort will be made possible. Accept the invitation."

The naked man started laughing. He said, "I have dropped all wandering. I don't go anywhere any more. I have come home."

They said, "Don't be stupid. The great Alexander can force you to go. If you don't go as a guest, you will go as a prisoner. The choice is yours. Anyway you will have to go."

He started laughing again. He said, "I have dropped the very thing that can be imprisoned. Nobody can make me a prisoner. I am freedom."

Alexander himself came. He took his sword out and he told the sannyasin, "If you don't come with me, this sword is here and I will cut your head."

The sannyasin said, "You can do it. In fact I have done it

already. I have cut my head myself. And if you cut my head, you will see it falling down on the ground and I will also see it falling on the ground because I have become a witness."

It is said that Alexander could not gather courage to kill this man. He was so happy, he was so fearless, he was so blissful.

When Buddha says, *Meekness is most powerful*... he means one who does not exist as an ego is meek. One who does not exist as an ego cannot be conquered, cannot be defeated, cannot be destroyed. He has gone beyond.

By going beyond the ego, you go beyond death. By going beyond the ego, you go beyond defeat. By going beyond the ego, you go beyond powerlessness. This is a totally different concept of power – the power of a sannyasin.

This power is no longer out of conflict. This power is not created out of friction. You say electricity is created out of friction. You can create electricity out of friction, you can create fire out of friction. If you rub both your hands, they will become hot. There is a power that comes out of friction by conflict. And there is a power that comes by cooperation – not by friction but by harmony. That's what Buddha says: "One who is in accord with the way is great." One who is in accord with the way is powerful. But to be in accord with the way, one has to be meek.

Blessed are the meek. Certainly they shall inherit the earth. History will never know about them because history has nothing to do with them. History knows only friction, history knows only mischief. History knows only mischief-mongers. History knows only mad people because history records only when something goes wrong. When everything is absolutely in tune, it is out of time and out of history also.

History does not report much about Jesus, in fact, nothing. If the Bible was not in existence, there would have been no record about Jesus. And I would like to tell you that many people like Jesus have existed, but we don't have any record about them. History never took any note. They were so meek, they were so silent, they were so in tune, so deep in harmony that not even a ripple was created around them. They came and they left, and they have not left even a footprint.

History has not been recording buddhas. That's why when you hear about a Buddha or a Mahavira or a Zarathustra, they look like mythological figures, not historic. It appears that they never existed, or they only existed in the dreams of man, or they existed only in the poetries of a few imaginative, romantic people. They look like wish fulfillments. They look like how man would like man to be, but not realities. They were real. They were so real that no trace has been left behind them.

Unless you create some mischief, you will not be leaving your signature on history. That's why history records only politics because politics is the mechanism of mischief. The politician is in conflict. The religious person lives in harmony. He lives like trees. Who records about trees? He lives like rivers. Who records about rivers? He moves like clouds. Who bothers about clouds?

The meek person is one who is in harmony. And Buddha says he is the most powerful. But this concept of power is totally different. To understand it, a few things will be good to remember.

In Japan they have a beautiful science – aikido. The word *aikido* comes from a word *ki. Ki* means power. The same word in Chinese is *chi*. From *chi* comes *t'ai chi* – that too means power. Just equivalent to *ki* and *chi* is the Indian word *prana*. It is a totally different concept of power.

In aikido they teach that when somebody attacks you, don't be in conflict with him. Even when somebody attacks you, cooperate with him. This looks impossible, but one can learn the art. And when you have learned the art, you will be tremendously surprised that it happens – you can cooperate even with your enemy. When somebody attacks you, aikido says go with him.

Ordinarily when somebody attacks you, you resist. You become stiff, you become hard. You are in conflict. Aikido says even take attack in a very loving way. Receive it, it is a gift from the enemy. He is bringing great energy to you. Receive it, absorb it, don't conflict.

In the beginning it looks impossible. How? Because for centuries we have been taught about one idea of power, and that is that of conflict, friction. We know only one power and that is of fight. We know only one power, and that is of no, saying no.

You can watch it even in small children. The moment the

child starts becoming a little independent, he starts saying no. The mother says, "Don't go out." He says, "No, I will go." The mother says, "Keep quiet." He says, "No. I want to sing and dance." Why does he say no? He is learning ways of power. "No" gives power.

Aikido says, "say yes." When the enemy attacks you, accept it as a gift. Receive it, become porous. Don't become stiff. Become as liquid as possible. Receive this gift, absorb it, and the energy from the enemy will be lost and you will become the possessor of it. There will be a jump of energy from the enemy to you.

A master of aikido, without fighting, conquers. He conquers by non-fighting. He is tremendously meek, humble. The enemy is destroyed by his own attitude. He is creating enough poison for himself; there is no need for you to help him. He is suicidal. He is committing suicide by attacking. There is no need for you to fight with him.

You just try it sometimes. You have watched it, the same phenomenon happening in many ways. You see a drunkard walking on the road, and then he falls in the gutter, but he is not hurt. By the morning you will see him again going to the office, perfectly healthy and okay. The whole night he was in the gutter. He fell, but he has not broken his ribs or his bones, he has no fracture. You fall, and you will immediately have a fracture. What is happening when a drunkard falls? He falls so totally, he goes with it. He is drunk, he cannot resist.

It is said about Chuang Tzu…

He came across an accident. A bullock cart had turned upside down, had fallen in a ditch. The driver was hurt very much, the owner was hurt; he had fractures. But a drunkard was also traveling in the bullock cart with the owner, he was not hurt at all. He was not even aware of what had happened, he was snoring. He had fallen on the ground. The others were crying and weeping and he was fast asleep. Chuang Tzu said, "Seeing this, I understood what Lao Tzu means when he says 'let go.'"

Children are doing this every day. Watch children: the whole day they fall here and there, but they are not hurt. You do the same. It will be impossible for you, you will have to be hospitalized. Within a day, twenty-four hours, you will be hospitalized. The children fall in accord. When they fall they are not resisting, they are not going against the fall, they are not trying to protect themselves. They don't go stiff. In fact, they fall in a very relaxed way.

Aikido, *t'ai chi*, or what Jesus calls meekness, what Buddha calls meekness, depend on the same principle – the principle of harmony. You try it in your life, you just try in small experiments. Somebody slaps your face. Try to absorb it, receive it. Feel happy that he has released energy on your face and see how it feels. You will have a totally different feeling. And that has happened many times unawares. A friend comes and slaps you on your back. You don't know who it is – then you look. He is a friend and you are feeling happy. It was a friendly slap. You look back and he is an enemy, and you feel hurt.

The quality of the slap immediately changes with your attitude. If it is a friend you accept it. It is beautiful, it is a loving thing. If he is the enemy, then it is not loving, it is full of hate. The slap is the same, the energy is the same, the same impact of energy, but your attitude changes.

You can watch it many times. Just now it is raining. You will be going back home. You can take it in an aikido way, or you can take it in the ordinary way. The ordinary way is that you will see that your clothes will become wet, or you may get cold, or this may happen, or that may happen. And you will be against the rains. You will be running towards home in a bad mood, antagonistic.

This has happened many times. You try aikido. You relax, you enjoy the falling drops of water on your face. It is tremendously beautiful. It is so soothing, so cleansing, so refreshing. What is wrong in your clothes getting wet? Why be so worried about it? They can be dried. But why miss this opportunity? The heaven is meeting with the earth. Why miss this opportunity? Why not dance it?

Don't rush and don't run. Slow down, enjoy. Close your eyes and feel the drops falling on your eyelids, moving on your face. Feel the touch of it. Accept it, a gift from heaven, and suddenly you will see – it is beautiful, and you have never looked at it that way.

Try it in ordinary life experiences. You have always been in conflict, now try accord, and suddenly you will see, the whole meaning changes. Then you are no longer in antagonism with nature. Suddenly the sun arises, the clouds have disappeared, and a great light falls on your face. Take it easily, take it as a love gift from the sun. Close your eyes, absorb it. Drink the light. Feel happy, blessed, and you will see it is a totally different energy.

Otherwise you start perspiring. You may still perspire because heat is heat, but deep down the meaning has changed. Now you perspire, but you feel good. Nothing is wrong in perspiring. It cleanses you, it takes toxins outside, it releases poison from the body. It is a purifying fire. Just the attitude...

Meekness is most powerful... And meekness means the attitude of no-friction, no-conflict – the attitude of harmony. "I am not, God is" is what meekness is. "I am not, the whole is." That is the meaning of meekness.

Ordinarily we live through the ego and we suffer. And the ego goes on misinterpreting. Last night I was reading a beautiful anecdote...

Some years back a senator from the Interior Committee visited an Indian Reservation in Arizona, where he made a fine speech full of promises of better things, as politicians always do. "We shall see," he said, "a new era of Indian opportunity."

To this the Indians gave a ringing cry of "Hoya! Hoya!"

Encouraged, the senator continued, "We promise better schools and technical training."

"Hoya! Hoya!" exclaimed the audience with much enthusiasm.

"We pledge better hospitals and medical assistance," said the senator.

"Hoya! Hoya!" cried the Indians.

With a tear running down his cheek, the senator ended, "We come to you as equals, as brothers, so trust us."

The air shook with one long mighty "Hoya!"

Greatly pleased by his reception, the senator then began a tour of the reservation. "I see you have fine breeds of beef cattle here," he said. "May I inspect them?"

"Certainly, come this way," said the chief, "but be careful not to step in the hoya."

Get it?! The ego is just hoya, a misunderstanding. It is non-existential, yet the dirtiest thing possible. The very idea that "I am separate from existence," is dirty. The very idea that "I have to fight with my own energy source," is foolish and absurd.

But sometimes, what happens – sometimes you seem to conquer. That is a misinterpretation. When your ego sees that it is conquering, it is not the ego that is conquering. In fact, it is just a coincidence. Sometimes you are going to the left and the whole existence is also going to the left – you coincide. But you think you are succeeding, you think, "I am gaining power." Sooner or later you will be in trouble because it cannot always be so. It can be always so only if you are meek.

A meek person becomes so sensitive that he is never against the whole. He is always sensitive to feel where the whole is going. He rides on the horse and goes with the horse. He does not try to give a direction to the horse. He trusts the horse.

It happened...

With a grinding of brakes, the officer pulled up in his car and shouted to a little boy playing in the field, "I say, sonny, have you seen an airplane come down anywhere near here?"

"No, sir," replied the boy, trying to hide his slingshot. "I have only been shooting at that bottle on the fence."

A small child can be forgiven. He is afraid that maybe because of his slingshot the airplane has fallen. He can be forgiven if he is hiding his slingshot. But this is what your so-called great personalities are doing. That's what all egoists are doing. They go on thinking that things are happening because of them.

It happened...

Drought struck the countryside, and the parson of the church prayed for rain. Rain came in such torrents that a flood followed. A rescue party in a boat spied the parson sitting on the roof of his house watching the current swirl by. "Your prayers were sure answered," shouted one.

"Yes," said the careful, stranded one. "I figure it ain't bad for a little church like ours."

Sometimes your prayers are fulfilled not because of your prayers, but just because by a coincidence the whole was also going in that way, in that direction. Your prayers coincided. Sometimes your efforts are fulfilled because they coincide. Ego is coincidental. You go on collecting your ego just out of coincidences.

But this cannot always happen, that's why one feels miserable. One day you are succeeding, another day you are failing, and you cannot figure it out – what is happening? Such a great intellectual, such a great man of understanding, power, strength, logic, reason – failing? What is happening? You cannot believe it because just now it was succeeding.

Ego is always in trouble because it cannot always be a coincidence. Sometimes you are with the whole, unknowingly; sometimes you are not with the whole. When you are with the whole, you succeed. The whole succeeds always, you never.

The meek person is one who says, "I am not, only the whole is." He drops himself completely. He does not become a barrier. He allows the whole to have its way.

Buddha says this is real power.

> *Meekness is most powerful for it harbors no evil thoughts, and moreover it is restful and full of strength.*

When you fight, you dissipate energy. When you fight, you lose energy. Buddha says, don't fight, preserve your energy, and you will be powerful.

A man who goes on preserving his energy becomes such a tremendous pool of energy that his very being is powerful. Just his presence is powerful, his presence is magical, miraculous. Coming close to him, you will start feeling that you are being changed and transformed. Coming close to him, you will feel your darkness disappearing. Coming close to him, you will feel a silence descending. Just coming close to him, you will feel you are being lifted to another plane of being, to another altitude of being, to another dimension.

People come to me and they ask how to find the right master. The only way to find is just to be close, and be silent, be in harmony. And if in that harmony and silence you start feeling that you are soaring higher and higher, then this man is your master. Then this man is going to become your door for the ultimate. Then your energy fits with his energy. Then something between you and him falls in tune. Then something between you and him transpires, becomes a solid force.

You cannot decide by your intellect who is your master. You cannot decide by argumentation, and you cannot decide by your prejudice. You have heard many definitions – that the master should be like this or like that. Those definitions won't help because a person may be fulfilling all the definitions and still he may not fit you; your and his energies may not be complementary. And unless your energies are complementary, compensatory, completing each other, making a circle, then you cannot go high with that man. Going high has to be felt.

Meekness is powerful for it harbors no evil thoughts... When you have evil thoughts – evil thoughts mean thoughts of violence, of destruction, thoughts of aggression, egoistic thoughts, ego-oriented thoughts – then you dissipate energy. Then these thoughts take too much energy out of you. They are never going to be fulfilled. You are sowing stones; they are not going to sprout. Your whole energy will be wasted.

...and moreover it is restful and full of strength. Rest should be the criterion of power. A man of power is absolutely at rest, he has no restlessness in him because restlessness is nothing but dissipation of energy. When you are feeling restless, you are dissipating energy.

Hence in the East, the meditator became the symbol of power. When a person meditates, he loses all restlessness. His thinking stops, his body movements stop; he becomes like a marble statue: totally still, unmoving. In that moment he is a pool of energy. He is tremendously powerful.

If you see somebody meditating, sit by his side, and you will be benefited. Sitting by the side of someone who is in a meditative mood, you will move into meditation also. His energy will pull you out of your mess. Meditation is nothing but absolute rest.

How you bring that absolute rest depends on many things. There are a thousand and one methods to create that rest. My own methods are such that first I would like you to become as restless as possible, so nothing is hanging inside you – restlessness has been thrown out. Then move into rest, and there will be no disturbance, it will be easier.

In Buddha's time, such dynamic methods were not needed. People were more simple, more authentic. They lived a more real life. Now people are living a very repressed life, a very unreal life. When they don't want to smile, they smile. When they want to be angry, they show compassion. People are false, the whole life pattern is false. The whole culture is like a great falsity. People are just acting, not living. So, much hangover, many incomplete experiences go on being collected, piled up inside their mind.

So just sitting directly in silence won't help. The moment you sit silently, you will see all sorts of things moving inside you. You will feel it almost impossible to be silent. First throw those things out so you come to a natural state of rest. But real meditation starts only when you are in rest.

All the dynamic meditations are preparatory to real meditation. They are just basic requirements to be fulfilled so that the meditation can happen. Don't treat them as meditations; they are just introductory, just a preface. The real meditation starts only when all activity has ceased – activity of the body and activity of the mind.

...it is restful and full of strength. Remember, this definition of power is different from the ordinary definition of power. The ordinary definition of power depends on comparison. You are more powerful than your neighbor, you are more powerful than this man or that woman. You are powerful in comparison with somebody else. The power that Buddha is talking about is non-comparative; it has nothing to do with anybody.

Power is your own state. When you are full of energy, you are powerful. When you are leaking energy, you are powerless. Evil thoughts are like holes through which energy leaks. Restlessness is like leaking, continuous leaking.

You create energy every day, a tremendous amount of it, but you waste – sometimes in anger, sometimes in sexuality, sometimes in greed, sometimes in competition, sometimes for no reason at all – just because you have it, what to do with it?

There is a famous Sufi story about Jesus. Jesus comes to a

town and he sees a man drunk, shouting, lying down on the street. He comes close to him, shakes the man and says, "What are you doing? Why are you wasting your life in such a way?"

The man opens his eyes and says, "My Lord, I was ill – you cured me. Now what else can I do? Now I am healthy. I was always ill and confined to my bed – you cured me. Now what am I supposed to do? Now I have energy and I don't know what to do with it."

Jesus feels as if he has committed a crime by helping this man. He is throwing the responsibility on him. He becomes very sad. He goes into the marketplace of the town, but he is sad. There he sees a young man following a prostitute with lustful eyes, almost oblivious of the whole world.

Jesus stops the young man and says, "What are you doing? The eyes are not given for this. The eyes have been given to see God. What are you doing? Why are you wasting?"

The man looks at Jesus, touches his feet, and says, "My Lord, I was blind. You cured me. Now what to do with these eyes? I don't know anything else."

Jesus becomes very sad, he leaves the town. He comes out of the town and there he finds a man trying to commit suicide by hanging from a tree. His preparation is complete; he is just starting when Jesus comes. He says, "Wait! What are you doing? Such a precious gift of God – life! And you are going to destroy it. Are you mad?"

The man looks at Jesus and says, "My Lord, I had died. You resurrected me. Why did you resurrect me? Now I am in trouble, I don't want this life at all. What to do with it?"

You have energy and you don't know what to do with it. So one goes on wasting. There are people who say they are "killing time." Killing time means killing life. Killing time means killing the opportunity to grow, to mature, to come home.

The power that Buddha is talking about is the power when you don't do anything with your energy and you simply delight in its presence: a sheer delight in being full of energy, the sheer delight of a young green tree; the sheer delight of a cloud, a white cloud wandering in the sky; the sheer delight of a lotus flower, the sheer delight of the sun coming out of the clouds, the sheer delight of being so full of energy – vibrant, radiant, throbbing. When you don't put your energy to any purpose whatsoever, then energy itself starts moving in a vertical line.

If you put it to work, to some action, it moves in a horizontal line. Then you can make a big house, you can have more money, you can have more prestige, this and that. When you put energy to work, it moves in the horizontal line. When you don't put energy to work, you simply delight in its presence, you are happy that it is there, then it moves in a vertical line. I am not saying stop all work. I am saying find a few moments for vertical movement also. Horizontal movement is okay, but not enough. It is necessary for life – but man cannot live by bread alone.

You can get bread through horizontal work, but love, meditation, godliness, nirvana exist on the vertical line. So sometimes just sit, do nothing. Sitting silently, doing nothing, and something goes on growing within you. You become a reservoir, and you start throbbing with an unknown delight. When you are full of energy, you are in contact with the whole. And when you are in contact with the whole, you are full of energy.

> *As it is free from evils it is sure to be honored by all.*

The monk had asked: *What is most powerful and what is most illuminating?*

> *The most illuminating is a mind...*

says Buddha,

> *...which is thoroughly cleansed of dirt, and which, remaining pure, retains no blemishes. From the time when there was yet no heaven and earth till the present day there is nothing in the ten quarters which is not seen or known or heard by such a mind. For it has gained all knowledge and for that reason it is called "illuminating."*

The most illuminating is a mind which is thoroughly cleansed of dirt. Thoughts are like dirt, clinging to the mirror of the mind. Thoughts, desires, imaginations, memories – all are forms of dirt. Because of them the purity of the mind is lost. Because of them the capacity to reflect, the mirrorlike quality of the mind is lost. A continuous cleaning is needed.

So, meditation is not something that you do once and forget about, because each moment of life you go on gathering dust. It is just like a traveler who is traveling. Each day he goes on gathering dust on his clothes, on his body. Every day he has to take a bath to cleanse his body. Again the next day he will be gathering.

Meditation is like a daily bath. It is not something that once you have done it, you are finished. It should become like a natural thing, matter of fact. As you eat, as you go to sleep, as you take a bath, meditation should become a natural part of your life. At least twice a day you should cleanse your mind.

The best times are the morning, when you are getting ready for the day, the workaday world. Cleanse your mind so you have clarity, so you have transparency, so you don't commit errors, mistakes, so you don't have any evil thoughts, egoistic thoughts – you go in a purer way in the world, you don't go with corrupting seeds. And the next best time is before you go to sleep, again meditate. The whole day the dust collects. Clean the mind again, fall asleep.

If you really start cleaning it, you will see tremendous changes happening. If you clean it rightly before you go to sleep, dreams will disappear. Because dreams are nothing but the dust gathered the whole day – it goes on moving inside you, goes on creating fantasies, illusions.

If your meditation is going right, your dreams will, by and by, disappear. Your night will become a peaceful sleep with no dreams. And if the night is without dreams, in the morning you will be able to wake up very fresh, very young, virgin. Then meditate again because even if there have been no dreams, with the very passage of time, dust collects.

Even if you have not been traveling on dusty roads, just sitting in your house, dust collects. Even if your windows are closed, and doors are closed, in the morning you will find your room has gathered a little dust. Dust collects. The very passage of time is dust-collecting.

In the morning, again meditate. And if you meditate rightly and you become a silent pool of energy, you will move in the world in a totally different way – non-conflicting, non-aggressive, in harmony. Even if somebody hates you, you will transform that energy into love.

Then you will move in the world deeply skillfully with the attitude of aikido. Whatsoever is happening, you will take it, receive it, in deep love and gratitude. Even if somebody insults you, you will accept it in deep love. And then the insult will no longer be an insult, and then you will be nourished by it. By the insult he has thrown a certain amount of energy. He is losing it, you can gain it. You can simply receive it, welcome it.

And if this becomes your natural way of life – the way of the sannyasin, not the way of the soldier – every moment you will feel things are growing into a new light and your mind is becoming more and more illuminating. *The most illuminating is a mind which is thoroughly cleansed of dirt, and which, remaining pure, retains no blemishes. From the time when there was yet no heaven and earth till the present day there is nothing in the ten quarters which is not seen, or known, or heard by such a mind.*

When your mind is pure, uncontaminated, unpolluted, when not even a thought flickers in your mind and there is no smoke around your mind, your mind is like a clear sky without clouds, Buddha says you will be able to see everything that is. You will be able to know everything that is. Your sensitivity will be infinite. And whatsoever has existed from the very beginning of time will become available to you. Your knowing will become perfect.

For it has gained all knowledge and for that reason it is called "illuminating." And this illumination, this luminosity, does not come from anything outside you. It explodes from your innermost core. You are like a lamp which is covered by many curtains, dark curtains, and no light comes out of it. Then by and by you remove one curtain, then another curtain, then another curtain. And slowly rays start coming – not clear, but a glow. More curtains are removed; the glow becomes more penetrating, clearer. More curtains are removed and one day when all curtains are dropped, you suddenly see that you are a lamp unto yourself.

When Buddha was dying, this was his last message to the world. Ananda, his chief disciple was crying and weeping. Buddha said, "Stop! What are you doing? Why are you crying and weeping?"

Ananda said, "You are leaving us. I was with you for forty years. I walked with you, I slept with you, I ate with you, I listened to you – I was just like a shadow to you, and yet you were available and I could not become enlightened. Now I am crying that you are going, you are leaving.

"Without you it seems impossible for me to become enlightened. With you I could not become – I have missed such a great opportunity. Without you, now there is no hope. That's why I am crying. I am not crying because you are dying because I know you cannot die. I am crying because now for me there is no hope. Now, with your death, starts my dark night of the soul. For eons of time, millions of years, I will be stumbling in the darkness. Hence I am crying – not for you, for myself."

Buddha smiled and said, "Don't be worried about that because your light is in your own being. I am not taking your light away. I was not your light, otherwise you could have become enlightened if it was in my power to make you enlightened. It is your innermost capacity to become, so be courageous, Ananda, and be a light unto yourself: *appa deepo bhava*, be a light unto yourself."

Buddha died and after only twenty-four hours Ananda became enlightened. What happened? This is one of the mysteries. For forty years he lived with Buddha, and just twenty-four hours after Buddha died he became enlightened. The very death worked like a great shock. And the last message penetrated very deep.

When Buddha was alive, Ananda was listening so-so – as you listen to me. You listen and yet you don't listen. You say, "Okay. If I miss today, tomorrow I will be listening again, so what is the hurry? If this morning is missed, nothing is missed; other mornings will be following."

So he had listened half asleep, half awake. Maybe he was tired, maybe the night was not good and he had not slept. Maybe the journey was too long and too exhausting, and Buddha was saying the same thing again and again and again, so how long to listen? One starts feeling that one already knows. One starts feeling, "Yes, I have heard this before, so what is the point?

Why not take a little sleep? A little nap will be good."

But when Buddha was dying, Ananda must have been alert, utterly alert. He was really trembling – the very idea of millions of years again stumbling in darkness. And Buddha says, "Don't be worried, your light is within you." That struck home.

Maybe that was the first time he heard. Those forty years he must have been missing. That may have been the first time he was not deaf. He had clarity. The very situation was such that he was trembling to his roots, he was shaking to his very foundations. Buddha was leaving, and when you have lived with a man like Buddha for forty years, it is difficult. The very idea to be without him is difficult. It is impossible to believe.

Ananda must have thought of committing suicide. It is not reported in the Buddhist scriptures, but I say he must have thought about committing suicide. That idea must have happened to him; it is so human. Living forty years with Buddha, and then Buddha is dying and nothing has happened to him. He has remained desert-like, not even an oasis. He has missed the opportunity.

His eyes must have become clear. This death must have penetrated him like a sword. Sharp must have been this moment. And Buddha said, "Be a light unto yourself," and he died. He died immediately. This was his last utterance on this earth: "Be a light unto yourself." This struck home, this penetrated his heart, and within twenty-four hours he became enlightened.

That source of luminosity is within you. It is not outside you. If you seek it outside, you seek in vain. Close your eyes and go within yourself. It is there, waiting since eternity. It is your innermost nature. You are luminosity, your being is luminous. This luminosity is not borrowed, it is your innermost core. It is you.

You are light, light unto yourself.

From the time when there was yet no heaven and earth till the present day there is nothing in the ten quarters which is not seen, or known, or heard by such a mind. For it has gained all knowledge and for that reason it is called "illuminating."

Meekness is power and meditation is illumination. Both are two aspects of the same coin. On one side it is meekness, egolessness; on another side it is purity of mind, illumination. They both go together.

You will have to work on both these things together, simultaneously. Become more and more egoless, and become more and more meditative. And the greatest power will be yours, and the greatest knowing will be yours, and the greatest light will be yours.

Enough for today.

6

A QUESTIONLESS MIND

Osho,
Some months ago when I left you for the first time I was feeling strong, excited, confident in myself, and yet I spent my time speaking with you, inside or outside about some problems, trying to find a solution.
Now I am leaving again probably for a longer period, and I feel calm, peaceful, detached – even if more and more weak, confused, and without any answer. And yet I don't feel that I have any specific question to be answered by you, but only and above all, your hand on my head and your blessing.
Please, what is happening? It seems nonsense.

The question is from Nagarjuna. He is a psychoanalyst, a trained rationalist. His whole discipline of the mind is that of analysis. Coming to me, being with me has transformed him tremendously, but his old mind goes on lingering somewhere in the unconscious. It goes on throwing judgments. The old mind goes on saying, "What are you doing? It is nonsense."

It is nonsense in a way because it is beyond sense. Just to think that you ask only for the hand – somebody's hand on your head – is so irrational, so fanciful. Just to ask for blessings only is so unreasonable. The reasonable person asks questions, waits for answers, analyzes those answers, judges whether they are right or wrong, creates more questions, and so on, so forth.

To ask for blessings is difficult for the modern mind, but it is beautiful that it is happening to you. You are getting into contact with a deeper world which goes beyond sense and reason. You are asking for something which is not of this world. It cannot be understood by intellect alone. It can be understood only by the heart. You can feel it. There is no way to figure it out by reasoning. Allow it, go with it.

To be capable of nonsense is to be alive because all that is beautiful is nonsense: love is nonsense, meditation is nonsense, God is nonsense, poetry is nonsense, beauty is nonsense. All that is beautiful, true is far beyond sense.

Sense is very narrow. Nonsense is vast. Remain sensible, but don't be confined by it. Use your sense, your reason, but never be a slave to it. One should be capable of putting reason and sense by the side whenever one wants.

When you are watching a full moon in the night put your reasoning aside, be a child again. When you go to the sea and you listen to the roar of the waves put your reason aside, be primitive again. Those roaring waves are primitive, you be primitive also so that a deep contact becomes possible, so you become *en rapport* with them. When you go to the trees, please don't take your reason and sense with you, otherwise you will miss much which was there just for asking.

When you come to me, by and by you will have to put your reason aside because only then will you be able to enter deeper. Once you have known the beauty of nonsense, the truth of nonsense, then you will not call it nonsense; you will call it supra-sense. Then you will not think in terms condemnatory and negative, you will start thinking in more positive terms.

Good that you have no more questions. That's my whole effort here – to help you to become questionless. I am not here to supply you with answers because no answer can be the answer. All answers in their own turn will create more questions. It is a nonending process, it goes on ad infinitum. One question is answered, the answer creates more questions. They are answered and those answers create still more questions.

The whole history of philosophy is nothing but creating more and more questions. The old ones are not solved. The questions remain the same as they were in the days of Solomon, as they were in the days of Vedas. They remain the same as they were in the days of Manu, Mahavira and Mohammed; they have not changed. Of course, they have become multiplied. The old are there, new have bubbled up. And those new have bubbled up out of the old questions. The old questions were answered, those answers created new ones.

This is the difference between philosophy and religion. Philosophy tries to answer your questions. Religion tries to make you aware that questions cannot be solved, they have to be dropped. And in their dropping is the solution. A questionless mind is a mind who has arrived home.

So the real thing is to look deep into your questioning. They are all absurd. From the very beginning they are doomed. They cannot be answered, their very formulation is such.

For example you ask, "Who created the world?" Now this is a foolish question, it is absurd. It cannot be answered. The way it is asked prohibits its answer. If somebody says, "God created the world," you will ask the same question about God: "Who created God?" And if the person becomes angry – as so-called religious people become angry if you ask them "Who created God?" –

then they are simply showing that they are afraid.

They are afraid that you may be bringing the question back again. Somehow they have tried to solve it, somehow they pretend that they have solved it – and you are bringing the question again. Again the anxiety, again the worry. They become angry. They don't want you to open that Pandora's box again. Somehow they are sitting on the lid, they have closed it – God created the world. They also know that the question still remains relevant.

If asking who created the world is relevant, then who created God is also relevant. The question is the same. Now if you say "*A* created God," then you ask, "Who created *A*?" Say *B*. Then who created *B*? It goes on and on. It is a foolish question. I am not here to answer your foolish questions. I am here just to show it to you – that they are foolish. In that understanding they drop.

When I am answering you, in fact I am not answering you. I am just trying to make you a little more aware about your question, so that you can see that in the very asking of it you are entering into a ditch, and you will never be able to get out of it unless you drop the question.

Religion is the art of dropping questions. So, good that now you don't have any questions. I am happy, my blessings are with you. My hand is on your head. And be careful, sooner or later you will find only my hand is there, your head has disappeared. That is the whole effort. If you don't believe me, you can ask Yatri our cartoonist. A few days ago he made a beautiful cartoon for me. He has understood the point – that this is the whole magic.

If you allow me to put my hand on your head, beware. Sooner or later you will find only the hand is, and the head is gone. I am trying to behead you. And once your head disappears, you have arrived home. Then there is nowhere to go.

It is all in your head this going, searching, inquiring, questions, problems, believing this, not believing that, Islam, Hinduism, Christianity, Jainism, Buddhism. This is all in your head. When the head disappears, you are suddenly there. The old man is there. The essential man is there. God is there.

Call it whatsoever you like, but there is no problem, there is no question – you are there full of wondering eyes, you are there full of awe. Suddenly a tremendous "Aha!" arises in your being and spreads all over you and goes on spreading into the existence, what psychologists call the "Aha!" experience, the peak experience.

That's what ecstasy is, such a great "Aha!" that you are completely dissolved into it. It becomes your very song, your celebration, your dance. Life is a mystery to be lived, not a problem to be solved. Life is a mystery to be lost in, not a problem to be handled. Good that you are becoming more and more capable of not asking questions. But I can understand the puzzlement.

"Some months ago when I left you for the first time, I was feeling strong, excited, confident...and yet all my time I was asking questions, problems, trying to find a solution." When for the first time you come to me, you start feeling very strong because whatsoever you hear from me, your ego feeds on it. You start feeling very confident, very superior. You start feeling that you know, that you are somebody. Those are the honeymoon days. If you want to remain in that honeymoon, never come back again. Once is good, twice is dangerous, thrice – and you are finished!

When you listen to me for the first time, you listen as you can listen. You don't know how to listen. Your whole life has been nothing but an effort to enhance the ego, so whatsoever you get goes on feeding the ego. If you get money, your ego immediately exploits it. If you get knowledge, your ego jumps on it and becomes more knowledgeable. If you succeed in anything, the ego – whatsoever you do – the ego goes on absorbing everything that comes to it. It goes on eating it, and goes on becoming bigger and bigger.

When you come to me for the first time and take sannyas, I know very well the ego will jump on it also. It is its old habit, you have trained the ego for it. But this time it is getting into danger because sannyas is like poison to the ego. But the ego jumps on it, as it has been jumping on everything.

So for the first time you will feel everything getting better and better and better. Next time you come, the poison has started working, it has entered into your very guts – the ego starts dying. Then you understand me more. You listen to me rightly. Then you understand what the game is – the ego has to be dropped. Then you are no longer so confident, then you don't feel so strong. Then you are not so excited. Then you start shrinking because the ego starts shrinking. Then you feel weak. It is natural and good. It indicates growth.

When Nagarjuna comes for the third time, I hope he will become even more capable, more receptive. Then again he will feel a new confidence arising, but this will not be of the ego any more. It will be of his being.

You cannot call it confidence. The best way to say it is to say that there will be an absence of no-confidence. You cannot say that he will feel strong. The only way to say it is that he will not feel weak. You cannot say that he will feel more knowledgeable. You can only say that he will not feel that he lacks anything, or he needs anything. Not that there will be knowledge – there will be knowing. Not that there will be confidence because all confidence is based somewhere on fear. There will be no confidence, no no-confidence. One will simply be there, just there, with no idea.

In Zen they call these three steps. Bokuju is reported to have said, "When I came to my master, rivers were like rivers and mountains were like mountains. Then everything got confused. I lived with my master and rivers were no longer rivers and mountains were no longer mountains. Everything was confusing, everything got entangled into each other, everything trespassed each other's boundary, everything became a mess. But I remained. Again one day rivers became rivers, mountains became mountains. But what a difference." Again one day you will become the same as you were before, and yet not the same. It will be a totally different phenomenon in a way.

For example, a person who feels very strong must be aware somewhere deep down that he is weak. Otherwise who will feel strong? A person who feels that he is confident must be alert at some level of his being that he lacks confidence. Otherwise who bothers about confidence? A person who feels superior must have some inferiority somewhere.

We always project the contrary. Our projections are complementary. Whatsoever is lacking we project. An ignorant person becomes knowledgeable, an egoistic person becomes humble, a person who feels inferiority starts projecting superiority in some way or other. Because it is so difficult to live with inferiority, with no confidence, with weakness, we project the other. We project something opposite and we pretend, and we start believing in it.

But when some day one comes really home, becomes aware, then there is no inferiority, no superiority – and that is real superiority. Then there is no strength and no weakness – and that is real strength. Then there is no ignorance and no knowledge – and that is real knowing.

"Now I am leaving again, probably for a longer period, and I feel calm, peaceful, somehow detached – even if more and more weak, confused, without any answer." He has been able to understand his situation very correctly: calm, serene, tranquil; he is growing. But the calmer you become, the more you feel that all your strength was just your belief, that all your declarations were just bogus. They were efforts to hide behind, they were like masks.

So those masks are falling down and you will feel weak, confused, without an answer. Live through it. Don't start falling back. Go through it. It will be hard, it will be arduous, but if you can go through it, soon the morning is coming closer. The dark night is going to end. But remember, before the morning comes the night becomes very dark.

Now, that is exactly the case with Nagarjuna. The night will become very dark, but don't be afraid. That is simply indicative that the morning is not very far. And still he is feeling he is more calm, more tranquil.

Always remember that whenever you are feeling calmer, you are on the right track. Whatsoever else is happening, don't be bothered. Feeling calm, quiet, silent, is enough indication that you are coming closer and closer to the garden of God. The very calmness shows that you are coming closer to the cool garden. Shady trees are just waiting for you. The breeze has become cool, fragrant. You can feel it in the winds, you can feel it in the atmosphere. Calmness is the first indication of blissfulness. Silence, the first glimpse of the far away peak of bliss.

So whenever you feel silent, whatsoever else is there – confusion, weakness – don't be worried, it will disappear. If calmness is not there and you are confused, then there is trouble. That means you are not growing, you are even regressing.

So this has to be remembered by all. Whosoever is working with me, whosoever is in the work with me, should remember –

keep your eyes alert for calm, tranquility, silence. If that is happening, then don't be worried whatsoever else is happening. Let it be. It will disappear on its own accord. Maybe before it disappears it will create the last bout, it may create the last trouble that it can create. It has been there for so long, for millennia. Now suddenly you are ousting it.

These diseases, these illnesses, have lived in the house so long that they have completely forgotten that they are guests. They think they are hosts. And you are going to turn them out. They are not going to leave you easily. They will create trouble, that is accepted, agreed. You just go on listening to the silence that is happening, the calmness that is arising in you, and you will be able to transcend them.

My hand is on your head, my blessings with you.

Osho,
Empathy comes and goes. When it goes I am a wreck.
I am falling apart in fear and yearning. The yearning
is getting deeper, twisting in my gut.
Sometimes I know I am a fool and in those moments
can hear the birds and see the sky.
I have written questions for months and not handed
them in because they all seemed foolish when the
moment passes.

First, all questions are foolish. I have never come across a question which is wise. How can there be a wise question? Questions are foolish. All questions are childish.

One of the very important therapists in the West was Fritz Perls. He used to say to his friends, patients and disciples, that only children ask questions. That seems to be perfectly true. Only children ask questions.

Have you ever walked with a child, just a morning walk? And see, he will not allow you to walk at all. A thousand and one questions – each step brings questions. "Why is this tree green, papa?" Now who knows why this tree is green?

Everything becomes a question for a child. Put anything in a child's mind and out comes a question. The whole mechanism is question producing. Anything, any small thing and the child immediately makes it a question.

Questioning is childish. The more your maturity comes, the more you grow in maturity, the more questions disappear. And when there are no questions there is a possibility to see. Otherwise questions are clouding the eyes and the mind so much.

This is my experience answering so many people, and in their questions I have come to observe that it almost always happens that the person who has asked the question never listens to my answer. Everybody else listens but he is so much concerned with his question, he is so worried with his question. Others listen and understand better because they are not involved at all. This is not their question so they can listen silently. There is no worry about it. Their ego is not involved at all. But the questioner becomes very much involved. His ego is involved. He goes on looking from the corner of his eyes – what am I saying? He has asked the question to be appreciated. He has asked the question in search – not of the answer, but in search that people will think he is very knowledgeable: look, what a beautiful question he has asked!

If I don't answer questions, a few people go on asking. For example, Madhuri: she goes on asking every day, and I go on throwing her questions. She is more interested in asking than in listening to the answers because it is not a question – it has to be your question. Anybody's question is your question also. Any question that has happened to any human mind is part of you. If you listen rightly, it will solve many problems for you. It will give you insight, clarity.

But there are people who are interested only in their questions. If I am answering their questions they cannot listen because I am answering their questions, and they get into excitement and fever. If I don't answer their questions they are sitting there limp and dead: "Again this man is not answering my question."

Questioners are in trouble. The very effort to question is a little immature. In the old days it was the custom, it was the tradition to go to a master and to be with him – not to ask anything, just to be with him because what is there to ask? Even to ask, one has to know something and one knows nothing. So what to ask? One has to just be with the master, to imbibe his being, just to be soaked by his presence. One has to be like a sponge. One has to be open and receptive.

This was the tradition in the old days – that a disciple had to wait. When the master said, "Now you can ask," then the disciple could ask. And almost always it used to happen that when the master would say, "Now you can ask," the disciple would laugh and he would say, "Now it is too late. My questions are finished. There is nothing to ask now." In fact the master would ask the disciple to ask only when he would say, "Now there is nothing to ask. Now the mind is absolutely clean. There are no question marks in the mind."

Question marks are like clouds. Behind those question marks your inner luminousness gets lost. When there is no question, all clouds disappear, the sky is clean, the sunrise is clear.

The answer is in your inner illumination. The answer cannot come from the outside. I cannot answer you. The answer is in your certain state of centering.

So the questioner has felt rightly: all questions are foolish. But I am not saying, "don't ask," because I know the modern mind is not the old mind. Great changes have happened. Now if you say to somebody to wait for years, then nobody can wait. The modern mind is in such a hurry that it is not in a state of patience, and the modern mind has been trained to ask. The modern mind has not been trained to be.

That's why I go on answering your questions. Not that your questions are worth answering, or that answers are needed, or that I *can* answer your questions. No, nothing of the sort. I go on answering you questions because questioning has become part of the contemporary mind. Only by and by will you become able not to ask.

Listening to your questions and their answers, you can wait. Not doing anything, just simply sitting there in silence, you cannot wait. Silence will be too much, intolerable. So I go on answering you just to give you a few toys to play with. Meanwhile you are growing, and I am waiting for that.

The child is growing while he is playing with the toys. I go on giving you toys every day. You play, but my interest is in your growth. One day I know you will go beyond the toys and you will come to me and you will say to me, "Thank you Osho, for all the toys you gave us to play with, but no more are needed."

That will be the day, when for the first time you will fall in harmony with me and the answer will start flowing. It will not be a verbal answer, it will be a transfer of energy, a transfer beyond the scriptures. It will be a transmission, a jump, because in that moment you will be perfectly open.

Questioning shows doubting. Doubt creates barriers. A question is nothing but doubt in a very civilized dress. It looks very mannerly, but it is doubt. It is as if you go and you catch hold of a primitive man and take him to the barber, and the barber shaves and cleans him and shampoos him and gives him a bath, and then you take him to the dresser and give him a beautiful dress – and then you bring that primitive man to me. He looks a perfect gentleman, but he is not. Deep down he is the same primitive man. A question is doubt pretending not to be doubt. A question is doubt in a very mannerly, gentlemanly way.

When questions disappear, doubts disappear. Or when doubts disappear, questions disappear. Then you are in tune with me, *en rapport*. Then we are not two. Then I can look into your eyes, and you can look into my eyes and you can see a meeting happening, a meeting of two souls. And then it is very difficult to understand who is the master and who is the disciple because the energies meet and mingle and become one. In that moment, in that intimate moment, the real answer will be heard.

This is a paradox. What I am saying is this – can be summarized into this paradox – if you ask, you will not get the answer; if you don't ask, the answer is available.

Go on asking and you will go on missing the answer. Stop asking and the answer has always been waiting for you to receive it. A mind that goes on questioning never comes to the answer, and a mind that drops questioning suddenly finds the answer has always been there, luminous in one's own being. You had never lost it. Good that you could feel "I have written questions for months and not handed them in because they all seemed foolish when the moment passes."

"Sometimes I know I am a fool and in those moments can hear the birds and see the sky." Let that be your key. Then be a fool. Then that is your path. If when you are a fool you can see the sky and you can hear the birds, then being foolish is your meditation. Then be a fool, then don't try to be anything because whenever you become knowledgeable, clever, cunning, intelligent, you miss.

The sky is there, the birds are singing – they have always been singing. Since eternity, existence has been in celebration. The dance continues, it is an ongoing process, a continuum. It is a river flowing and flowing and flowing. Sitting on the bank, what are you doing?

Yes, there are moments, the questioner says, and exactly he has caught, he has found some deep intuition – that whenever he is foolish, the sky is there and the birds are singing, and the celebration can be felt. Whenever he becomes intelligent it is lost. So be a fool.

When I say be a fool, I mean don't be a mind, I mean don't be cunning and clever. Don't be calculating. You have come across a beautiful intuition, an insight. Then be more and more like a fool.

There is a beautiful novel of Fyodor Dostoevsky, *The Idiot*. Read it, meditate upon it. In that novel the main character is a fool, but a fool like St. Francis; a fool, but like Lao Tzu, Chuang Tzu. He has dropped, or he has no calculating mind.

Of course, if you are a fool you will be cheated. Of course, if you are a fool you will not be an achiever in this world. If you are a fool you will be poor, but you will be tremendously rich with godliness. In this world you will not succeed, that's certain. In this world only calculating and cunning people can succeed. But what is their success? Finally death comes and their whole success is nullified. It comes to be zero. In the end they see that it has always been a dream. They were befooled by their own cunningness.

If you are a fool you will have god within you. If you are a fool you will have all the beauties of life, tremendous riches of life. Your whole life will be a precious thing. Nobody can cheat you out of it because that is your innermost core. Nobody can take it away.

Remember it: it is better to be cheated than to cheat. If there is a choice, always choose to be cheated rather than to cheat. Because in the ultimate analysis of things the cheater is the cheated, and the cheated has not been cheated at all. In the ultimate analysis of things it is exactly as Jesus says: "Those who are last in this world will be the first in the kingdom of God, and those who are first will be the last."

The first will be the last and the last will be the first? The logic of existence is totally different from the logic of the marketplace. That is the difference between politics and religion. So I cannot conceive of a religious person being political, and I cannot conceive of a political person being religious. It is impossible, it cannot happen in the nature of things.

A politician has to be cunning. A politician has to be always ready to rob and cheat. Of course he cheats and robs in such a way that it is very difficult to catch hold of him. Rarely it happens that a Nixon is caught. But all the politicians are exactly the same – caught or not caught, that is not the point. Maybe Nixon did a little too much, he went beyond the limits. There are limits. If you remain below a hundred degrees you will not evaporate, ninety-nine will do.

The very clever politicians remain nearly ninety-nine. They never go beyond that. Nixon got a little too self-confident, went a little further, got himself into trouble. But all politicians are cunning. If they were not politicians they would be criminals. They belong to the same category. The criminals, if they were somehow brought up in a better way, would have been politicians. The quality of the mind is the same.

A religious person is one who is virtually a fool in the eyes of the world. Accept that, and you will not be a loser. I promise you, you will not be a loser. Be a fool and enjoy it. Sometimes it is wisdom to be foolish, it is foolish to be wise.

And what the questioner says – the question is from Dayal. He has tremendous capacity to become like St. Francis. He is a very simple man, very simple. He has come to a great understanding. "Sometimes I know I am a fool and in those moments can hear the birds and see the sky." Then stick to it. Then relax more and more and let those foolish moments come more and more to you. Allow them to enter you deeper. You have nothing to lose. What is there to be lost? Drop calculations and cunningness.

People think that they are not calculating. But there are a few people who are calculatingly non-calculating. They think they don't calculate.

I was reading an anecdote:

Mrs. Meyerowitz was having tea with Mrs. Abramowitz. "These cookies of yours are so delicious," raved Mrs. Meyerowitz, "I have already had five of them."

"Seven," smiled Mrs. Abramowitz, "but who is counting?"

People go on counting by the side, and they go on thinking, "Who is counting?"

Be a fool. Nothing is like it. Jesus is a fool. Buddha is a fool. In India we have a word *buddhu*: *buddhu* means fool. It comes from buddha. People must have thought that Buddha is a fool. So in Indian languages the very word for fool has become *buddhu*.

When Buddha started sitting under his *bodhi* tree where he became enlightened, everybody must have thought that he was a *buddhu*, a fool. People must have come to him and said, "What are you doing? Have you gone mad? You were meant to be the king." He was the only son of his father, he was going to be the king. There was no competition even – he was simply going to be the king. He had lived in tremendous riches, and suddenly he escaped. What to call this man?

Everybody must have said that he was a fool. People must have come to him and said, "What are you doing here, sitting like a fool?" His name, "Buddha," became associated with foolishness. Now *buddhu* means the fool. Nobody bothers to go into the history of the word, but it is tremendously meaningful.

Buddha was a fool. What else can you say? Everybody was trying to become the king, and he escaped. He was just on the verge. He had all the beautiful women possible. His father had brought all the beautiful girls from his kingdom for him. He was surrounded continuously with beautiful girls. Beautiful palaces were made for him, one for each season. In summer he had one palace, in winter he had another palace, in the rains he had another palace. And the father really looked after him because he was born when the father was very old; he was his only hope. And suddenly one night he escaped. To all practical purposes he is a fool: Jesus is a fool, so is Francis, so is Lao Tzu, so is Chuang Tzu. Listen to your heart and be simple, be a fool. Let that be your very style of life, and more and more godliness will penetrate you.

"Empathy comes and goes. When it goes I am a wreck. I am falling apart in fear and yearning. The yearning is getting deeper, twisting in my gut." But, "Sometimes I know I am a fool and in those moments can hear the birds and see the sky." Empathy comes, compassion, love comes, but it comes only when you are a fool. That's why everybody thinks that lovers are foolish, blind, hypnotized by each other. Love is a sort of foolishness. In the world where money seems to be the only goal, where name and fame seem to be the only goals, love is foolish, meditation is foolish, compassion is foolish.

That's why I insist – be a fool. That's why I have given you these ochre robes to make a fool out of you. Now you will be moving in the world and everybody will laugh that here goes a madman. Children will follow you and they will laugh and they will think, "What has happened to this man or this woman?" They will ridicule you. When they ridicule you, laugh. Laugh with them. Enjoy.

People come and ask me, "Why do you insist on orange robes?" It is a trick, a device to force you to become fools. You can have it only if you are ready to surrender your so-called ideas of ego, respectability; your so-called ideas which society's approval gives to you. The society will disapprove of you. You will become strangers.

That's the whole purpose. I want you to become strangers in this world so you become guests in the house of God. If you become too worldly, you will miss God.

Compassion comes; there are moments when you are flowing, when nothing holds you, when you are open. Allow it, enjoy it. Make it a point that it comes more and more. Don't close your heart. Float with it. Let it stream. In season, out of season, let it stream. With people, without people, let it stream. In the crowd, alone, let it flow over you. And by and by you will see that you have been missing. Without compassion, there is no truth.

Buddha has said that truth and compassion come together – aspects of the same energy. If you become true, you will have compassion. Or if you have compassion, you will start becoming true. A man of compassion, how can he be untrue? Just think of it. It is impossible.

If you love a person, how can you be untrue, inauthentic; how can you be false? How can you wear masks if you love a person? When you love a person you are naked, nude. You drop all curtains. You don't carry any masks. You are simply there, whosoever you are, whatsoever you are; in your simplicity, in your truth.

Compassion or love brings truth. Truth brings compassion and love. Start from anywhere – the same will be the goal, the same will be the outcome.

For Dayal I would like to say, start by being a fool and by being compassionate. And everything will happen to you. Then you need not worry.

> *Osho,*
> *The other day I felt "Hell is myself." I am in hell. Hell!*
> *Do I have to accept hell before I can find bliss? I don't understand how.*

Listen to the question very deeply. "The other day I felt 'Hell is myself.' I am in hell." No, you are not in hell. You are hell. The very ego is hell. Once the ego is not there, there is no hell. The ego creates structures around you which make you miserable. The ego functions like a wound, then everything starts hurting it. The "I" is hell. That is why Buddha says attain to no-self. Self is hell, no-self is heaven. Not to be is to be in heaven. To be is always to be in hell.

"Do I have to accept hell before I can find bliss?" You have to understand hell because if you don't understand hell you will never be able to get out of it, and for understanding, acceptance is a must. You cannot understand anything if you go on denying it. That's what we have been doing. We go on disowning parts of our being. We go on denying: "This is not me." That's what Jean-Paul Sartre says, "The other is hell." When you deny something in you, you project it on the other. Look at the mechanism of projection. Whatsoever you deny in yourself, you project it on others. You have to put it somewhere. It is there, you know.

Just the other night a sannyasin told me that she has become very afraid that her husband is going to kill her. Now she has a very simple and beautiful husband, a very simple man. Rarely can you find such simple people. It is almost absurd, the idea that he is going to kill her.

When she was saying it the husband started crying. The very idea was so absurd tears started falling from his eyes. It is very rare to see a man crying because men have been trained not to cry. He felt it, what to do? And the woman thinks that any moment the husband is going to suffocate her. She feels his hands on her neck in the darkness. Now, what is happening?

Then, by and by, she talked about other things. She has no child, and she desperately needs a child. And she told me that looking at others' children she feels that she would like to kill them. Now things are clear. Now nothing is complicated.

She said she would like to kill the children, others' children, because she has no child and she would not like anybody else to be a mother. Now this murder is in her, and she does not want to accept it. It has to be projected on somebody else. She cannot accept that she has the murdering instinct in her; it has to be projected. It is very difficult to accept that you are a murderer, or that you have ideas of murdering children.

Now, the husband is the closest person, the most available to be projected on, almost like a screen – you can project. Now the poor man is crying and the woman thinks he is going to murder her.

In the deep unconscious she may even have ideas of murdering the husband because she must have this logic inside – that because of this man she is not getting pregnant. If she were with some other man she would have become a mother. She will not accept it on the surface. Deep down because of this man, because of this man being her husband, she has not been able to become a mother. Somewhere in the unconscious there is a lurking shadow that if this man dies she will be able to find another man, or something like that. And then the idea that she would like to kill others' children – she is projecting it. Now, you project your ideas on others, then you become frightened. Then this man looks like a murderer.

This we all do. If you have some part of your being denied, disowned, where will you put it? You will have to put it on somebody. So Hindus go on projecting on Mohammedans. Mohammedans go on projecting on Hindus. Mohammedans think Hindus are very cunning. Hindus go on thinking that Mohammedans are very dangerous, murderous, violent rascals. India goes on projecting on Pakistan; Pakistan goes on projecting on India. China goes on projecting on Russia; Russia goes on projecting on China. Russia goes on projecting on America; America goes on projecting on Russia. And they all deny that they have these things inside them.

Just look, America goes on piling up armament, Russia goes on piling up armament. Now the competition has gone to foolish extremes. The people who understand it, they say, "Now it is absolutely foolish to go on accumulating more armaments because already we have more than we need – seven times more! This earth is too small: we can destroy seven earths like this, we can kill every person seven times. Of course this is not needed. One person dies once. There is no need. We have overkill capacity." But still we go on.

So now the problem is that Russia goes on piling up armaments; looking at the absurdity – now where to, how to put it, how to make it understandable? She projects that America is after her, is getting ready to destroy her. The murderer is there, that's why we have to prepare, get ready. The same is happening in America. Both project on each other, then they become frightened.

Wars have continued, conflicts continue, violence continues – unless man comes to understand not to deny anything in himself, but to accept it. Reabsorb it into your organic unity because the denied part will create many troubles for you. Whatsoever you deny, you will have to put somewhere else, you will have to project on somebody. The denied part becomes a projection, and the eyes which project live in maya, illusion. Then they are not realistic.

Jean-Paul Sartre says, "The other is hell." This is something to be understood. You always think in that way. He is simply saying a very common misunderstanding, expressing a very common illusion. If you are miserable you think somebody else is making you miserable. If you are angry you think somebody is making you angry – but always somebody else.

If you are angry, you are angry. If you are miserable, you are miserable. Nobody is making you. Nobody can make you angry unless you decide to become angry. Then everybody can be a help, then everybody can be used as a screen and you can project. Nobody can make you miserable unless you decide to be miserable. Then the whole world helps you to be miserable. Self is hell, not the other. The very idea that "I am separate from the world" is hell. Separation is hell. Drop the ego and see suddenly all misery disappears, all conflict disappears.

"Do I have to accept hell before I can find bliss?" Certainly, absolutely. You will have to accept and understand. In that acceptance and understanding, the hell part will be absorbed back into the unity. Your conflict will dissolve, your tension will dissolve. You will become more of one piece, you will be more together. And when you are together, there is no idea of ego at all.

Ego is a disease. When you are pulled apart, when you live in a split way moving in many dimensions – directions simultaneously against each other – when you live in contradiction, then the ego arises.

Have you ever felt your head without a headache? When the headache is there you feel the head is there. If all headache disappears, head disappears. You will never feel that it is there. When you are ill you feel the body. When you are healthy you don't feel the body. Perfect health is bodilessness. You don't feel the body at all. You can forget the body, there is nothing to remember it. A perfectly healthy person is one who is oblivious of the body, he does not know that he has a body. A child is perfectly healthy. He has no body. The old man has a big body. The older one becomes, the more illness, disease, conflict settles in. Then the body is not functioning as it should function, is not in harmony, is not in accord. Then one feels the body.

All younger cultures accept the body, old cultures deny body. Old cultures reflect the old minds, old man's mind; younger cultures reflect the young man's mind. For example in India, it is one of the ancient-most cultures, the body is denied. Your so-called monks, *munis*, saints, sadhus – they are anti-body, they are enemies to the body. They have the old man's attitude towards the body. In America, it is a very young country, the body is accepted, enjoyed. When a country is young, the body is enjoyed, when the country is old, the body becomes the enemy. It simply shows the old man's attitude.

If you understand this simple phenomenon, that headache

makes you aware of the head, illness makes you aware of the body – then it must be something like illness in your soul which makes you aware of the self. Otherwise a perfectly healthy soul will not have any self. That's what Buddha says, "There is no self, no atman, *anatta*." No-self is, and that is the heavenly state. You are so healthy and so harmonious that there is no need to remember it.

But ordinarily we go on cultivating the ego. On one hand we go on trying not to be miserable, on another hand we go on cultivating the ego. All our ways are contradictory.

I have heard...

A haughty socialite died and arrived at the gates of heaven. "Welcome, come right in," was Saint Peter's greeting.

"I will not," sneered the snob. "If you just let anyone in without a reservation, this is not my idea of heaven."

If the egoist, even by chance reaches to the gate of heaven, he will not enter. This is not his idea of heaven – without reservation, anybody is welcome? Then what is the point? Only very chosen persons, very few rare persons should be allowed. Then the ego can enter in heaven. In fact the ego cannot enter in heaven, it can only enter in hell. It will be better to say the ego carries its own hell wherever it goes.

It happened...

Mulla Nasruddin fell into a cesspool in the countryside and was not able to work his way out. So he stood there yelling, "Fire! Fire!" and in a couple of hours the firemen finally arrived.

"There is no fire here!" exclaimed the chief. "What are you yelling 'Fire' for?"

"What did you want me to yell?" demanded the Mulla. "Shit?"

The ego is such that even if it is in hell, it will not accept, it will not accept it. The ego goes on decorating itself.

You ask me, "Do I have to accept hell before I can find bliss?" There is no other way. You will have not only to accept, you will have to understand and penetrate. You will have to suffer the pangs and the pain of it so that you become perfectly aware what it is. Only when you know what it is will you be able to know how you create it. And only when you know how you create it, then it is for you whether you want to create it anymore or not. Then it is your choice.

"I don't understand how." Yes, it is difficult to accept hell. Our whole effort is to deny it. That's why you may be crying within, you go on smiling on the outside. You may be sad, but you go on pretending you are happy. It is hard to accept that you are miserable. But if you go on denying it, it will by and by become disconnected from your awareness.

That's what happens when we say something has become unconscious. It means it has become disconnected from consciousness. You have denied it so long that it has receded back into the shadow part of your life, it has moved into the basement. You never come across it, but it goes on working from there and affecting you and poisoning your being.

If you are miserable you can smile, but that smile is painted. It is just an exercise of the lips. It has nothing to do with your being. You can smile, you can persuade a woman to fall in love with your smile. But remember, she is doing the same. She is also smiling and she is also miserable. She is also pretending. So two false smiles create the situation that we call love. But how long can you go on smiling? You will have to relax. After a few hours you will have to relax.

If you have a penetrating eye, you can see. If you live with a person for three hours you can see his reality because to pretend for even three hours is very difficult. How to go on smiling for three hours if there is no smile coming from you? You will forget again and again, and your miserable face will show.

For moments you can deceive. That's how we deceive each other. And we promise that we are very happy persons, but we are not. The same is done by the other. Then every love affair becomes a misery, and every friendship becomes a misery.

By hiding your misery you are not going to get out of it, you will create more misery. The first thing is to encounter it. Never move unless you have encountered your reality, and never pretend to be somebody else because that is not the way happiness ever happens. Just be yourself.

If you are miserable, then be miserable. Nothing wrong is going to happen. You will be saved many troubles. Of course nobody will fall in love with you. Okay – you will be saved many troubles, you will remain alone, but nothing is wrong in being alone. Face it, go deep into it, take it out, uproot it from the unconscious and bring it to the conscious.

It is hard work, but it pays – it pays tremendously. The pay-off is immense. Once you have seen it, you can simply throw it. It exists unseen, it exists only in the unconscious, in the darkness. Once you bring it to light, it starts withering.

Bring your whole mind to light and you will see all that is miserable starts dying, and all that is beautiful and blissful starts sprouting. In the light of consciousness, that which remains is good, and that which dies is bad. That's my definition of sin and virtue. Virtue is that which can grow with absolute awareness, there is no difficulty. Sin is that which cannot grow with awareness, it needs unawareness to grow. Unawareness is a must for it.

Osho,
About a year ago I heard of an enlightened Buddhist master south of Korea and walked three days to his temple from the nearest town. He was ninety-four years old, with a face like a child, a smile like a baby, and most compassionate eyes.
His first question was, "How did you get here since there is no road?" I sit here often and wonder how I got to you, Osho, since there is no road.

There is no need for a road because your master is where you are. You can come to me only when you stop traveling, when you drop out of all paths and ways and roads. When you are simply there, where you are, you are with me. That is the only way to be with me. No path is needed. All paths lead astray. To come home no path is needed. You have to stop traveling and rushing here and there.

The old man really asked a beautiful question to you. "How did you get here since there is no road?" He was talking in a Zen way. In Zen they have a koan that a man had a goose. When the goose was very small he put it into a bottle. Then the goose started growing. He continued to feed the goose in the bottle. Then the goose became too big, so big that the mouth of the bottle was very small and it could not come out.

Now the problem is, the bottle has not to be broken, and the goose has to be taken out otherwise it will die. Now there is no space to grow and it is growing. The bottle has to be saved, it is very precious, and the goose has to be taken out, and the mouth is so small that it cannot get out. What to do?

This is a Zen koan. It is given to disciples to meditate over. Now it is absurd. What can you do about it? Whatsoever you do, again and again the same problem. The bottle has not to be broken. That seems to be the only way to bring it out. And the goose cannot be allowed inside any more because now there is no space left and it will die. Now what to do? The question is urgent. And the disciple is told to meditate as intensely as possible.

The disciple meditates twenty-four hours. Then he comes to the master, he finds some way – but what way can you find? All ways are impossible. There is no other way, this is the only alternative. And the disciple becomes desperate and more desperate, and he thinks and meditates, and his mind starts reeling around. He cannot sleep because the master says, "The question is very urgent. The life has to be saved. The goose is dying – and what are you doing sitting there? Be more intense, be more alert, and find out the solution." The master is walking around with his staff, and you cannot relax and you cannot sleep. Even in sleep the disciple thinks only of the bottle and the goose. And it continues day in, day out.

And one day it happens. The disciple is sitting silently, relaxed. There is no worry. And the master comes and says, "So, it has happened?"

The disciple says, "Yes, the goose is out because it has never been in."

But this is not an intellectual answer. I have given it to you. You cannot deceive a Zen master. He will beat you badly if you try to deceive because your whole being has to show it, your very being, your tranquility, your silence, your relaxation has to show it. It is not a question that you have to answer.

The disciple goes on thinking and thinking and thinking. And thinking becomes almost mad. His whole mind moving, moving, moving. And there comes a point where no more thinking is possible. He has come to the very end of it.

Every tension has to come to a point where you cannot go any more. Try it by closing your fist and making it as tense as possible, and go on making it tense and tense and tense. One moment suddenly you will see the fist is opening, you cannot make it any more tense. And you cannot open it, you cannot close it. It is simply opening on its own accord because to remain open is natural. When the extreme is touched, relaxation settles in.

The same happens in the mind. The worry goes to a climax, a peak, and then suddenly all thoughts fall away, and the disciple is sitting there on a lotus flower, as if on a lotus flower: no worry, no problem, no koan, nothing. The goose is out because the disciple is out. That constant thinking was the bottle in which one was confined. Now the goose is out because the disciple is out.

The old man must have asked you, "How did you get here since there is no road?" like a Zen koan.

In fact there is no road to reach to God because God is where you are. The goose is already out, the God has never been missed.

And now you ask, "I sit here often and wonder how I got to you." You may have forgotten me, but I have been always there. I am not separate from you. If I am separate then I am worthless. If I am separate from you and you have to come to me, and there is a path that connects you to me, then you will never reach to me. Then I will be like a mirage. You will be coming and coming and you will never reach to me.

One day you will understand that you are just sitting here, sitting here doing nothing, and you are in me and I am in you. And that will be the beginning of a totally new dimension of life.

Then God is in you and you are in God, and the world is in you and you are in the world. Then you are floating with the clouds and clouds are floating within you. Then you are flowering in the flowers and the flowers are flowering in you. Then division disappears. Then only one is. The goose is out. There is no road to it. The bottle is not to be broken, the bottle does not exist. The bottle is illusory. The bottle is just a belief. That you are far away and you have to travel is just a belief. That you have never gone anywhere and you have always been in the home is the truth.

A small anecdote...

A traveler hundreds of miles from home was walking across a flat, featureless desert. It had been twelve hours since he left the last oasis and he was beginning to feel a tinge of fear that he was lost and soon night would come.

Far off in the distance he saw a dust trail, hardly visible, and watched with relief as it drew nearer. Finally recognizing a figure walking towards him, as they drew nearer he shouted, "How far to the nearest oasis?" And the oncoming figure did not respond.

"How far to the nearest oasis?" he cried as the man passed beside him and still no answer. "How far to the nearest oasis?" he yelled, nearly hysterical as the dusty-robed figure disappeared in a cloud of windswept sand, and still no sign of an answer or even that the figure had heard.

He walked on. Five minutes later he heard a distant sound. Turning, he heard the figure shout, very faint in the evening winds, "Two hours."

"Why didn't you tell me before?"

"Because I did not know how fast you walked."

It depends. But this journey is just the opposite journey. If you walk very fast, you will never reach me. If you don't walk at all, if you simply sit there inside you, you have arrived. In fact you had never departed.

Enough for today.

7

REFLECTIONS OF EMPTINESS

The Buddha said:
Those who have passions are never able to perceive the way, for it is like stirring up clear water with hands. People may come there wishing to find a reflection of their faces, which however they will never see. A mind troubled and vexed with passions is impure, and on that account it never sees the way. O monks, do away with passions. When the dirt of passion is removed the way will manifest itself.
The Buddha said:
Seeing the way is like going into a dark room with a torch. The darkness instantly departs while the light alone remains. When the way is attained and the truth is seen, ignorance vanishes and enlightenment abides forever.

Who is a buddha? Or what is buddhahood? Unless you have a clear concept about it, it will be difficult to understand the sayings of Buddha. To understand those sayings, you will have to understand the source from where they arise. To understand the flower you will have to understand the roots. Unless you understand the roots, you can appreciate the flower, but you will not be able to understand it.

Who is a buddha? Or what is buddhahood? The word *buddha* means pure awareness, a state of absolute awareness. A buddha is not a person but a state – the ultimate state, the ultimate flowering. Buddha has nothing to do with Gautam the Buddha. Before Gautam the Buddha there were many buddhas, and after Gautam the Buddha there have been many buddhas. Gautam the Buddha is only one who has attained to that ultimate consciousness.

The word *buddha* is just like *christ*. Jesus is only one of the christs – those who have attained to the ultimate flowering. There have been many christs and there will be many. Remember it, that buddhahood is not in any way confined by Gautam the Buddha. He is just only one example of what buddhahood is.

You see a roseflower. It is not *the* roseflower, it is only one of the roseflowers. Millions have existed before, millions are existing right now, millions will exist in the future. It is simply a representative. This roseflower is simply a representative of all the roseflowers that have been, are, and will be.

A buddha is not defined by his personality; he is defined by the ultimate state of his being, which is beyond personality. And when a buddha speaks, he does not speak like a person. He speaks through his ultimate awareness. In fact to say that he speaks is not good, not right. There is nobody to speak, there is no self in him to speak. And in fact he has nothing to say. He simply responds. Just as if you go and start singing in a valley the valley responds. The valley simply echoes you.

When you come to a buddha, he simply mirrors you. Whatsoever he speaks is just a reflection. It is an answer to you, but he has nothing to say himself. If another buddha comes to him, they both will remain absolutely silent, two mirrors facing each other – nothing will be reflected. The mirrors will reflect each other, but nothing will be reflected. Two mirrors, just think of two mirrors facing each other. If Christ comes to see Buddha, or Buddha comes to meet somewhere on the roads of life, and he comes across Lao Tzu, they will be absolutely silent, there will be no echo.

So when Buddha is speaking, remember it. He is not saying anything in particular. He is simply reflecting the people, that's why a buddha can never be very consistent. A philosopher can be very consistent. He has something to say. He remembers it, he clings to it, he never says anything that goes against it, he manages. A buddha is bound to be contradictory because each time somebody faces him, something else will arise. It will depend on the person who faces him.

It is just like a mirror: if you come before the mirror, it is your face. Somebody else comes, then it is his face. The face will go on changing. You cannot say to the mirror, "You are very inconsistent. Sometimes you show a woman's face and sometimes a man's face, and sometimes a beautiful face and sometimes an ugly face." The mirror will simply keep quiet. What can he do? He simply reflects. He reflects whatsoever is the case.

So Buddhist sayings are very contradictory: Jesus is contradictory, Buddha is contradictory, Krishna is contradictory, Lao Tzu is tremendously contradictory. But Hegel is not contradictory, Kant is not contradictory, Russell is not contradictory, Confucius is not contradictory, Manu is not contradictory. They have a certain dogma. They don't reflect you. They have something to say. They go on saying. They are not like mirrors, they are like a photograph. It doesn't bother who you are, it remains the same. It is dead. It has a clear cut definition and form.

Buddhahood is a formless awareness. Remember it, otherwise many times you will come across contradictions and you will not be able to figure out what is happening.

When Buddha died, immediately there was much controversy and the followers divided into many sects because somebody had heard Buddha saying this, and somebody had heard something absolutely contradicting it. So there was no possibility. How can one man say all those things? So, somebody must be lying, and people started sorting out. They sorted out into many different schools. Buddha was cut: somebody carried his hand, somebody his head, somebody his legs; but he was no longer an alive phenomenon.

Now, these philosophies are very consistent – very consistent, very logical, but dead. A buddha is not a philosopher, he is not a systematizer. A buddha is not logical in any way, he is simply alive and he reflects everything that is.

So when you come to a buddha, he answers you. He has no fixed answer to give to you, he answers you. He has no public face. All his faces are private and they depend on you. If you bring a beautiful face to him, you will see your own face reflected. And if you come without any face, pure, mirrorlike, nothing will be reflected, then Buddha disappears, he has nothing to say.

Those who lived with Buddha, they knew. When they had their own minds, those minds were reflected in him. When their minds dropped they really became meditators, and when they looked at Buddha there was nobody, just emptiness, a valley, pure silence, primal innocence – but nobody there.

These sayings are collected, compiled by a certain school. They are very consistent. Many sayings have been dropped which were apparently contradictory. Many have not been included which were ambiguous. These sayings were collected by a particular school. Later on I will be discussing other sources, and many times you will come across contradictions – remember it.

Those who are near me, they have to understand this absolutely clearly because I will be contradicting myself every day. It depends on the climate. It depends – if the weather is very cloudy, I am cloudy. If the sun is shining bright and clear, I am that way.

You not only come to me with questions, you also come with the answers. Maybe the answer is not known to you, maybe the answer is hidden in your unconsciousness, lurking somewhere in the darkness of your soul. The question is conscious, the answer unconscious. My function is to make your answer clearly obvious to you, to bring it to light. I am bound to be contradictory.

I am not a public man. I am not interested in the crowds. I am interested only in disciples and devotees. That means I am interested only in intimate relationship. I am interested in you, and whatsoever I say to you is said to you and is irrelevant for others. When I talk personally, then I am talking to a particular person. To others it may not be relevant. Even to the same person it may not be relevant tomorrow because he will be changing.

Life is continuous change. And I am only consistent with life and nothing else. So I am bound to be contradictory. So if sometimes you come across contradictions, don't be in a hurry, and don't try to figure out somehow, and don't try to fix them. Let them be as they are.

A man like Buddha has to be contradictory. He has to contain all contradictions because he contains all the possibilities of humanity. He contains all possible questions and all possible answers. He contains all the possible faces and all the possible phases. He contains the whole past of humanity, the present and the future.

That is the meaning when Buddha says, "When you have come home, when your innermost being is luminous, all will be known – all that was past, present and future. Nothing remains unknown. In that knowing light everything is revealed." But everything... and things are not consistent.

That's the beauty of the world, that things are not consistent. Things have different qualities, different personalities. All things are beings in their own way, and Buddha is simply reflecting: a reflection, a mirror.

These sayings always start with, "The Buddha said:" Remember it. When it is said, "The Buddha said:" it simply means he has nothing to say. He reflected, he reflected you back. He simply showed you who you are. He revealed you to yourself. He brought you to your own center.

> *Those who have passions are never able to perceive the way, for it is like stirring up clear water with hands. People may come there wishing to find a reflection of their faces, which however they will never see. A mind troubled and vexed with passions is impure, and on that account it never sees the way. O monks, do away with passions. When the dirt of passion is removed the way will manifest itself.*

Many things of tremendous import are said in this sutra. First Buddha says, *Those who have passions are never able to perceive the way*... What is passion? Passion is a sort of fever, a sort of trembling of your being, a sort of inner wavering. Passions mean you are not content as you are. You would like something else, you would like something more, you would like a different pattern of life, a different style. Then you think you will be happy and contented.

A mind full of passion is a mind full of discontent with the present. A mind with passion, desires, hopes – but never lives; it postpones. It says tomorrow, always tomorrow. It is never here and now. A mind full of passion always goes on missing the present, and the present is the only reality there is. So a mind full of passion goes on missing reality. It cannot reflect that which is, it cannot reflect the truth, it cannot reflect the *dhamma*, the way. It cannot reflect the real that surrounds you because you are never here.

Watch your mind: whenever there is a desire you have gone astray. You cannot be in the future, remember; you cannot be in the past, remember – that is impossible. That doesn't happen in the way things are. That simply doesn't happen. You cannot be in the past. Past is no more. How can you be in the past? But more or less you are always in the past. You are in the memory of the past. That is a way of not being, that is not a way of being. That is a way of not being. Or you are in the future, which is impossible because future is not yet. How can you live in a house which is not yet?

But you live. Man goes on doing miracles. These are the real miracles. He goes on living in the past which is no more, and he starts living in the future which is not yet. You love the woman you have not found yet, or you go on loving the woman who is dead.

The mind either clings to the past or to the future. This is a way of not being. This is how we miss existence. This is how by and by we become phantoms, shadows, ghosts. Watch yourself. As I see people, millions of people remain in the life of a ghost.

A woman was here just a few days ago, and she said she is very much afraid of ghosts. I said, "This is something because sometimes ghosts come to me and they say that they are very afraid of you. You are also a ghost. Why should you be afraid of ghosts?" I looked into her face. It was of the past, it had something of the future, but there was no real content of the present.

Living in the memories or living in imagination – that is the way of passion. Passion is a wavering either to the left or to the right, but never in the middle. And middle is the truth, the present is the truth, the door to reality.

Buddha says: *Those who have passions are never able to perceive the way...* We are always on the way, there is no other way to be, but we never perceive that which we are always together with. We are always in God, but we never perceive God. God is so obvious. But we perceive everything except God, and he surrounds you, within and without. He is pulsating in everything. Only he is, but you cannot see him because you are never in the real. You are unreal, so how can the unreal meet the real? A mind full of passion cannot meet with the real. And this continues.

Children are full of passion. One can understand, they are childish, they don't know life yet. Young people are full of passion. One can forgive them too; they are yet too young. That means they are yet too foolish, they will have to learn. But even old people, dying on their deathbed, but still full of passion? – then it is too much. An old man cannot be forgiven.

A child is okay, a young man can still be forgiven, but an old man? – impossible to forgive. He has lived his whole life and he has not come to understand a simple fact, that you cannot be in the future and you cannot be in the past. He has lived his whole life and he has been frustrated each moment of it, and yet he goes on expecting. He has lived his whole life, desiring and desiring and desiring, and nothing has come out of it. Death has come and life has not yet arrived. He has been waiting only, preparing for life, it has not happened. Yet he goes on hankering for more life.

As I see many people, I have watched people dying – it is very rarely that a person dies without passion. When a person dies without passion the death is beautiful. It has tremendous significance, it has intrinsic value. But people die ugly deaths. Even death cannot shake them out of the dreams and passions and fevers. Even death cannot make them realize what is happening.

I have heard a very beautiful anecdote...

There is a whorehouse. The doorbell rings and the madam

answers it, but she sees no one. Then, looking downstairs she sees a man with no arms or legs sitting on a platform with wheels. She says to the guy, "What could you possibly want here?"

The guy looks up at her, smiles and says, "I rang the doorbell didn't I?"

Now that's enough! To the very end dying people think of sex. There is some interconnection because sex means birth. So death and sex are really very deeply connected. If you have not been able to sort it out while you were fully alive, it will be very difficult to sort it out while you are dying because when death comes it also brings its polarity, its shadow.

Life starts with sex, life ends with death, and when death comes, the sex energy has a last bout. It becomes a flare. That very flare leads you into another life, the wheel starts moving again. Dying with a sexual, passionate mind, you are again creating a new life, a new birth. You have started seeking a womb. Sex means the search for a womb has started. You are not dead yet, but the search has started. Your soul is already preparing to take a jump into another womb.

Buddha says if you can die without passion you have broken the circle. You may never be born again. Or even if you are born it is going to be only once. Maybe a little karma is left, accounts have to be closed, things finished, but basically you are free.

When the mind is free of passion, the mind is free. Freedom means freedom from passion. And only a free mind can see what is real. Only a free mind, free from passions, can see what is here.

Those who have passions are never able to perceive the way, for it is like stirring up clear water with hands. Have you watched sometimes, on a full moon night you go to the lake – everything is silent, not even a ripple on the surface of the lake and the moon is reflected so beautifully. Shake the water, create a few ripples in the water with your hands and the moon is divided into fragments, the reflection disappears. You may see silver all over the lake, but you cannot see the moon. Fragments and fragments, the totality is broken, the integration gone.

Human consciousness also can be in two states. One state is the state of passion: when there are many ripples and waves hankering for some shore somewhere in the future, or still clinging from some shore in the past. But the lake is disturbed, the surface is not calm, quiet and tranquil. The surface cannot reflect the reality, it distorts. A mind full of passion is a mechanism for distortion. Whatsoever you see, you see through distortion.

Go to a lake on a full moon night and watch these two things in the lake. First see everything quiet, calm, the moon reflected, a tremendous beauty, and everything so still as if time has stopped. And everything so present, as if only present is. In a moonlit, full moon night, being on a faraway lake, just sitting there, you are going a little out of time and space. Then create ripples, or wait for a wind to come and distort. Then all reflection is gone or distorted. Then you go on looking – you cannot find the moon, you cannot figure out what the moon is like. You cannot make it out from the reflection.

These are the two states of the mind also. A mind without any thought, desire, passion, is quiet – quiet like a lake. Then everything as it is, is reflected. And to know that which is, is to know God, is to know truth. It is all around you, you are just not in a state to reflect it.

When your passions drop, by and by things start falling in line, they become integrated. And when the reflection is perfectly clear, you are liberated. Truth liberates; nothing else liberates. To know that which is, is to be free, is to be absolute freedom.

Dogmas cannot liberate you, creeds cannot liberate you, churches cannot liberate you. Only truth liberates. And there is no way to find the truth unless you have come to create a situation in yourself where that which is, is mirrored.

Those who have passions are never able to perceive the way... Consciousness has to become without content. That is the meaning of being passionless. When you are, simply you are. I call it primal innocence. You are not hankering, desiring for anything; you are just in this moment, absolutely here and now. A great content arises into your being, a tremendous satisfaction arises into your being. You feel blessed.

In fact that is what you are seeking. In all your desires you are seeking a state of contentment. But desires cannot bring it. Desires create more ripples on your lake. Desires create more restlessness in you. You are desiring only one thing: how to come to a state where everything is just contentment, nowhere to go, one is simply delighted. Just by being, one is blissful. Just by being, one can dance and sing.

That is what you are seeking. Even in your desires, in your greed, in your sexuality, in your ambition, that's exactly what you are seeking. But you are seeking in the wrong direction; it cannot happen that way. It has never happened that way. It can happen in only one way: the way of the Buddha, the way of Krishna or Christ. The way is the same, it belongs to nobody.

That way is right now here available to you, you just have to come to meet it here. You are escaping somewhere else, you are never found at your home. Whatsoever address you give, you are never found there. You are always somewhere else.

God comes and seeks you, of course he trusts you, and he comes to your so-called address, but you are never there. He knocks at the door and the room is empty, the house is empty. He goes into the house, looks everywhere, but you are not there. You are somewhere else. You are always somewhere else, your house is somewhere else. Ordinarily people think that they have to seek God. The truth is just the opposite: God is seeking you, but you are never found.

What Buddha is saying is, if you are passionless you will be found. You will immediately be found because you will be sitting in the present moment. Your mind will not be wavering, your flame will be absolutely unwavering. In that very moment of meditation you meet God, you meet truth. You become free.

Those who have passions are never able to perceive the way... But one thing has to be remembered, you can drop the worldly passions – many people do. They become sadhus, monks, they move to the monasteries, but they don't drop the passion as such. Now they start thinking of God. Now they start thinking how to achieve in the other world. Their achiever's mind still continues, only their language has changed. The content remains the same, only the container has changed. Now they no longer desire money, they no longer desire a bank balance, but still they desire security, security in the hands of God.

When you are seeking a bank balance, or when you are going

to an insurance company to be insured, these are just languages for a deep search for security. You leave them, then you become a Christian or you become a Hindu. By becoming a Christian, what are you seeking? You are again seeking security. You are thinking, "This man Jesus is the begotten son of God, I will be more secure with him."

Or you are seeking to become a Hindu. You think, "These Hindus, they have been longest in the profession of religion. They must know. They must know all the secrets of the trade. They must be having keys. Many civilizations have come and gone, but these Hindus have some trick, they continue: Babylon is no more, Assyria is just ruins, the old civilization of Egypt is just in the museums. Many civilizations have existed on this earth and gone, only traces are left here and there. But these Hindus are something. They have persisted, they have not been destroyed by time, they have a certain quality of eternity. They must be knowing some secret. Become a Hindu." But you are seeking security.

If you are seeking security, your mind still carries the same passion, desire, fear. You may not be interested in this world. There are many people who come to me and they say, "This is impermanent, momentary; this world is not worth. We are seeking something like permanent bliss." So nothing has changed. In fact, they seem to be more greedy than ordinary people.

Ordinary people are satisfied with momentary things. These people seem to be very dissatisfied. They are not satisfied with momentary things: a beautiful house and a garden, a beautiful car, a beautiful woman and a husband, and a wife and children; they are not satisfied. They say, "These are all momentary, sooner or later they will be taken away. We are seeking something which cannot be taken away." These people are more greedy. Their passion knows no bounds. They think they are religious. They are not. A religious person is one who has dropped all passion, passion as such. Just by changing the language, nothing is changed.

I have heard...

Mulla Nasruddin was saying to his friend, "I never called you a son of a bitch."

"Yes you did!" The friend was very angry. He insisted, "Yes you did!"

"No I didn't!" Mulla repeated. "All I said was, 'When you get home throw your mother a bone.'"

But it is the same. Just by changing your language, nothing is changed.

The so-called religious people are as worldly as worldly people, sometimes even more so. I have come across many religious people, many Jaina monks, they seem to me more worldly than their followers because the world does not mean the world. The world simply means passion, desire, greed. They are hankering for *moksha*, hankering for the other world, the heaven, the paradise. Their dreams are full of future.

Your dreams are also full of future, but your future is not so big. You think only a few days ahead, or at the most a few months. If you are very, very imaginative, at the most a few years ahead, that's all. Your passion is not so strong. Their passion seems to be mad. They are not only thinking a few years ahead, they are thinking a few lives ahead – the other world. Their desires have gone berserk, they are mad. They can leave and renounce the world, but that renunciation is false because they are renouncing for better worlds.

When you renounce for something better it is a bargain, it is not a renunciation. You go to the film, to the movie. Of course, you have to renounce five rupees. You have to sacrifice five rupees immediately. But nobody calls it renunciation. It is a bargain. If you want to live in heaven, in paradise, you have to pay for it.

Remember this – that whenever you are paying something for something, it is not renunciation. The very idea of paying makes it immediately clear that it belongs to the world of desire because life is free and nobody needs to pay for it. Let me repeat it: life is absolutely free, nobody needs to pay for it. The moment you start paying for it, it is not life. It must be something like a commodity in the market – maybe in the religious market, but it must be some commodity.

If somebody asks you to renounce because that is the way to gain, then he is asking you to pay for it, sacrifice for it. He is talking economics, not religion. He is talking finance. He is telling you, "This much you have to pay. If you want to be in God's paradise you will have to pay these things. You will have to sacrifice."

Of course it appeals to you because you know the logic. How can you get anything free? You have to pay for it. And when you see God, you have to pay tremendously. You have to pay with all your pleasures. You have to become frozen, dead. You have to renounce life, so you become a "good boy," a "nice boy." And now God feels very happy. "Look, this man has renounced everything for me. Now he should be allowed."

God never asks any sacrifice from you. How can he ask any sacrifice from you? It is not a market. Paradise is not to be earned. You are not to pay for it. You have only to learn to enjoy it, that's all. If you know how to enjoy it, it is available right now. You are not to pay for it.

But our whole mind has been trained by economists and politicians. They say you will have to pay. Sacrifice your childhood in education so that when you are young you can have a beautiful house, a family, respect, a respectable job. You will have to pay for it, so sacrifice your childhood so when you are young you have all the pleasures of the world.

Then when you are young your wife says, "Take out insurance because the children are growing and they will need it. And we will be growing old – and old age? What are you going to do?" Sacrifice your youth for old age so that in old age you can retire, and comfortably.

So you sacrifice your youth for your old age. And then what do you do when you retire? Now the whole life is gone, always just preparing for something else. And the more you prepare, the more you become skillful in preparing – that's all. Then you can prepare more. A man who becomes more skillful in preparing is never ready to live. He becomes more ready to prepare more, that's all.

That's how the whole life is missed. And then in the old age they say, "Now prepare for the other world. What are you doing? Pray, meditate, go to the church. Now become religious. What are you doing? Death is coming. Prepare for the afterlife."

Now this whole logic is foolish. The childhood sacrificed for youth, the youth sacrificed for old age, the old age sacrificed for after-life. So everything is just a sacrifice. When comes the time to enjoy? Let me say to you, if you want to enjoy, never prepare. If you want to enjoy, enjoy! Do it right now because there is no other way to do it.

If you become a great preparer, a great, skillful, efficient man in preparations, you will always prepare but you will never go for any journey. You will become so skillful in preparing, packing and unpacking, that you will not know how to go for the journey. You will only know how to pack and unpack again.

That's what people are doing in life. Life is free, it is a gift – gift of God. Enjoy it. Let this go as deep as possible in your heart. Let this secret be now no longer a secret. Life is a gift. Let there be dancing in the streets.

There is no need to prepare. Preparation is always a shadow of passion. When you desire for the future, of course you have to prepare for it. In the present, no preparation is needed. The present has already arrived. The trees are already green, and the roses have flowered and the birds are calling you. Where is the point in preparing?

This craziness of preparation is absolutely human. You will never find it anywhere. Have you ever seen any animal preparing for anything, any tree preparing for anything, any star preparing for anything? They must all be laughing. Man is so ridiculous an animal. They must be all laughing. What has gone wrong? They are enjoying, just now they are enjoying. Reality must be more clearly reflected in animals, in birds, in rocks, than in man. Man's mind is full of ripples. These ripples have to be dropped.

Man is in a very strange situation. Below man is nature, absolutely unconscious and blissful. Above man are buddhas, absolutely conscious and blissful. Man is just in between: a passage, a bridge, a rope stretched between two eternities. Man is neither as happy as the cuckoo in the garden, nor as happy as the buddha. He is just in between, stretched, tense, wants to move both the ways together, becomes more and more split.

That's why I say schizophrenia is not a special disease; it is a very common phenomenon. It is not unusual. Everybody is schizophrenic, has to be. The very situation of humanity is schizophrenic.

Man is not unconscious so he cannot be like trees, enjoying without preparation. And he is not yet buddhalike, so he cannot enjoy without preparation. He is not in the present. He is just in the middle.

But nothing to be worried about. You can never be as happy as the tree now, there is no way of going back, that world is lost. That is the meaning of Adam's expulsion from the Garden of Eden – he is no longer part of the unconscious bliss. He has become conscious by eating the fruit of the tree of knowledge. He has become man.

Adam is man, and every man is Adam-like. Every childhood is in the Garden of Eden. Every child is as happy as the animals, as happy as the primitive, as happy as the trees. Have you watched a child running in the trees, on the beach? – he is not yet human. His eyes are still clear, but unconscious. He will have to come out of the Garden of Eden.

It is not that Adam was once expelled – every Adam has to be expelled again and again. Every child has to be thrown out of the God's garden; it is part of growth. The pain is that of growth. One has to lose it to gain it again, to gain it consciously. That is man's burden and his destiny, man's responsibility; his anguish and his freedom, man's problem and man's grandeur – both.

Buddha is nothing but Adam, Adam coming back, re-entering the Garden of Eden. But now he comes with full awareness, now the circle is complete. He comes dancing, he comes absolutely blissful. He is as blissful as any tree, but not unconscious. He has gained consciousness, he has risen towards consciousness. Now he is not only blissful, he is aware that he is blissful. A new quality has entered.

That's what is trying to enter in you – knocking your head from everywhere. That's what I mean when I say God is searching you. I mean that consciousness wants to happen to you. Allow it to happen. Recognize that God is searching you. Let go, fall in accord with him. That's what Buddha calls *dhamma* – being in accord with nature, fully accord, fully in accord, but aware.

And don't wait. Don't wait for some age when the whole humanity will become aware and passionless. That will be a very futile waiting, you will be waiting in vain.

I have heard...

A drunkard was walking home when he came upon a group of men digging a big hole in the middle of the street. "Watcha doing?" he asked.

"We are building a subway," came the answer.

"When you gonna finish it?" he asked.

"Ah, in about eight years."

The drunk thought for a while and then shouted back, "Ah, the heck with it. I will take a taxi."

The humanity will someday become collectively conscious, that possibility exists, but nobody knows when. Millions of years will pass, and millions of individuals will have to become buddhas before it can happen. Then one day it is possible that buddhahood may become a natural phenomenon.

But before it, you have to strive individually. And you cannot wait for it. That waiting will be very suicidal. And if everybody waits for it, it will never happen because for it to happen a certain amount of individual souls are needed to become buddhas.

Now a few experiments are being done about meditation. It has been found that if in a village, a small village of four hundred people, the number of meditators rises at least one percent – for example, if in a village of five hundred people, five persons start meditating – the crime rate in the village falls immediately. People commit fewer crimes just because one percent of the village is meditating. It affects the whole consciousness, just one percent. And just meditating; they are not buddhas.

If one percent of humanity becomes buddhas, the whole quality will change. Consciousness will become easier, may become almost natural and spontaneous.

So if you are waiting, you are waiting in vain. And if you are waiting and everybody goes on waiting, it is never going to happen. Do something about it because by doing something about it, you will be creating a situation in which it will become easier and easier for it to happen to others.

Those who have passions are never able to perceive the way, for it is like stirring up clear water with hands. People may come there wishing to find a reflection of their faces, which however they will never see. That's why you don't know who you are. You have not been able to see your own face in your mind. What to say of other things? What to say about the face of God? You have not been able to look at your own face in your mind, even that much reflection is not possible. The face does not become a reality, you see only fragments because the mind is continuously shaking, wavering.

The flame is never in a state of tremendous rest, so everything is flickering. Sometimes you see one of your eyes, sometimes you see your nose, sometimes you see one of your hands, sometimes you see a part of your face, but everything is muddled. And if you want to figure it out, it becomes a Picasso painting. You don't know what is what.

I have heard that Picasso made a portrait of a friend. The friend came, he looked from all sides. He said, "Good, beautiful, but I don't like the nose. You will have to change at least that much."

Picasso said, "Okay, come after one month."

He said, "One month! It will take so long?"

Picasso said, "I cannot be even certain whether I will be able to do it in one month."

He said, "What do you mean?"

Picasso said, "Now don't force me to say the truth. In fact I don't know where I have made the nose. I will have to search and meditate upon it. I have made your nose certainly, somewhere, but where?"

If you look about yourself you are a Picasso painting. Everything is muddled, in a mess. You don't know your identity, who you are. So you cling to outer supports: your name, your father's name, your family name, your certificates from the university, your degree. These are outer supports. They help you somehow to give some idea who you are. But really you don't know who you are. Because how can you know yourself if you know that you are a doctor or an engineer or a plumber? What has that to do with your being?

You can be a plumber, you can be a doctor, you can be an engineer – that has nothing to do with your essential being. These are all accidents. You can be white or you can be black, but that has nothing to do with your essential being. These are just accidents, nothing essential. The difference between a white man and a black man is just of a small pigment. If you go to the market, the pigment will not cost more than four *annas*. That is the only difference between a Negro and a white man – very nonessential, but it has become so tremendously important.

What is the difference between a rich man and a poor man? – just accidents. Between a successful man and a failure? – just accidents. They don't really define you. But we don't know how to define in any other way, so we go on clinging with this fragment and we go on making something out of it.

The reality of your being is within you. You just need a little silent mind, it will be reflected. You will know who you are, and that will become your first step to know what this reality is.

What is this whole game? What is this magical world? By knowing yourself, you will have taken the first step of knowing God. By knowing yourself absolutely, you have taken the last step of knowing God. By knowing yourself, you know what God is. There is no other way because you are gods, but you have not been able to see your face. *A mind troubled and vexed with passions is impure, and on that account it never sees the way. O monks, do away with passions. When the dirt of passion is removed the way will manifest itself.*

...the way will manifest itself. There is no need to discover it. All that is needed is you should have an innocent, pure mind. And when Buddha says pure, he does not mean a mind which is moral. He does not mean a mind which is religious. His definition of purity is more scientific. He says a mind which is without thought, because a moral man is moral, but he has moral thoughts. An immoral man is immoral, but he has immoral thoughts. As far as the mind is concerned, both are full of thoughts. A worldly man has worldly thoughts, a religious man has religious thoughts. Whether you are singing a song from the latest movie or you are chanting a religious prayer, it makes no difference – your mind is wavering, your mind is not silent.

So by pure, Buddha does not mean moral. No, he simply means a mind which has no content. All content brings impurity.

Whatsoever the content, it is impure. He is not saying impurity in any condemnatory sense. He is saying it only in a very scientific sense: anything foreign, anything alien, makes the mind impure.

Mind is just pure reflection, the capacity to reflect. If the mind has some ideas in itself, they will not allow its reflection to be pure. Then projection starts and the reflection is distorted. So whether you have religious ideas or non-religious ideas, whether you are a Communist or a Democrat, it makes no difference. Christian, Mohammedan, Hindu, Sikh – it makes no difference. If you have ideas, your mind is impure.

A mind full of consciousness will be empty of all contents. He will be neither a Christian nor a Hindu nor a Jew. He will not be a moral man nor an immoral man. He will simply be. That being, that be-ness, is purity. That's what I call primal innocence. Then all dust is washed and you are just a reflective force.

O monks, do away with passions. When the dirt of passions is removed the way will manifest itself. And then suddenly you will see, the way has always been herenow, only you were missing it. It is impossible to lose the way, it is impossible to lose God. You can try, that's what you have been doing. You can try, and for moments you can also believe that you have succeeded. But in fact it never happens.

You cannot lose the way, there is no way to lose the way. There is no way to go astray. You can only believe in your dreams that you can go astray, but in reality you cannot go astray. Any time when you become awake, you will simply laugh that you have been thinking you have gone far away. You have never even gone out of your home. You have always lived here, just with closed eyes you go on dreaming and dreaming and dreaming.

In dreams you can go as far away as you like, but in reality there is no way to go anywhere except God because wherever you are, reality is. You are part of reality and you exist only as an organic part to reality. You cannot go away. You cannot separate yourself. You are intermingled with existence, you are interwoven with existence. We are not dependent, we are not independent, we are interdependent. We are members of each other. There is no way to go anywhere.

So when the mind is pure, *When the dirt of passion is removed the way will manifest itself.* Suddenly you will see, G standing before you. Suddenly you will recognize that you ha always been standing in the door, on the threshold. You will start laughing. The whole game has been so ridiculous.

A really religious person never loses the sense of humor. And if you see a religious person who has no sense of humor, you can be certain he has not come home yet. Because a religious person, the more he understands, the more he sees the ridiculousness of the game, the more he starts laughing. How did it all become possible? How did I dream? How long have I been in dreams? – and those dreams were looking so real.

> *The Buddha said:*
> *Seeing the way is like going into a dark room with a torch.*
> *The darkness instantly departs while the light alone remains. When the way is attained and the truth is seen, ignorance vanishes and enlightenment abides forever.*

A beautiful maxim to be remembered. *Seeing the way is like going into a dark room with a torch.*

If you go into a dark room with a torch, with a lamp, the darkness immediately disappears – immediately. Buddha says instantly, it does not take time. It is not that you bring light in, then the darkness lingers a little while, decides whether to leave or not, takes a little time and then goes; no! No time is needed because darkness is not real.

If it was real, it will take a little time – maybe a split second, but it will take a little time to go out. It will have to travel; traveling will take time. Sometimes it may be a lazy darkness, it may take a little longer time. Sometimes it may be a fast runner; then it will go fast. But anyway it will take time if it is real.

When you bring light, the very bringing of the light is the disappearance. Darkness is not, only light is. When darkness is, in fact there is nothing. It is only the absence of light, that's all. Darkness has no positive being; it is just absence of light, so when you bring presence, the absence is no longer there.

Buddha says this world is just like darkness. Once you bring light to it, once you become aware, once you drop your passions and become meditative, once the mind attains to the purity of meditation, suddenly the light is there. Darkness dissipates, disappears instantly, immediately, within no time. *Seeing the way is like going into a dark room with a torch. The darkness instantly departs while the light alone remains. When the way is attained and the truth is seen, ignorance vanishes and enlightenment abides forever.*

Enlightenment is that which has always been the case. Enlightenment is that which has always been there. You were not aware. You were fast asleep. It was just sitting by your side waiting for you to awaken. Enlightenment is your nature, is your very being. From the very beginning it has been there. It is there right now. If you can flare up in awareness you can attain to it immediately. It is a sudden illumination.

But if you want you can take your time, you can move slowly, gradually. You can turn over and go to sleep again and wait a little more. But whenever you open your eyes you will find it. It has always been there. Just for asking's sake it would have been achieved any time. It was never difficult. It seems difficult because you are asleep. Once you are awakened, you will laugh. How was it difficult? Why was it difficult? It was something that was present, only you had to claim it.

The way is. Waves come and go, the ocean is. Minds come and go, no-mind is. Roles come and go; Buddha is. Buddha is your original face, your originality, your very being.

O monks, do away with passions. Drop desiring. Our desiring culminates everything. Our desiring becomes our interpretation of everything. The more you desire, the more miserable you will be because the more you desire, the more your expectation will be. The more you desire, the less grateful you will be because the more you desire, the more you will feel man proposes and God disposes. The less you desire, the more grateful you will be because the less you desire, the more you will see how much is given without desiring, without asking. If you don't desire at all, you will be in tremendous gratitude because so much is given already. Life is such a gift, but we go on with our mind.

I have heard...

A man was reckoned to be the laziest man in the country and

naturally spent most of his time sleeping. He was so inactive and so useless that at one time the townspeople thought it would be a good idea to bury him regardless of whether he was dead or alive.

They made a crude coffin, came around with it to his house, put him in it without any protest from his family, and started off with the live old critter for the cemetery. Of course there was no resistance from him; he was so lazy. He said, "Okay." Or he may not have even said that. He may have just watched what was going on.

But before they got to the cemetery, they were stopped by a stranger who had heard of the grim proceedings. They told the stranger the man would not work and had not a grain of corn on his place, and the town was sick of providing him with food. "Enough is enough," they said, "and we are fed up."

"If you boys will hold off, I will gladly give that man a wagonload of corn," said the stranger. Before the townspeople could reply, a head was raised out of the coffin, and the almost deceased asked, "Is that corn shucked?"

The lazy man is worrying about the corn, whether it is shucked or not. He is ready to die, but if he has to shuck the corn, then it is too much effort.

A man who is surrounded by laziness looks at everything through his laziness. His laziness becomes his interpretation of things.

If you are sleepy, you will look at life with sleepy eyes, naturally. And if you miss life, it is natural because life is possible only if your eyes are fully alive, if your eyes are radiant with life. If you look at life with alive eyes, there is a meeting, a communion.

We live surrounded by clouds of desire. Then those desires become our interpretation. Then we go on thinking according to those desires.

It happened...

Applicants for a job on a dam had to take a written examination, the first question of which was: What does hydro-dynamics mean?

Mulla Nasruddin, one of the applicants for the job, looked

at this, then wrote against it: It means I don't get the job.

Whatsoever meaning we give to life, *we* give it to life. And Buddha is saying if you want to know the real meaning of life, then you have to drop giving all meanings to it, then the way reveals itself, then life opens its mysterious doors. You stop giving meaning to it – your desires are giving meaning to it; they are defining the indefinable. And if you remain clouded with your desires, whatsoever you know is nothing but your own dreaming. That's why we say in India that this life, this so-called life lived through desires, is maya, it is a magical thing. You create it, you are the magician. It is your maya, your magic.

We don't live in the same world, remember. We live in separate worlds because we don't live in the same desires. You project your desires, your neighbor is projecting his desires. That's why when you meet a person and you want to live with a person, with a woman or with a man or with a friend, difficulties arise. That is a clash of two worlds.

Everybody is good alone. Together, something goes wrong. I have never come across a wrong person, but every day I come across – I have to watch and see and observe – wrong relationships. I never come across a wrong person, but every day I come across wrong relationships. It seems almost all relationships are wrong. Because two persons live in two desire worlds, they have their own magical worlds. When they come together those worlds clash.

It happened…

One night Mulla Nasruddin was sitting on one side of the fire and his wife on the other. Between them lay the cat and the dog, lazily blinking at the fire. The wife ventured this remark, "Now dear, just you look at that cat and dog. See how quietly and peacefully they get along together. Why can't we do that?"

"That's all right," said Nasruddin, "but just you tie them together and see what will happen."

Tie two persons together – that's what a marriage is – and see what happens: suddenly two worlds. It seems almost impossible to understand the woman you love. It should not be so, you love her, but she seems impossible to understand. It is impossible to understand the man you love. It should not be so, you love him, but he seems impossible to understand.

It is very easy to understand strangers, it is very difficult to understand people who are very close. To understand your mother, father, brother, sister, friend, is very difficult. The closer you are, the more difficult because the worlds are clashing.

These worlds surround you like a subtle aura. Unless you drop this magical creation that you go on feeding, you will remain in conflict. You will remain in conflict with persons, and you will remain in conflict with God because he has his own world, and you have your own private world. They both never go together. You have to drop your private mentation.

Dropping mentation is what meditation is all about. You have to drop your thinking, desiring. You have just to be, and suddenly everything falls into an organic whole, becomes a harmony.

These desires are the root of the darkness that is surrounding you. These desires are the support, the foundation of the darkness that surrounds you. These desires are the hindrances that don't allow you to become alert.

Beware of these desires. And remember the word *beware* means be aware. That is the only way. If you really want to get rid of these desires, don't start fighting them. Otherwise you will miss again because if you start fighting with your desires, that means you have created a new desire – to be desireless. Now this desire will clash against other desires. This is changing the language, you remain the same.

Don't start fighting with the desires. When Buddha says, "Do away with passions, O monks," he does not mean to fight with the passions. Because you can fight only if there is a prize, if you are going to attain something. Then again a desire has arisen – a new shape, a new form, but the same old desire. Don't fight, just be aware.

Beware of desires. Become more watchful, more alert and you will see the more alert you are, the fewer desires are there. Ripples start subsiding, waves start disappearing and one day, suddenly any moment it can happen because all moments are as potential as any other. There is no auspicious moment for it to happen. It can happen in any ordinary moment because all ordinary moments are auspicious. There is no need for it to happen under a *bodhi* tree. It can happen under any tree, or even without a tree. It can happen under the roof of your house. It can happen anywhere because existence is everywhere.

But by and by become aware. Create more and more awareness, collect more and more awareness. One day the awareness comes to such a point, the energy is so much that it simply explodes. And in that explosion darkness disappears and light is. Immediately darkness disappears, instantly darkness disappears and light is. And that light is your own luminosity, so you cannot lose it. Once known it becomes your eternal treasure.

Enough for today.

8

WHATSOEVER YOU CHOOSE, YOU BECOME

Osho,
When life itself is so fulfilling, overflowing, so blissful, then what is that which makes a man miserable?

Life is overflowing, life is blissful, but man has lost contact with life. He has become too self-conscious. That self-consciousness functions as a barrier and one remains alive, yet not truly alive. Self-consciousness is the disease.

The birds are happy, the trees are happy, the clouds and the rivers are happy, but they are not self-conscious. They are simply happy. They don't know that they are happy. Buddha is happy, Krishna is happy, Christ is happy, but they are pure consciousness. They are happy, but they don't know that they are.

There is a similarity between the unconscious nature and the supra-conscious beings. Unconscious nature has no self, the supra-conscious beings also have no self. Man is just in between: he is no longer an animal, no longer a tree, no longer a rock, and yet not a buddha. Hanging in between is the misery.

Just the other day a new seeker from the West wrote me a letter saying: "Osho, I don't want to become a sannyasin. I don't want to become superhuman – Buddha or Christ. I simply want to become just human. Help me to become just human."

Now, this is too ambitious, and it is impossible. Just to be human is impossible. Try to understand it because that means you are saying "Let me just remain the process, in the middle." Man is not a state, man is only a process. For example, if a child says, "I don't want to become young, I don't want to become old, let me just remain a child," is it possible?

He is already becoming young, he is on the way. Childhood is not a state. You cannot remain in it, you cannot stick to it. It is a process. Childhood is already going, youth is already coming. And so is youth, howsoever hard you try to remain young, your efforts are doomed to fail because the youth is already turning into old age.

Just to be human, you ask – you ask the impossible. You are too ambitious. You can become a buddha, that is simpler. You can become a god, that is simpler. But to ask that you would like to just remain human is impossible because humanity is just a passage, a voyage, a journey, a pilgrimage. It is a process, not a state. You cannot remain human. If you try too hard to remain human you will become inhuman. You will start falling. If you don't go ahead, you will start slipping backwards. But you will have to go somewhere. You cannot remain static.

To be human simply means to be on the way to being a god – nothing else. "God" is the goal; to be human is the journey, the way. The way can never be permanent, it cannot become eternal otherwise it will be very tiring. The goal will never arrive then, and you will be just on the journey, on the journey, on the journey.

To hope is to be human. But to hope means to hope to go beyond. To hope means to desire beyond. To hope means to hope to surpass, to transcend. This is really the state of a human being – that he is always surpassing, going, going; somewhere else is the goal. The person who has asked it must be a beautiful person. In fact, ready for sannyas, but he does not understand what he is saying.

Man is miserable because man has to be miserable. It is not your fault, it is not like you are in some error. To be human is to be miserable because to be human is to be in the middle: neither here nor there, hanging in limbo. Anguish arises because of the tension.

One home is lost – the home where birds are still singing, animals still moving, trees still flowering, the Garden of Eden; that home is lost. Adam has been turned out. Adam has become human. When Adam was in the Garden of Eden he was an animal; he was not an Adam, he was not a man. God turned him out of the garden. That very expulsion became humanity.

Man is expelled from one home so that he can search another home: bigger, higher, deeper, greater. One home is lost; there is a nostalgia, man wants to become animal. It is very difficult to forget that Garden of Eden, it was so beautiful. And there are moments we become animal-like: in deep anger, in violence, in war, we become animal-like. That's the enjoyment of being angry.

Why do you feel so happy in being angry? Why do you feel such a rush of energy in destroying something? Why in wartime do people look more radiant, healthier, sharper, more intelligent; as if life is no longer a boredom? What happens? Man falls back. Even for a few days, a few months, man again is an animal. Then he knows no law, then he knows no humanity, then he knows no God. Then he simply goes, drops his self-consciousness, becomes unconscious; murders, kills, rapes – everything is allowed in war. That's why man needs war continuously. After every ten years a big war is needed, and small wars have to be continued continuously otherwise it will be difficult for man to live.

Man becomes a drunkard, becomes a drug addict. Man tries to reclaim the lost home, the lost paradise, through chemical drugs.

When you are under LSD, you are back in the Garden of Eden, from the backdoor; LSD is the backdoor of the Garden of Eden. Again life seems psychedelic, colorful; again trees look luminous as they must have looked to Adam and Eve, as they must be right now for cuckoos and tigers and monkeys. The green has a luminosity in it, everything looks so beautiful. You are no longer human. You have fallen back. You have forced your being to fall back. Hence tremendous appeal exists for alcoholic beverages.

Since the very beginning of human history, man has been after drugs. In the Vedas they called it soma, now they call it LSD. But it is not a different thing. Sometimes it was ganja, bhang, now it is marijuana and other things, but it is the same old game.

Chemically it is possible to fall back, but you cannot really go back. There is no going back, time does not allow that. One has just to go forward. You cannot move backwards in time. The reverse gear does not exist. When Ford made his first car there was no reverse gear. Only later on they thought that it was very difficult to come back home. You had to take long turns, unnecessary miles, then you could come back. Then the reverse gear was added as a later thought. But in time, God has not yet added the reverse gear, you cannot go back.

Man has dreamed about it, fantasized about it. There are science fiction stories in which man can go back into time. H. G. Wells has an idea of a time machine. You sit in the machine and you put it in the reverse gear and you start moving backwards. You are young, you become a child, then you become a baby, then you are in the womb. You start moving backwards. But no time machine exists. It exists only in poets' minds, fantasies.

To go back is not possible. There is only one possibility: to go ahead. Man has to remain in anguish. There are only two ways: either make it possible to go back, or to go beyond humanity. Humanity is a bridge. You cannot make a house on it. It has to be passed. It is not to be lived upon.

When the Mohammedan mogul emperor Akbar made a special city, Fatehpur Sikari, he asked his wise men to find out something: a maxim to put on top of the bridge that joins the city to the world. They looked, they searched and they found a saying of Jesus. It does not exist in the Bible; it must have come from some other source, from Sufis. There were many Sufis in Akbar's court. The saying is: "The world is like a bridge, don't make your house on it." The saying is still there on the bridge. It is beautiful; that's how it is.

Humanity is a bridge. Don't try to be just human, otherwise you will become inhuman. Try to become supra-human, that is the only way to be human. Try to become a god, that is the only way to be human; there is no other way. Have your goal somewhere in the stars, only then you grow.

Man is a growing phenomenon, a process. If you don't have any goal, growth stops. Then you are stuck, then you become stagnant and stale. That's what has happened to millions of people in the world. Look at their faces – they look like zombies, as if they are asleep or drugged, stoned.

What is happening to these people's hearts? They don't show any freshness, aliveness, no spurt of life, no flame – dull. What is happening to them? They have missed something. They are missing something. They are not doing that for which they are made, they are not fulfilling that destiny which has to be fulfilled.

A man is here to become superman. Let superman be your goal. Then only will you be able to be man, and at ease. The more you will be transforming into a superman, the more you will find you are not in anguish, not in anxiety. The buds are coming soon, there will be great rejoicing, soon there will be blossoms. You can wait, you can hope, you can dream.

When you are not going anywhere, when you are trying just to be human, then the river has stopped flowing. Then the river is not going towards the ocean because to go to the ocean means to have a desire to become the ocean. Otherwise why go towards the ocean? Going towards the ocean means merging into the ocean, becoming the ocean.

God is the goal. You can be human only if you go on making all efforts, all possible efforts to become divine. In those very efforts, your humanity will start shining. In those very efforts, you will become alive.

"When life itself is so fulfilling..." Life is fulfilling, but you are not in contact with life. Old contact is lost, new has not been made. You are in a transition, hence you are so dull, hence life looks so mediocre, sad, boring – even futile.

Jean-Paul Sartre says: "Man is a useless passion, futile impotent passion, unnecessarily making much fuss about life, and there is nothing in it; life is meaningless." The more you become enclosed in your self, the more life becomes meaningless. Then you are miserable.

But then misery has some other payoffs.

When you are happy you are ordinary because to be happy is just to be natural. To be miserable is to become extraordinary. Nothing is special in being happy: trees are happy, birds are happy, animals are happy, children are happy. What is special in that? It is just the usual thing in existence. Existence is made of the stuff called happiness. Just look – can't you see these trees? – so happy. Can't you see the birds singing so happily? Happiness has nothing special in it. Happiness is a very ordinary thing.

To be blissful is to be absolutely ordinary. The self, the ego, does not allow that. That's why people talk too much about their miseries. They become special just by talking about their miseries. People go on talking about their illness, their headache, their stomach, their this and that. All people are in some way or other hypochondriacs. And if somebody does not believe in your misery, you feel hurt. If somebody sympathizes with you and believes in your misery – even in your exaggerated version of it – you feel very happy. This is something stupid, but has to be understood.

Misery makes you special. Misery makes you more egoistic. A miserable man can have a more concentrated ego than a happy man. A happy man cannot really have an ego because a person becomes happy only when there is no ego. The more egoless, the more happy; the more happy, the more egoless. You dissolve into happiness. You cannot exist together with happiness, you exist only when there is misery. In happiness there is dissolution.

Have you ever seen any happy moment? Watched it? In happiness, you are not. When you are in love, you are not. If love has ever made its abode in your heart, even for a few moments, you are not. When you see the beautiful sun rising, or a full moon night, or a silent lake, or a lotus flower, suddenly you are not. When there is beauty, you are not. When there is love, you are not.

Hearing someone, if you feel there is truth, you simply disappear in that moment. You are not, truth is. Whenever there is something of the beyond, you are not; you have to make space for it. You *are* only when there is misery. You are only when there is a lie. You are only when there is something wrong. You are only when the shoe does not fit.

When the shoe fits perfectly, you are not. When the shoe fits perfectly you forget the feet, you forget the shoe. When there is no headache there is no head. If you want to feel your head, you will need a headache, that is the only way.

To be is to be miserable. To be happy is not to be. That's why Buddha says there is no self. He is creating a path for you to become absolutely blissful. He is saying there is no self so that you can drop it. It is easy to drop something when it is not. It is easy to drop something when you understand that it is not, it is just imagination.

One day Mulla Nasruddin was telling his friends in the tavern about his family. "Nine boys," he said, "and all good except Abdul. He learned to read."

Now when a person learns to read difficulties arise, now the self is arising. In villages, people are happier, they are closer to animals. In big cities, they are far away. In primitive societies the aboriginals are happier. They are closer to trees and nature than in London, Tokyo, Mumbai, New York: trees have disappeared, only asphalt roads, absolutely false; concrete buildings, all man-made.

In fact, if suddenly somebody from outer space comes to Mumbai, New York, Tokyo, London, he will not find any signature of God there. All is man-made. Looking at Tokyo or Mumbai, one will think man made the world. These concrete buildings, these asphalt roads, this technology – all is man-made. The farther away you go from nature, the farther away you go from happiness – the more and more you are learning to read.

God expelled Adam because he ate from the tree of knowledge: he started learning to read. He threw him out. Adam became knowledgeable. A man is bound to be more miserable if he is more knowledgeable. The misery is always in exact proportion to your knowledgeability.

Knowledgeability is not knowing. Knowing is innocence;

knowledgeability is cunningness. It is very difficult for an educated person not to be cunning. It is almost impossible because the whole training is cunning. The training is of logic, not of love. The training is for doubt, not for trust. The training is to be suspicious, not to be trusting. The training is that everybody is trying to deceive you, so be aware. And before somebody else tries to cheat you, cheat because that is the only way to be protected.

Machiavelli says: "The best way to defend oneself is to be aggressive." Just see, all the governments of the world call their military organization, army, "defense." They are all arrangements for attack – they call it "defense." Even Hitler called his military "defense." Nobody down the ages has ever said, "I am attacking." They say, "We are defending." They all follow Machiavelli. They all respect Mahavira, Mohammed, Moses, and they all follow Machiavelli. As far as respect is concerned, go to the temple, read the Bible. But as far as actual life is concerned, read *The Prince*, read Machiavelli, read Chanakya.

In Delhi, the Indian capital where politicians live, they call it Chanakya Puri – the city of the Machiavelli. Chanak is the Indian counterpart of Machiavelli, even more dangerous than Machiavelli. The more a person becomes educated, the more Machiavellian, cunning.

When Machiavelli's book *The Prince* was published, he was thinking that all the kings of Europe would invite him, and he would be posted on a high post as an advisor to some king. But nobody called him. The book was read, the book was followed, but nobody called Machiavelli. He was surprised, he inquired. Then he came to know that reading his book they had become afraid of him. He was so cunning that to give him a big post was dangerous. If he followed his own book, he would destroy, he would throw the king away. Sooner or later he would become the king. He lived a poor man's life, he could never get into any powerful post.

Education makes you more cunning. Of course, education makes you more miserable. To be religious is to wipe out all this nonsense. To be religious means to learn how to unlearn, how to uneducate yourself again. Whatsoever the world has conditioned you for, you have to uncondition it. Otherwise you are in clutches.

Man is miserable because man is caught in his own net. He has to come out of it, and only a distant star will be helpful.

Maybe there is no God – I'm not worried about it. But you need a God, a distant star to move towards. Maybe by the time you reach there you will not find God, but you will have become a god by that time. Reaching to that star you will have grown.

Man is miserable because man has learned the tricks to be miserable. Ego is the base of it. Man is miserable because bliss, happiness, is so obviously available – that creates the trouble.

The first time I met Mulla Nasruddin happened this way:

I saw him fishing in a lake. I had not heard about him. I watched him. Hours passed, not a single fish. I asked him, "What are you doing here? Just close by there is another lake, and don't you know? – there are many fish there."

He said, "I know. There are so many fish in that lake that it is even difficult for them to swim. The lake is full of fish."

"But then why are you sitting here? I don't see any fish at all."

He said, "That's why I am sitting here. What is the point of fishing in the other lake? Any fool can do that. To fish here is something!"

The ego goes on fishing in lakes where fish are not. That which is obvious, that which is available is not attractive. That's why we miss God. God is available, God is your very surround. He is the very atmosphere we breathe in and out. He is our very life. He is the ocean in which we live, are born, and will dissolve. But he is so close, no distance. How to feel him?

Watch it in your own life. Whatsoever you have loses interest for you. You have a beautiful house. It is beautiful only for your neighbors, not for you. You have a beautiful car. It is beautiful only for others who don't have cars, it is not beautiful for you. You have a beautiful woman or a beautiful man, it does not have any appeal. You have it, that's enough. People are attracted only to that which they don't have. The nonexistential attracts.

I have heard...

"Say, Ramon," said Mulla Nasruddin, as they met in the street one day, "I have been meaning to ask you something."

"Go ahead, Mulla," said his friend.

"My wife is kind of fat. In fact when she takes off her girdle at night she is one great big blob. Is your wife like that?" questioned Nasruddin.

"Ah, no. My wife has a gorgeous figure. In fact she is so trim she does not wear anything underneath, and she is a real knock-out," replied Ramon.

"Well," continued Nasruddin, "my wife is so ugly, she covers her face up at bedtime with creams and curlers. Does not your wife do that?"

"Ah, no. My wife does not need any creams or makeup, and her hair is magnificent," replied the friend.

"Well, Ramon, I have only one more question. How come you are chasing my wife?" demanded Nasruddin.

That's the way of the ego: always chasing somebody else's wife, always chasing something that you don't have. Once you have, all interest is lost.

So an egoist remains miserable, because to be happy one has to be happy with that which one has. You cannot be happy with that which you don't have; you can only be unhappy with that. You can be happy only with that which you have. How can you be happy with that which you don't have? And ego is always interested only in that which you don't have.

You have ten thousand rupees, ego is no longer interested in it. It is interested in twenty thousand. By the time you have twenty thousand, it is no longer interested in it. It is interested only in thirty thousand. And so on, so forth, it goes on.

The ego only gives you goals; but whenever those goals arrive, it does not allow you to celebrate. One becomes more and more miserable. As life passes, we go on gathering misery, we go on piling up misery. And it is very difficult to realize this – that you are causing your own misery. That is against the ego, so you throw the responsibility on others.

If you are miserable you think the society is such, your parents were wrong. If you listen to Freudians, they will say it is because of your parents, your parental conditionings. If you listen to Marxists, they will say it is because of the social structure, the society. If you listen to the politicians, they say because it is the wrong type of government. If you listen to the educationist, they say because some other type of education is needed.

Nobody says that you are responsible; the responsibility is thrown on others. Then it is impossible to be happy, because if others are making you miserable then it is beyond you to be happy, unless the whole world is changed according to you.

Now it is difficult to choose your parents. It has already happened. What to do?

Somebody asked Mark Twain, "What does one person need to be really happy?"

He said, "The first thing is that one should choose his parents rightly."

Now that is impossible, it has already happened. You cannot choose your parents now. One should choose a right society. But you are always in a society. You don't choose it, you are always in the middle of it. And if you want to create it to your heart's desire, your whole life will be wasted. And it will never be changed because it is such a big phenomenon, and you are so tiny.

The only hope of any transformation is that you can change yourself. That is the only hope, there is no other hope.

But the ego does not want to take the responsibility. It goes on throwing the responsibility on others. In throwing responsibility on others, you are throwing your freedom also, remember. To be responsible is to be free. To give the responsibility to somebody else is to be a prisoner.

That is the religious standpoint. Religion says you are responsible. That's why Marx was so much against religion. His reasoning is clear-cut. He knew it perfectly well – that either religion can exist in the world or communism. Both cannot exist together. And he is right, both cannot exist together. I also agree with him.

Our choices are different. I would like religion to exist, he would like communism to exist, but we agree that both cannot exist together because the whole standpoint of communism is that others are responsible for your misery. And the religious standpoint is that except you, nobody else is responsible. The communist says a social revolution is needed for a happy world. The religious person says a personal revolution is needed to be a happy person.

The world is never going to be happy; it has never been so, and it is never going to be so. The world is bound to remain unhappy; only individuals can be happy. It is something personal.

It needs consciousness to be happy, it needs intensity to be happy, it needs awareness to be happy. The world can never be happy because it has no awareness. Society has no soul, only man has it. But it is very difficult for the ego to accept this.

It happened...

Mulla Nasruddin made life very difficult for his associates because he believed he was infallible. Finally one of his workers spoke up. "Nasruddin," he said, "you surely have not been right all the time?"

"There was one time I was wrong," admitted the Mulla.

"When was that?" asked the surprised worker. He could not believe that Nasruddin would ever admit that he was ever wrong, even one time. He could not believe his own ears. He said, "When was that?"

"The one time," recalled Mulla Nasruddin, "when I thought I was wrong, but I was really not."

Ego is tremendously defensive. Ego is never wrong, hence you are in misery. Ego is always infallible, hence you are in misery.

Start looking in the loopholes. Make your ego fallible and it will fall and disappear. Don't go on supporting it, otherwise you are supporting your own misery. But we go on supporting it. In good ways, in bad ways, we go on supporting it.

You call somebody a good man, a moral man, a very respectable man. He has his own supports and props for his ego. He goes to the temple every day, to the church, reads the Bible or the Gita, follows the rules of the society. But he is just trying to find props for his ego: he is a religious man, a respectable man, a moral man.

Then there is somebody else who never follows the rules of society – never goes to the church. Whenever he finds any opportunity to break any rule, he enjoys it. He is enjoying another sort of ego: the ego of the criminal, the ego of the immoral person. He says, "I don't care." But both are finding supports for the same miserable thing. Both will be in misery.

As Muldoon walked down the street, he pinched a strange woman on the behind, threw a brick through the jewelry store window, and cursed a poor old lady. "That should do it!" he said to himself. "When I make my confession I will have enough to talk about."

Even when people go to confess, they don't want to confess small sins, they are not worth confessing. This is the experience of many priests of many religions, that people exaggerate their sins. When they come to confess, they exaggerate. They may have killed an ant and they think they have killed an elephant. They exaggerate because it is not ego-fulfilling to do such a small thing.

The ways of the ego are very subtle. If you go to the jail and you listen to the talk of the people confined there, you will be surprised. They all go bragging that they have done so many robberies, and they have killed so many people. They may not have done at all, but there, that is the way of the ego. Then you are miserable and then you become worried. Why? You create a barrier between you and life. Ego is nothing but barrier.

When I say drop the ego I mean drop all demarcation lines. You are not separate from life. You are part of it; like a wave, you are part of the ocean. You are not separate at all. Neither as a saint are you separate, nor as a sinner are you separate. You are not separate at all. You are one with life. You are neither dependent on life, nor are you independent of life – you are interdependent.

When you understand that we are all interdependent, linked with each other – life is one, we are just manifestations of it – then you start becoming blissful. Then there is nobody who can prevent you from bliss.

Bliss is very obvious. Bliss is very close. Bliss is so natural and so close that mind tends to forget it. Every child is born in a blissful state, and every person, almost every person, dies in tremendous misery. Only rarely someone, a Buddha, a Jesus, dies in a blissful state. What happens? What goes wrong?

When a child is born he is not separate. When the child is in the mother's womb he is part of the mother, he does not exist separately. Then he is born, then too he remains part of the mother. He goes on being fed by the mother. Then he goes on hanging around the mother. Then, by and by, he grows.

This growth can be of two types. If he grows as ordinarily people grow, then he grows into an ego, he becomes hard, he gathers a hard crust around himself and that will make him miserable. That is not the right way to grow. Something has gone sour, something has gone wrong.

To me, if the mother is religious, if the father is religious, if the family is religious… And when I say religious, I don't mean that they are Christians or Hindus or Mohammedans or Jainas or Buddhists; that has nothing to do with religion. In fact, all these things never allow religion to evolve. If the child is forced into a dogma, into a dogmatic ideology, then the ego will gather, then the ego will become Christian, and the ego will be against the Hindu and against the Mohammedan. Then the ego will become Hindu, and will be against the Christian and against the Mohammedan.

But if the parents are really religious – by religion I mean meditative, loving – they help the child to be, but yet without the ego. They help the child to feel more and more the affinity, the unity that exists. The child has to be helped. He is helpless, he does not know where he is, he does not know where he is going. If he is loved and there is a meditative rhythm in the family and the family vibrates with silence, understanding, the child will start growing in a more organic way. He will not feel himself separate, he will start learning how to become part.

That has not happened. I am not telling you to have any grudge about it – but you can do it right now. You can stop helping your ego and you can start dropping the burden. Make it a point not to miss any opportunity where you can feel one with anything. If it is a full moon night, feel one with the moonlit night, allow a flow, stream with it, dance, sing and drop your ego.

There is nothing better than dance for dropping the ego. Hence I insist that all meditators should dance because if you go really in a whirlwind, if you are really a whirling pool of energy, if you really are in the dance, the dancer is lost. In the dance the dancer is always lost. If the dancer is not lost then you are not dancing. Then you may be performing, then you may be manipulating, then you may be doing some bodily exercises, but you are not dancing.

Dancing means to be lost, to be drunk and enjoying the energy that is created by dance. By and by you will see your body is no longer as solid as it was before. By and by you will see that you are melting; the boundary is losing its sharpness, it is becoming a little vague. You cannot exactly feel where you end and where the world starts. A dancer is in such a whirlpool, he becomes such a vibration, that the whole life is felt as in one rhythm.

So whenever you can find a time, a place, a situation – you are in love with somebody – don't miss this opportunity. Don't talk nonsense, don't bring your ego and bragging. Drop that. Love is tremendously divine, God has knocked at your door. Be lost. Hold hands with your woman, or with your man, or with your friend. Get lost! Sing together, or dance together – but get lost. Or sit together, but get lost. And feel that you are no longer an individual. Sitting by the side of a tree, get lost.

That's how it happened to Buddha. In that moment the *bodhi* tree and Buddha became one. For five hundred years after Buddha, Buddha's statues were not built. Instead, only the *bodhi* tree's picture was worshipped. It was tremendously beautiful. Those people must have understood. Just the *bodhi* tree was worshipped. In Buddhist temples there was just a symbol of the *bodhi* tree because in that moment Buddha completely disappeared. He was not there, only the *bodhi* tree was. He was completely lost.

Disappearing, *you* appear. Nonbeing is your way of real being. And this can happen in ordinary life. You need not go to the Himalayas or to a monastery. There are millions of chances in ordinary life, millions of momentous situations where this can happen. You just have to be a little watchful and a little courageous to use them. Once you start using them, more and more situations will be coming. They have always been coming, but you were not aware so you missed them.

Sitting on the beach taking a sunbath, melt with the sun. It is an energy experience. Suddenly you see you are nothing but sun energy. Melting and meeting with the sun, Hindus came to worship the sun. They said, "The sun is God." They said, "The moon is God." They worshipped trees, they worshipped people as divine. They worshipped rivers, mountains.

It is very significant. Wherever it happened that they met God – sitting by the side of a river, listening to the beautiful music of the river, seeing the beautiful patterns of ripples – if they got melted, dissolved, the river became the God. It happened there. Sitting on a lonely mountain, they dissolved and disappeared, that mountain became their God.

God comes in millions of ways to you, but your ego never allows you to see him. And he comes in such ordinary ways that you miss. He never comes like a monarch with a great procession, with a great band and noise and fuss. He never comes like that. Only foolish people do that. God comes very silently, he never comes shouting, he comes whispering. You will have to be very quiet to understand his message. It is a love whisper. And man tends to forget the natural.

I have heard a very beautiful joke…

A very naive American went to Paris and got into an argument with a French Jew about the number of ways to make love.

"There are sixty-nine ways to make love, monsieur," said the French Jew.

"I thought there was only one – a man on top of a woman," said the American.

The Jew apologized, "Monsieur," he said, " I am very sorry. I miscalculated. There are seventy ways to make love."

Now the most simple, the most natural the mind tends to forget. The mind is always interested in something exceptional because that is the interest of the ego. The ego is not interested in the common, and God is very common. The ego is not interested in the simple, and God is very simple. The ego is not interested in the near, and God is very near. That's how you go on missing bliss and you become miserable.

It is up to you to change it. It is your choice. Each moment of life brings you two alternatives: to be miserable or to be happy. It depends on your choice. Whatsoever you choose you become.

It is said about a Sufi mystic, Bayazid, that he was a tremendously happy man, almost ecstatic. Nobody had ever seen him unhappy, nobody had ever seen him sad, nobody had ever seen him doing anything like grumbling, like complaining. Whatsoever was, and he was happy. It was not always good, it was not always right for others. Sometimes there was no food, but he was happy. Sometimes for days he would live without food, but he was happy. Sometimes there were no clothes, but he was happy. Sometimes he had to sleep under the sky, but he was happy. His happiness remained undisturbed. It was unconditional.

He was asked again and again, but he would laugh and never say. When he was dying somebody asked, "Bayazid, now give us your key, your secret. You will be leaving soon. What was your secret?"

He said, "There is nothing like a secret. It was a simple thing. Every morning when I open my eyes, God gives me two alternatives. He says, 'Bayazid, do you want to be happy or unhappy?' I say, 'But God I want to be happy.' And I choose to be happy and I remain happy. It is a simple choice, there is no secret."

You try it. Every morning when you get up, the first thing, decide. If you decide to be unhappy, nothing is wrong in it. It is your decision. But then stick to it, remain unhappy whatsoever happens. Even if you win a lottery, don't be worried, remain unhappy. Even if you are chosen as the prime minister or the president, remain unhappy, stick to your choice. And then you will see, you can remain unhappy if you choose. The same is also true about happiness. If you choose, you can remain happy.

The day you decide that it is your decision to be happy or unhappy, you have taken your life into your hands, you have become a master. Now you will never say that somebody else is making you unhappy. That is a declaration of slavery.

Buddha was passing. A few people gathered and they insulted him very much. He listened to them very attentively, very lovingly.

When they were finished, he said, "If you have said all that you wanted to say, can I go now because I have to reach the other village by the time the sun sets. If you still have something more to say I will be coming back again after a few days; you can tell me at that time." But he was absolutely undisturbed, his silence remained the same, his happiness the same, his vibration the same.

Those people were puzzled. They said, "Are you not angry with us? We have been insulting you, we have been calling you names."

Buddha said, "You will have to remain puzzled. You came a little late. You should have come ten years before, then you would have succeeded in disturbing me. Then I was not my own master. Now, it is your freedom to insult me, it is my freedom whether to take it or not. I don't take it. You insult me, true. That's your decision. I am free to take it or not to take it, and I say I don't take it. What will you do with it? I am also puzzled because in the last village people had come with sweets, and I said that I don't need them, so they had to take them away. I ask you, what must they have done with the sweets?"

Those people said, "They must have distributed them in the village or they must have eaten them themselves."

Buddha said, "Now think about you. You come with these insults and I say, 'Enough. I am finished with this. Nothing doing.' What will you do? You will have to take them. I am so very sorry for you."

It is your decision. Life is your decision, your freedom. That's why I call my sannyasins *swamis. Swami* means a master. It is just an indicator that from this moment you will try more to be a master than to be a slave.

Osho,
You say by just being here right now is all we need to know truth. Why do I find it the hardest thing to do? And if I do it, who is here?

Truth is! You have nothing to do for it, you have just to be. Truth is already there. You are not to invent it, you have only to discover it. Even that word is not right because truth is not covered, your being is covered.

It is as if the sun has risen but you are sitting with closed eyes. The sun is not covered, only your eyes are covered. Open your eyes and the light is there. If you are in darkness it is because you are keeping your eyes shut.

When I say just be, I mean be open. I mean don't try to be something else. Because in the very effort of being somebody else you will be strained, you will be tense, you will be under a stress, and you will remain closed. You can open only when you accept whatsoever you are.

If a rose is trying to be a lotus, it will not be possible for it to be a rose. The whole effort will make it so tense. A rose is a rose, that's why it opens and becomes a rose. There is no problem about it. Don't try to be something else other than you are. Don't try to become some ideal. That's what I mean when I say just be.

Being is a state of tremendous opening, of immense silence, of no desire, no effort. You are just here, present. You are just a presence. In that presence all happens because in that presence you are so alert that nothing bypasses you. In that silence you start hearing God, you start seeing God. In that silence visions open, doors of the unknown open. The mystery is clear. But you have to be in that state. That's what meditation is all about, just to be.

You ask: "You say by just being here right now is all we need to know truth." Yes, I repeat it again. "Why do I find it the hardest thing to do?" Because your whole life you have been training yourself to be somebody else. Your whole life you have been carrying some ideology in the head that has become a mechanical pattern. You want to be more beautiful, you want to be more intelligent, you want to be this, you want to be that. You are carrying great politics in you, you are ambitious; that ambition makes you tense.

Remember, these are the two dimensions of life: to be political or to be religious. To be political means compete, struggle, fight; you have to prove that you are somebody. That's why all politicians are in a subtle way, stupid. They have to be.

I have heard...

Fondly, Mulla Nasruddin and his wife looked into the cradle of their child. "I think he is going to be a politician," said the Mulla.

"Ah, how can you say that?" asked the wife.

"Well, he says more things that sound good and mean absolutely nothing than any other human being I ever saw. He is going to be a politician."

A politician is a mess. He is always striving to prove that he is somebody. That means that he must be suffering from inferiority complex. Every politician suffers from inferiority complex. In a better world they will not be in the capitals, they will be on the psychological couches. They should be put in madhouses. Mad people are not so dangerous, they have never done anything wrong.

Have you ever heard of any mad people doing anything wrong like Adolf Hitler or Josef Stalin or Tamerlane or Genghis Khan, or Mao Zedong? Mad people have never done anything wrong. But politicians, their very effort to prove that "I am somebody" shows that deep down they suffer from inferiority, they feel they are nobody. They have to prove and perform. They feel they are nobody if they are not on a big power post. They think they are nobody if they don't have power to crush, destroy people. This is a deep inferiority complex that is seeking to be superior.

A religious person is one who is immensely satisfied, who says, "I am; there is no need to perform, there is no need to prove." A religious person is one who says, "Life is and I am. Why not enjoy? Why not delight in it? Why not celebrate?" A religious person is one who says, "God is and I am. Now why not hold his hands and have a dance, have a little party? Let there be a deep orgasm between you and existence."

That's what I mean when I say just be herenow. This is the only time to be, there is no other time. And this is the only place to be, there is no other place. All that has ever happened has happened only in the now and here. Now is the only time and here the only space. Don't think of then and there.

A politician thinks of then and there. He says, "Yes, one day I will enjoy. But wait, let me first arrange." He prepares. He is a maniac in preparation. He goes on preparing, he goes on preparing.

I have heard about a man who collected millions of books. He had no time to read because it took so much time to collect. He collected and collected, his library became the best in the world, but he had not read anything. Then came his death, and doctors said, "You will not be surviving more than one week."

He said, "But this is unjust. For my whole life I have been collecting and waiting that one day I will retire and read, but now there is no time. What to do?"

Somebody suggested, "You can hire scholars. They can read all the books and in a summary form before you die, they can give you the gist." So scholars gathered, they read all the books, and they prepared short notes, but still it was too big a thing. Again it was like a Bible, and the man was dying.

On the seventh day they brought the book. He said, "Are you mad? There is no time! Make it shorter!"

By the evening they came. They had shortened it to only one paragraph, but the man was getting unconscious. So they said, "Wait! We have shortened it." But he was not there, he was relapsing into unconsciousness. He died without ever enjoying a single book.

Don't think that this is just a parable. This is the story of millions of people. You go on collecting. I have seen rich people collecting money, never enjoying it. Even poor people are not so poor sometimes. Rich people are very poor, they never enjoy. They say, "A little more. Let us first collect enough." But it is never enough, it can never be enough. Mind never says, "Enough." It says, "A little more, a little more, a little more." It goes on demanding more and more. It is a mad demand.

You can collect money; that will not make you rich unless you enjoy it. You can have millions of books; that will not make you learned unless you enjoy them. You can have many flowers; that will not give you the sense of beauty unless you dance with them in the air, in the wind, in the rain – unless you have a little dance with them.

Life is, God is, bliss is. God is never in the past tense: you cannot say "God was." God is never in the future tense: you cannot say "God will be." God is only in the present tense: God is, life is, bliss is, truth is. Now you also be. Immediately there will be a meeting. Immediately you will be facing him, you will be encountering him. Not even a split second is needed to be wasted.

But I know your difficulty. All your life you have been trained and you have trained yourself for something which never happens. You are not ready for that which is, you are always getting ready for that which should be. You are suffering from the disease called "should."

From the very childhood the mother, the father, the society, the education, the priest, the politician, they are always saying, "You should be like this." Nobody says, "You are already, rejoice!" Except sometimes a Jesus comes to people and says, "Rejoice! God is!"

You have always been told to become something, to prove something, that you are worthy; to struggle, be ambitious. And of course you resent it deep down, but still you have to follow it because you don't know what else can be done. You never come across a man who says simply, "Rejoice!" That voice has become almost absent from the world – from the world of humanity, from the world of human beings. You resent, but still you go on doing.

People come to me and they say, "We resent discipline, we resent somebody saying to us 'Do this!'" And in the next breath they ask me, "Osho, tell us what should we do?" Now what to do with these people. They resent, they say, somebody telling them, and still they have come to me to ask, "Osho, what to do?"

You have been trained, so you go on resenting. You don't want to follow, still you go on asking "What to do, what to follow, whom to follow, where to go, what is the ideal?" You have never been taught that you are original, you need not be a carbon copy. The habit can become so ingrained that even when you want to rebel, you want somebody to teach you how to rebel.

It happened...

Mulla Nasruddin lost his faith once and became a hard-bitten atheist. Now it is very difficult for a Mohammedan, very difficult, but he became an atheist. His new credo was – he came to me and he said, "This is my new credo: There is no God, and Mohammed is his prophet."

The old habit – Mohammed has to be the prophet whether there is God or not.

You come to me and say, "We resent discipline, and Osho, tell us what to do." Mohammed is your prophet and there is no God. Now if you are always in a conflict, it is simple to understand.

It happened...

The two seven year olds were watching a movie. One of them kept sniffing loudly. A woman nearby finally advised him, with irritation in her voice, to blow his nose. The kid sniffed again.

"You better do what she says," his pal advised. "After all, she ain't your mother."

Listen to what he says: "After all, she ain't your mother. You better do what she says!" Who bothers to listen to a mother? Who bothers to listen to a father? One simply pretends to listen. But still, even in that pretension, the poison is entering in you.

You have always been taught not to be yourself, be somebody else: be a Buddha, be a Krishna, be a Jesus – never be yourself. But have you watched? Jesus is never repeated, never again. Buddha is never repeated, neither is Krishna repeated. God is such an original creator, he never repeats, he always creates new people. He peoples the earth with new beings. He is not looking towards you to become somebody else, he is looking at you to become you.

A Hassid fakir, Joshua, was dying. Somebody said, "Joshua, are you reconciled with Moses?" He was a Jew, a Hassid. Joshua opened his eyes and he said, "Stop nonsense. Enough is enough! Why should I get reconciled with Moses? In fact, I was deep down worried that when I go before God – and soon I will be present before him – he is not going to ask me, 'Joshua, why were you not like Moses?' He will ask me, 'Joshua, why were you not Joshua?' That is my trouble. I have missed my being. Trying to be somebody else, I have missed my goal."

You can be only yourself, you can never be anybody else. You are an original person, you are not a carbon copy. When I say *be*,

I mean just be yourself, love yourself, accept yourself. Don't go on denying, don't go on hating yourself. If you hate yourself, you will never be able to love anybody. Love yourself, I say to you. I say respect yourself. Be happy that you are the way you are. Thank God for your being the way he has made you. Don't complain.

That's what I mean by the religious dimension. Don't be political, don't be ambitious, don't be competitive. You are alone like you. Like you, you are the only one. You are incomparable. Don't be stupid, don't be competitive.

A politician at a cocktail party said to Mulla Nasruddin, "I keep hearing you use the word *idiot*. I hope you are not referring to me?"

"Don't be so conceited," said the Mulla, "as if there were no other idiots in the world."

I am reminded of another joke. There was a case, a politician sued a man in the court. He said, "In a hotel, this man called me an idiot." Mulla Nasruddin was there to support the politician. "Yes, he is right, this man called him an idiot."

In India the leaders, the political leaders, are called *netaji*. Once it was a respectable term. In the days of the fight for freedom before 1947, *netaji*, the leader, was a very respectable word. Then it deteriorated. Now it has just gone down the drain. Now to call somebody *netaji* is to insult him. Now *netaji* means some crook, a fraud, a cunning fellow.

Somebody had called *netaji*, the leader an idiot. The magistrate asked Mulla Nasruddin, "in the hotel there were so many people – how can you say that this man called *netaji* an idiot? There were so many people, he may have been calling somebody else an idiot. How can you prove it?"

Nasruddin said, "Absolutely it can be proved. There were almost two hundred people in the hotel, I know that, but this man called *netaji* an idiot."

The magistrate said, "You tell us, what is your proof?"

Mulla Nasruddin said, "Because there was no other idiot present at that time."

Don't be stupid. Just be yourself and you will be intelligent.

That's what I mean. If you are just yourself, you will be an intelligent being. If you are yourself, totally accepting of yourself – not only accepting but welcoming, happy, grateful just being the way you are – your intelligence will start blooming. If you are competing, you will become stupid, you will become mediocre because you will be going against nature. If you compete and you try to become somebody else, you will destroy your inner spontaneity. That's what stupidity is. You will be retarded.

Be religious, never be political. And when I say never be political, I don't only mean don't be a member of a political party; by political I mean don't be ambitious. All ambition is politics, all struggle to be the first is politics. A non-struggling, non-conflicting mind is religious. Just be.

You have not been taught, I know. It is hard now to unlearn old habits, but they can be unlearned. Whatsoever is learned can be unlearned. It is difficult, but not impossible.

"You say by just being here right now is all we need to know truth. Why do I find it the hardest thing to do?" Everybody finds it, because your whole conditioning goes against it, all your habits go against it. It is hard, difficult, but not impossible. And once you understand the point, it will become easy. And once you allow your nature to flow, to be, it will become the easiest thing in the world.

In fact, to be somebody else is the hardest thing. It needs tremendous effort to be somebody else. Then too, failure is certain. One never succeeds in being somebody else. That is the misery. That's why there are so many failures all around. You don't see so many failures in the trees, in the birds, in the animals because they are not political.

Sometimes in a Buddha, Mahavira, Moses, Mohammed, you see the flowering of a natural being; spontaneous, animal-like, innocent. Just be, God is already there waiting for you. Calm down a little; don't be in such a hurry to go somewhere else. Don't miss this moment, this tremendous blissful moment, delight in it. Rejoice! And let your joy be your prayer. And let just being still, silent, just being, be your meditation and God will come rushing towards you.

Nobody need seek God, God is seeking you. Just you be silent, quiet, so he can find you. You are rushing, running, and

God goes on trying to find you. But you are never found because you are never in the present. The ambitious mind lives in the future, the religious mind lives in the present. The religious mind knows no other time. His only time is now, his only space is here. *Now-here!* – let that be your mantra.

If you miss now, you will miss always. If you miss here, you will miss there. Let now-here be your whole mantra. If this is not your mantra then God is nowhere.

Swami Ram used to tell a simple story about an atheist. He was a professor, a very logical, learned man, and he was very against God. He had written on his wall a small sentence to deny God: God is nowhere. Then a child was born to him, a small child, and the child was learning to read. "Nowhere" was too big a word for him, so he split the word in two. He was reading "God is" – nowhere he could not read; it was too big a word, so he read, "God is now-here."

Be that child. God is now-here. If you are not that child, then God is nowhere. Yes, Jesus is right when he says "Only those who are like small children, only they will be able to enter into my kingdom of God."

Enough for today.

9

THE DISCIPLINE BEYOND DISCIPLINE

The Buddha said:
My doctrine is to think the thought that is unthinkable, to practice the deed that is non doing, to speak the speech that is inexpressible, and to be trained in the discipline which is beyond discipline. Those who understand this are near, those who are confused are far. The way is beyond words and expressions, is bound by nothing earthly. Lose sight of it to an inch or miss it for a moment, and we are away from it forever more.

This sutra is one of the most important, one of the very central to Buddha's message. The very essence of his message is there like a seed. Go patiently with me into it, try to understand it because if you understand this sutra, you would have understood all that Buddha wants you to understand. If you miss this sutra, you miss all.

The Buddha said:
My doctrine is to think the thought that is unthinkable, to

practice the deed that is non doing, to speak the speech that is inexpressible, and to be trained in the discipline that is beyond discipline.

The choice of the word *doctrine* is unfortunate, but there are difficulties in translating. Buddha must have used the word *siddhanta.* It has a totally different meaning. Ordinarily it is translated as doctrine, it should not be translated so. But the problem is that in the English language there is no equivalent to *siddhanta*. So I will have to explain it to you.

A doctrine is a consistent logical theory. A *siddhanta* has nothing to do with logic, theory, consistency. A *siddhanta* is a realization, a *siddhanta* is an experience. A doctrine is intellectual, *siddhanta* is existential. You can make a doctrine without being transformed by it. You can make a great doctrine without even being touched by it. But if you want to achieve a *siddhanta* you will have to be totally transformed because it will be a vision of a totally different person.

The word *siddhanta* means the assertion of one who has become a *siddha*, one who has achieved, one who has arrived – his statement. You can be a great philosopher, you can figure out intellectually many things, you can systematize your inferences and you can make a very consistent logical syllogism which almost appears like truth, but is not truth. It has been manufactured by your mind. A doctrine is man-made, a *siddhanta* has nothing to do with man and his effort. A *siddhanta* is a vision; you come upon it.

For example, a blind man can think about light and can try to figure out what it is all about. He can even listen to great treatises on light and he can make a certain idea about it – what it is. But he will be as far away from light as he was before. He can even expound the doctrine about light, he can explain its physics, he can explain its structure. He can go deep into the constituents of light, he can talk about it, he can write a PhD on it, a thesis. He can be declared a doctor by a university because he has propounded a doctrine, but still he does not know what light is. He has no eyes to see.

A *siddhanta* is one which you have seen, which has been revealed to you, which has become your own experience, which you have encountered. A doctrine is almost imaginary, it is not real. A doctrine is almost always borrowed. You can hide your borrowing in many ways – subtle, cunning ways. You can reformulate, you can take from many sources and you can rearrange everything, but a doctrine is a borrowed thing – nothing original in it.

A *siddhanta* is absolutely original, new. It is your authentic experience. You have come to see what reality is. It is an immediate perception, it is a benediction, it is a blessing, it is a grace, a gift. You have arrived and you have seen what truth is. The statement of a realization is *siddhanta*. Propounding a doctrine is one thing, giving expression to a *siddhanta* is totally different.

I have heard...

Once Mulla Nasruddin was talking to a few of his friends. He was telling his pals about the wonderful vacation he and his family had just had in the United States.

"It is a wonderful country," he exclaimed. "Nowhere in the world is a stranger treated so well. You walk along the street and you meet a well-dressed fellow with lots of dollars. He tips his hat and smiles at you and you talk together. He invites you into his big car and shows you the town. He buys you a fine dinner, then takes you to the theater. You have more fine food and plenty of drinks, and he invites you to his house and you sleep nice all night. Next morning..."

"What, Nasruddin," a listener said, "did all this really happen to you?"

"No, not exactly, but it all happened to my wife," said Nasruddin.

A doctrine is that which has happened to somebody else. You

have heard about it. It has not happened to you, it is borrowed, dirty, ugly. A *siddhanta* is virgin.

A doctrine is a prostitute. It has been moving through many minds, through many hands. It is like dirty currency, it goes on changing its owner. A *siddhanta* is something absolutely fresh. It has never happened before, it will never happen again. It has happened to you. A *siddhanta* is deeply individual, it is a personal vision of reality.

What happened to Buddha is a *siddhanta*, what Buddhists propound is a doctrine. What happened to Christ is a *siddhanta*, what Christians talk about is a doctrine. What happened to Krishna is a *siddhanta*, what Hindus go on bragging about is a doctrine. What I am saying to you is a *siddhanta*, if you go and repeat it, it will be a doctrine. That's why I say it is a very unfortunate choice of words to put into Buddha's mouth.

My doctrine is to think... No, let it be: My *siddhanta* is to think, my realization is to think, my own understanding is to think. He is not proposing a theory, he is simply expressing an experience.

A few more things before we enter into the sutra.

A *siddhanta* is by its very nature paradoxical, it has to be so because life is paradoxical. If you really have experienced it, then whatsoever you see and say is going to be paradoxical. Life consists of contradictions. We call them contradictions, life does not call them contradictions. They are complementaries. Day and night dance together, life and death dance together, love and hate move hand in hand. We call them contradictions, in life they are not so. Life is big and vast, immense. It comprehends all the contradictions into it: they are complementaries.

When a person has realized, whatsoever he says is going to have the taste of paradox. That's why all great religious assertions are paradoxical. They may be in the Vedas, in the Upanishads, in the Koran, in the Bible, in the Tao Te Ching. Wherever, whenever you will find truth, you will find it paradoxical because the truth has to be total; totality is paradoxical.

A doctrine is never paradoxical; a doctrine is tremendously consistent because a doctrine is not worried about reality. A doctrine is worried about being consistent. It knows no reality. It is a mind game and the mind is very, very logical. The mind says

don't allow any contradiction in it. The mind says if you talk about light then don't talk about darkness because that will be inconsistent. Forget about darkness. The mind tries to prove that life is non-contradictory because that is the mind's choice.

Mind is very afraid of contradictions, becomes very shaky when it comes across a contradiction. It insists on its own pattern. Mind is logical, life is not. So if you find something very logical, beware, something must be wrong in it. It must not be part of life, it must be man-made.

Everything God-made is contradictory. That's why people go on arguing about God. Why, if he loves man so much, then why did he create death? The mind finds it very difficult to accept the idea that God created life and also death. If it was up to you, if you were the maker of the world, if mind was the creator, then you would have never done that.

But think of a life where no death exists. It will be sheer boredom. It will be tedium. Think, if death is impossible then you will be continuously in hell. If mind had created the world, then there would be only love, no hate. But think of a world where only love exists. Then it will be too sweet, sweet to the point of being nauseous. It will lose all taste, it will lose all color, it will be flat. Love is beautiful because of the possibility of hate.

If mind was to create the world, or Aristotle was asked to create the world, then there would have been only day, no night; only work, no play. Then think what would have happened. God in his compassion never took any advice from Aristotle. And maybe that's the reason he created man in the very end. First he created other things, otherwise man would start giving advice.

That has been a problem, why did he create man in the end? First he created trees and the earth and the sky and the stars and the animals and the birds and the whole, then he waited and waited. Then he created man. And first he created man, then he created woman. Because man, just out of politeness may have kept quiet, but a woman cannot keep quiet. He must have been afraid. Don't create man otherwise he will start giving advice – do this, don't do that. And for woman he waited last. And since he created woman he has disappeared, otherwise the woman would have nagged him to death.

One great industrialist was saying to me that for his new factory everything has been planned, agreed upon. The engineers, the architects, the planners, they have done everything and everything has been agreed. But then I asked, "Why do you repeat again and again that everything has been agreed? Has something gone wrong?"

He said, "Then I came home and talked about it to my wife – finished! Now she is suggesting things which will alter the whole idea. And if I don't do it now, then it will be a constant problem for my whole life. She will nag me to death."

If Aristotle was asked to create the world, or help the world to be created, then the world would have been absolutely consistent – absolutely consistent. But then it would have been a world of misery and hell. Life is beautiful because there are contradictions. Work is beautiful because there is play. Work means you are doing something to get something out of it. Play means you are simply doing it for its own sake.

No, Aristotle won't allow it. Plato won't allow it. In his *Republic*, Plato says there will be no possibility for any poets; we won't allow them. They are dangerous people, they bring contradiction in the world – poets, they are dreamers. And they talk in such ways which are vague, ambiguous. You cannot make anything out of it – what they are saying, what they mean. In Plato's world, in his *Republic*, logicians, philosophers will be the kings; they will decide.

It has not yet happened, only a few things like that have happened. For example, Soviet Russia is more Platonic, China is more Platonic. These two countries are run by logic. You cannot find more miserable people anywhere else. Well fed, well sheltered because logic is a great arranger of things; everything has been arranged, only life is missing. Somehow man is not happy because man cannot live by bread alone. You need the opposite also. The whole day you work, in the night you rest. You need darkness also.

A doctrine is a logical statement of a theory, and logic is like a chameleon – it goes on changing its color, it is not reliable. It is not reliable because it is not based in reality. It is not responsible because it is not based in reality. It is untrue because it is a partial

truth. Remember, a partial truth is more untrue than a total untruth because a partial truth gives a feeling of being true. It is only half-true and nothing can be half-true. Either it is true or it is not true. A half-truth is absolutely untrue, but logic gives it a feeling that it is true; at least on the way towards truth. It is not even on the way towards truth.

Logicians go on doing somersaults, they go on changing their standpoints because in fact they have not come to anything that is really real, just their mind games. One day one game, another day another game; they go on changing. They remain consistent, consistent with their own train of thought, but inconsistent with reality.

I have heard...

"It is difficult to explain what a course of logic will do for a person's thinking, but let me illustrate," said Mulla Nasruddin to his son. "Suppose two men came out of a chimney. One is clean, one dirty. Which one will take a bath?"

"The dirty one, naturally," answered the boy.

"Remember," chided Nasruddin, "that the clean man sees the dirty one and sees how dirty he is, and vice versa."

"Now I get it, Dad," answered the boy. "The clean one, seeing his dirty companion, concludes he is dirty too. So he takes the bath. Am I right now?"

"Wrong," said Nasruddin nonchalantly. "Logic teaches us this – how could two men come out of a chimney, one clean and one dirty?"

Once you start playing the game of logic there is no end to it, and you will never win. The logician will always win. The logician will always win because you can always find a way. And you have nothing to compare with, you have no reality. That's why so many philosophies exist, and all opposing each other, and not a single conclusion has been arrived at yet.

Down the centuries, for almost five thousand years, man has argued; man has not been doing much, but just arguing. Thousands of philosophies have been created, very neat and clean logic. If you read one philosopher you will be convinced. If you read his opponent you will be convinced. Read the third one, you will be

convinced – and you will be getting into a mess. By and by, you will be convinced by all and you will be mad because you will not know now what is true. They are all wrong because the logical approach is wrong.

There are two ways to know reality. One is: just close your eyes and think about it. I call it "about-ism." It is always about and about, it never goes directly. You go on beating around the bush. You never beat exactly the bush – just around. You never penetrate the center of a problem, you simply go round and round. It is a merry-go-round. You can enjoy it, logicians enjoy very much. It is so beautiful to come with a new theory which explains everything, but it is just in the mind. You close your eyes, sit on your easy chair and think about. This is not going to give you reality.

Reality is already there, you don't have to think about it, you have to allow it. You have to drop all thinking so that you can see what the truth is, so that you can see that which is. If you go on thinking, you cannot see that which is. It is impossible. Your thoughts will create smoke around you. Your consciousness will be covered by the smoke, your eyes will not have clarity, you will not have sensitivity. And you will be continuously searching and seeking your own ideas, imposing them, projecting them on reality. You will not give reality a chance to reveal itself.

A doctrine is arrived at through logical thinking. A doctrine comes through the process of "about-ism." A *siddhanta* is not arrived at by closing your eyes, not by thinking too much, but by dropping thinking as such, in toto; by opening your eyes with no prejudice, with no a priori conceptions, and looking direct into reality, facing reality directly. It is already there, it needs only you to be there.

And when you are absolutely without any thought, your mind is still, your memory is still, your thinking has completely ceased to be, then reality erupts, explodes. Then you become a receiver. Then *siddhanta* arises.

My siddhanta is to think the thought that is unthinkable... The first thing, Buddha says, is to think the thought that is unthinkable. It is a contradiction, a paradox. Now, no logician will ever utter such nonsense. It is from the very beginning nonsensical. That's why logicians go on saying that Buddha, Jesus, Bodhidharma, Lao Tzu, Zarathustra, these people are all nonsense. Their propositions are meaningless because they say one thing and in the next breath they contradict. Now look at this sentence: *My siddhanta is to think the thought that is unthinkable...* Now just in a small sentence absolute contradiction – to think the unthinkable. How can you think the unthinkable? If it is really unthinkable you cannot think. If you can think then how can it be unthinkable? Simple, illogical, but what Buddha means has to be understood. Don't be in a hurry, that's why I say go patiently.

When he wants to say something, he means it. He is saying there is a way to know things without thinking. There is a way to know things without mind. There is a way to see into reality directly, immediately, without the vehicle of thought. You can be connected with reality without any agent of thinking – that is what he is saying. He is saying that the mind can completely cease its activity, can completely drop its activity and yet be still, a reservoir, and see into reality. But you will have to experience it, only then you will be able to understand.

Sometimes try just to see. Sitting by the side of a rosebush, just look at the roseflower; don't think, don't even give names. Don't even classify. Don't even say that this is a rose because a rose is a rose is a rose; whether you call it rose or something else makes no difference. So don't label it, don't give it a name, don't bring language in. Don't bring any symbol in because symbol is the method of falsifying reality.

If you say this is a rose, you have already missed. Then you have brought in some past experience of other roses, which are not. Now your eyes are full of roses – rows of roses. In your life you must have come across many types of roses: white and black and red; all those roses are there floating in your eyes. Now you are crowded by your past memories. And then, beyond all those memories is this rose which is real. Now the crowd of the unreal is so much you will not be able to reach and touch the real.

When Buddha says drop thinking, he means don't bring the past in. What is the point of bringing it in? This rose is here, you are here. Let it be a deep meeting, a communion, a connection. Melt a little with this rose, let this rose melt a little in you. The rose is ready to share its fragrance, you also share your being, your consciousness, with it.

Let there be a handshake with reality. Let there be a little dance with this rose, dancing in the wind. You also move, be, look, feel, close your eyes, smell, touch, drink. This beautiful phenomenon that is facing you – don't go here and there, just be with it. No more right and left, just be direct like an arrow moving towards the target. If you bring words, language, you bring society, you bring past, you bring other people.

Tennyson has said something about the rose. Shelley has said something about the rose. Shakespeare has said something about the rose, or Kalidas. Once you bring language, Shakespeare and Kalidas and Bhavabhuti and Shelley and Keats – they are all standing there. Now you are too full of your own ideas, now you are in a crowd, lost. You will not be able to see the simple truth.

The truth is so simple. Yes, it is just like a roseflower in front of you. It is utterly there. Why go somewhere else? Why not move into this reality? Why go in time, past and future? Don't say this rose is beautiful because this rose needs no compliments from you. Let it be a feeling. This rose does not understand human language, so why puzzle this rose? Why say it is beautiful? Because this rose knows nothing of beauty and nothing of ugliness.

For this rose's life is not divided and split, this rose is not schizophrenic. This rose is simply there, with no idea of what beauty is and what ugliness is. Don't call it beautiful. When you call it beautiful you have brought a concept. The mind has started functioning. Now, you may have a little experience of the rose, but it will not be true – your mind will be a distortion. You will think of this rose just as a representative of all other roses.

Plato says that every real thing is just a representative of something ideal. Plato says that there with God exists the idea of rose – that is real. The idea of rose is real and this rose is just a reflection of that idea. This is nonsense, this is really absurd.

This rose exists here now with God. There is no idea in the mind of God. God has no mind as such. God is without mind. God is not a human being, and God has not been trained by any parents, and God has not been educated by any university. God has not been conditioned. There is no idea in the mind of God – and this rose is a real rose. God exists with this rose and this rose exists with God, and God has no barrier with this rose, no mind barrier.

But for Plato, the reality is unreal and ideas are real. For Buddha it is just the opposite: the reality is the real and ideas are unreal. If you follow Plato you will become a philosopher. If you follow Buddha you will become a religious man. Religion is not a philosophy, religion is an experience.

So try it: sometimes allow your no-mind to function. Sometimes push aside all your thinking. Sometimes let reality penetrate you. Sometimes let there be a blessing from reality. Allow it to deliver its message to you. But we go on living in words, and we pay too much attention to the words.

I had a teacher in the university and we used to go for a walk together. After few days I said, "I will not come. Better I should go alone."

He said, "Why?" Because he was so much obsessed with names. Every tree which he would see he had to say to which species it belonged. Every flower – what it contains, its history. If he would see a rose, he would not see a rose, he would see the whole history of rose: how it came from Iran, in what century, who brought it to India, it is not an Indian flower.

Now, he would never look at the flower, and I would pull him again and again back: "This flower is enough. What is the point? Flowers don't have histories, only human beings have. This flower does not bother whether it is in Iran or in India. This flower has no idea of any past, it lives just herenow. It is neither Hindu nor Mohammedan, nor Indian nor Iranian. It is simply there. It is not even a rose!"

But it was difficult for him. Any bird he would see he would say, "Wait, let me listen. What species of bird is this? From where has it come? Has it come from Siberia, or from Middle Asia, or is it a Himalayan bird?" After a few days I said, "You excuse me. You go alone because I am not interested from where this bird has come. This bird is here, it is enough. I am not interested in the scientific, historical explanation."

Explanation, to a few people, is almost a disease. Through their explanations they try to explain away everything. They are obsessed with explanation. They think that if they can name a thing, label a thing, they know it. They are very uneasy unless they can label a thing, know a thing by name, categorize it, pigeonhole it – unless they do it they are very uncomfortable. It seems as if a certain thing is just offending them: why are you there without any classification? Once they have categorized it, pigeonholed it, put a label on it, then they are at ease. They have known it. They are finished with the thing.

I have heard…

After the second world war a German soldier raped a French woman and told her, "In nine months you will have a son, you may call him Adolf Hitler." To which the French woman replied, "In nine days you will have a rash, you may call it gonorrhea."

But by calling names, it changes nothing. What you call is absolutely irrelevant. Whatsoever is, is! By your giving it a name it never changes. But for you it changes. Just by giving a name, reality becomes different to you.

It happened…

A lion and an ass made an agreement to go out hunting together. By and by they came to a cave, the abode of many wild goats. The lion took up his station at the mouth of the cave and the ass, going within, kicked and brayed and made a mighty fuss to frighten them out. When the lion had caught many of them, the ass came out and asked him if he had not made a noble fight and routed the goats properly.

"Yes indeed," said the lion. "And I assure you, you would have frightened me too if I had not known you to be an ass."

It may make a difference to you by calling names, but it does not make any difference to reality. It may make a difference to you because you live surrounded by your language, concept, verbalization. You immediately go on translating everything into language.

De-language yourself – that's what Buddha means. Un-mind yourself, un-wind yourself – that's what Buddha means. Otherwise you will never know what is true.

My siddhanta is to think the thought that is unthinkable...

You cannot think about reality. There is no way to think about it. All thinking is borrowed. No thinking is ever original. All thinking is repetitive, all thinking is mechanical. You can go on chewing and re-chewing the same things again and again and again, but nothing new ever arises out of thinking. Thinking is old, rotten. It is a junk-yard. You cannot think about reality because reality is every moment original. It is every moment so new that it has never been like that before. It is so absolutely fresh that you will have to know it. There is no other way to know it than knowing it.

The only way to know love is to love. The only way to know swimming is to swim. The only way to know reality is to be real. Mind makes you unreal. Mind makes you too much like thoughts: mind-stuff, words, concepts, theories, philosophies, doctrines, scriptures, isms. Mind does not give you the real thing, it gives you only reflections, and those reflections are also distorted.

Buddha says attain to a clarity: just see, just be. And then you will be able to think that thought which is unthinkable. You will be able to have a meeting with reality, a date with God. *...the thought that is unthinkable...* only that is worth thinking. All else is just wasting life energy.

...to practice the deed that is non doing... that is not doing. This is what Lao Tzu calls *wu-wei*. Action in inaction, again another paradox. But a *siddhanta* has to be paradoxical.

...to practice the deed that is non doing... Ordinarily we know only deeds which we can do. We are surrounded by our doing. We don't know that there are things which are beyond our doing and still are happening. You are born; you have not given birth to yourself, it has simply happened, and it could not happen in a better way. You are breathing, but you are not breathing as an act, it is happening. You can try to stop it and then you will see you cannot stop it. Even for a few seconds you cannot stop it; you will have to relax, you will have to allow it. Breathing is life, it is happening.

All that is essential is happening, and all that is nonessential, nonexistential, is to be done. Of course your shop will not be run if you don't run it. Of course you will not become a prime minister or a president if you don't struggle for it. Nobody has ever become a prime minister without struggling for it; without violence you cannot become a prime minister. You will have to compete, a cut-throat competition. You will have to be cruel. You will have to be aggressive. You will have to do it, only then it can happen. All that depends on your doing is accidental and all that goes on without you is essential.

Religion's whole concern is the essential, the world of the essential. You are there; not that you have done yourself, you are simply there for no reason. You have not earned it, it is nothing of your doing. It is a benediction, it is a gift. You are there, existence has willed you to be there, it is not your own will.

Watch it, understand it. When such a thing like life, so precious, can happen without your doing, then why bother? Then allow more and more the dimension of happening. Drop more and more doing. Do only that which seems needful. Don't be bothered too much with the doing.

That is the meaning of a sannyasin. The householder, the *grihastha*, is one who is simply possessed by the dimension of doing. He thinks that if he is not going to do, nothing is going to happen. He is a doer. A sannyasin is one who knows that whether he is going to do it or not, all that is essential is going to continue to happen. Nonessential may disappear, but that is irrelevant – but the essential will continue.

Love is essential, money is nonessential. To be alive is essential, to live in a big house or not is nonessential. To be fulfilled, contented, is essential; rushing, ambitious, always trying to reach somewhere, trying to perform, trying to prove that you are somebody, is nonessential. People live only in two dimensions: the dimension of the doer and the dimension of the non-doer.

Buddha says: *...to practice the deed that is non doing...* He says practice that. He says "practice," because there is no other way to say it. The word *practice* looks like doing, that's the paradox. He says, "Do that which cannot be done." Do that which only happens. Allow, he means – allow that which happens, allow God to be there. Allow life to be there, allow love to be there. Allow the existence to penetrate you, to infiltrate you. Don't continue to be a doer.

He does not mean don't do anything at all. He says don't emphasize it. Maybe it is needful. You have to clean your room.

Without your doing it, it is not going to happen. So do it, but don't get obsessed with it. It is just a minor part.

The major part of life, the central part of life, should be like a happening. As the lightning happens in the clouds, so God happens. As rivers go on rushing towards the ocean and dissolve, so love happens. So happens meditation – it has nothing to do with your doing. Your doing is not essential for it to happen. It can happen when you are sitting and not doing anything. In fact it happens only then, when you are not doing anything and you are sitting. I insist for you to do many things as methods, but the insistence is only this – that you have to be tired, otherwise you won't sit.

It is as if you tell a child, "Sit silently in the corner of the room," and he cannot sit; he is so restless, he is so full of energy. He wants to do this and that and run around. The best way is to tell him to go and have seven rounds – run around the house seven times, around the block – then come back. Then without your telling, he will sit silently.

That's the whole point of my insistence to do Dynamic, do Kundalini, do Nataraj – be spent, so that for a few moments you can allow happening. You will not reach to meditation by doing, you will reach to meditation only by non-doing. And in non-doing will happen the real thing.

The real thing cannot be produced; it always happens. One has to be just sensitive and open and vulnerable. It is very delicate. You cannot grab it. It is very fragile, fragile like a flower. You cannot grab it. If you grab it you will destroy it. You have to be very soft. It is not hardware, it is software. You have to be really soft, you have to be feminine.

Buddha says: *...practice the deed that is not doing...* That is the message of all the great ones, the really great ones. The greatest realization on this earth has been this: that we are unnecessarily creating too much fuss. That which is to happen is going to happen if we wait. In the right season, the harvest; in the right season, the fruition. In the right season everything happens. If a man can learn only one thing – how to wait prayerfully – nothing else is needed. Ecstasy is a *prasad*, a gift of God.

Just try. Practice what Buddha says. At least for one hour you become a non-doer. At least for one hour, deep in the night, sit alone. Don't do anything, not even chanting a mantra, not even Transcendental Meditation. Don't do anything. Just sit, lie down, look at the stars. That too should not be hard. Look very softly. Don't focus; remain unfocussed like an unfocussed photograph – hazy, blurred, not knowing where the boundaries are. Just remain silent in the darkness.

If thoughts come let them come. Don't fight with them either. They will come and they will go, you just be a watcher. It is none of your business whether they come or they go. Who are you? They come without invitation, they go without pushing. They come and go, it is a constant traffic. You just sit by the side of the road and watch.

When I say watch, don't misinterpret me. Don't make watching an effort. Otherwise people become very stiff and they start watching in a very stiff and tense way. Again they have started doing. What I am saying, or what Buddha is saying is: be in an attitude of not doing, be lazy.

Just be lazy and see what happens. You will be amazed. Some day just sitting, just sitting, not doing anything – some day, from some unknown source, a lightning flash, a benediction. Some day in some moment, suddenly you are transfigured. Suddenly you see a quiet descending upon you. It is almost physical.

If a real meditator, a person who can relax, sits silently and allows, even somebody who is not a meditator will feel the presence – that something is happening. You may not be able to figure it out what it is; you may feel strange or a little scared, but if you sit by the side of a meditator...

Now, it is difficult to use the right word because the word *meditator* again gives the impression as if he is doing something – doing meditation. Remember again and again, language has been developed by non-meditators, so the whole language is in a subtle way wrong. It cannot express.

When somebody is sitting there, just sitting there like a tree, like a rock, not doing anything, it happens: something from the above descends, penetrates his very core of being. A subtle light surrounds him, a glow, a blessing can be felt around him – even by those people who don't know what meditation is. Even passing by the side, they will also feel the impact of it. This benediction has been called God.

God is not a person, it is a deep experience when you are not doing anything and existence simply flows in you – the immensity of it, the beatitude of it, the grace of it.

You are not doing anything, you are not even expecting anything, you are not waiting for anything. You have no motive. You are just there like a tree standing in the winds, or like a rock just silently sitting by the side of a river. Or like a cloud perched on the hilltop – just there, no movement of your own.

In that moment you are not a self, in that moment you are a no-self. In that moment you are not a mind, you are a no-mind. In that moment you don't have a center. In that moment you are immense vastness with no boundaries – suddenly the contact, suddenly it is there! Suddenly you are fulfilled, suddenly you are surrounded by some unknown presence. It is tremendous.

That's what Buddha says: *...practice the deed that is not doing; to speak the speech that is inexpressible...* And if you want to say something, say that which cannot be said. Express the inexpressible. What is the point of saying things which can be said? – anybody knows them, everybody knows them. If you really want to express something, express the inexpressible.

What is the way to express the inexpressible? It can be expressed only through being. Words are too narrow. It can be expressed only by your existence, by your presence: in your walking, in your sitting, in your eyes, in your gestures, in your touch, in your compassion, in your love. The way you are – it can be expressed through it.

Buddha talks, but that is not very essential. More essential is his being, that he is there. Through his talking he allows you to be with him. The talking is just persuading you because it will be difficult for you to be in silence with a buddha. He has to talk because if he is talking you feel that everything is okay, you can listen. If he is not talking how will you listen? You don't know how to listen when nobody is talking. You don't know how to listen to that which cannot be expressed.

But by and by, living around a master, a Buddha, a Jesus, by and by you will start imbibing his spirit. By and by, in spite of you, there will be moments when you will relax, and not only that which he is saying will be reaching into your heart, but that which he *is* also will penetrate. And with him the whole dimension of happening opens. That's the meaning of *satsang*, being in the presence of a master.

...and to be trained in the discipline that is beyond discipline. Buddha says there is a discipline which is not a discipline. Ordinarily we think about discipline as if somebody else is trying to discipline you. Discipline carries a very ugly connotation – as if you are being disciplined, as if you are just to obey. The center that is disciplining you is outside you.

Buddha says that is not discipline, that is surrendering to slavery. Be free. There is no need to be disciplined from any outside source. Become alert, so that inner discipline arises in you. Become responsible, so that whatsoever you do, you do with a certain order, a certain cosmos in it; so that your being is not a chaos, so that your being is not in a mess.

So there are two types of discipline: one that can be forced from the outside. That's what politicians go on doing, priests go on doing, parents go on doing. And there is a discipline that can be provoked in you. That can be done only by masters: they don't enforce any discipline on you, they simply make you more aware so you can find your own discipline.

People come to me and they ask, "Why don't you give a certain discipline? What to eat, what not to eat. When to get up in the morning and when to go to bed." I don't give you any such discipline because any discipline that comes from outside is destructive.

I give you only one discipline – what Buddha calls the discipline of the beyond, the discipline of transcendence. I give you only one discipline and that is of being aware. If you are aware you will get up in the right time. When the body is rested you will get up. When you are aware you will eat only that which is needed, you will eat only that which is least harmful to you and to others. You will eat only that which is not based on violence. But awareness will be the decisive factor. Otherwise you can be forced to become obedient, but deep down you go on being rebellious.

I have heard a second world war story...

A sergeant and a private were up on a charge of kicking the colonel. When asked for an explanation, the sergeant replied, "Well, sir, the colonel came round the corner as I was coming from the gym. I only had my tennis shoes on, he was in riding boots, and he trod on my toe. I am afraid the pain was so great, sir, that I lashed out before I realized who it was, sir."

"I see," said the orderly officer. "And what about you soldier?"

To which the private replied, "I saw the sergeant kick the colonel, sir. So I thought to myself, 'The war must be over, so I can also kick.'"

Whenever somebody enforces a discipline on you, deep down you resent, deep down you are against it. You may surrender to it, but you always surrender reluctantly. And that's how it should be because the deepest urge in a human being is for freedom, for *moksha*.

To be free is the search. Down the centuries, for millennia, in many lives, we have been searching how to be free. So whenever somebody comes – even for your own sake, for your own good – and enforces something upon you, you resist. It is against human nature, it is against human destiny.

Buddha says there is no need to be obedient to somebody else; you should find your own awareness. Be obedient to it, be aware; that is the only scripture. Be aware, that is the only master. Be aware, and nothing can ever go wrong. Awareness brings its own discipline like a shadow, and then the discipline is beautiful. Then it is not like a slavery, then it is like a harmony. Then it is not as if enforced, then it is a flowering out of your own being, a blooming.

...and to be trained in the discipline that is beyond discipline. People ordinarily seek somebody to tell them what to do because they are afraid of their freedom, because they don't know that they can rely on their own sources, because they are not self-confident, because they have always been told what to do by somebody else, so they have become addicted to it. They are searching father figures for their whole life. Their God is also a father, nothing else. That God which is a father is false. And the search for a father figure is anti-life.

You should learn how to be free from all father figures. You should learn how to be yourself. You should learn how to be aware and responsible. Only then you start growing. Maturity is always maturity towards freedom. Immaturity is always a sort of dependence and a fear of freedom.

A child is dependent; it's okay, it can be understood, he is helpless. But why remain a child your whole life? That is the revolution Buddha brought into the world. He is one of the most rebellious thinkers of the world. He throws you to yourself. It is dangerous, but he takes that risk. And he says that everybody has to take that risk. There is every possibility you may go astray, but life is risk.

It is better to go astray on your own accord than to reach heaven following somebody else. It is better to be lost forever and be yourself, than to reach paradise as a carbon copy, as an imitator. Then your paradise will be nothing but a prison. And if you have chosen your own hell on your own accord, out of your own freedom, your hell will also be heaven because freedom is heaven.

Now here you will see the difference between Christianity and Buddhism. Christianity says Adam was expelled because he disobeyed God. Buddha says obey only yourself, there is no other god to be obeyed. Christianity calls disobedience the original sin, and Buddha calls obedience the original sin. Tremendous is the difference. Buddha is a liberator, Christianity created an imprisonment for the whole humanity.

Buddha's liberation is pure. He teaches you rebellion, but his rebellion is not a political rebellion. He teaches you rebellion with responsibility, with awareness. His rebellion is not a reaction. You can be obedient, you can be disobedient. What is Buddha saying? Buddha is saying neither be obedient nor be disobedient because disobedience is again being conditioned by somebody else. You go on doing something because your father says don't do it, but again he is manipulating you in a negative way. You go on doing something because the society says don't do it, but again the society is determining what you should do.

Buddha says rebellion is not reaction. It is neither slavery nor reaction, neither obedience nor disobedience. It is an inner discipline. It is a discipline, it is a tremendous order, but it comes from your inner core. You decide it.

We go on throwing our responsibility on others. It is easier. You can always say that your father said to do it, so you have done it – you are not responsible. You can always say the leader said to do it, so you have done – you are not responsible. The whole country was going to do it, was going to war and was killing other countries; you have done it because you simply obeyed orders, you simply obeyed.

When Adolf Hitler's colleagues were caught after the second world war they all stated before the court that they were not responsible, they were simply obeying orders. Whatsoever order was given they were obeying. If the order was given, "Kill a million Jews!" they killed. They were simply following orders, they were simply obedient. They were not responsible.

Now look and watch: you may be simply trying to find out someone who says "do this" so you can throw the responsibility on him. But this is no way to throw the responsibility on anybody else. Life is yours and responsibility is yours.

If you understand Buddha, the world will be totally different. Then there cannot be any more Hitlers, then there cannot be any more wars because there cannot be any obedience from the outside, and everybody responsible will think on his own. Not that "Hindus are killing Mohammedans, so I have to kill," nor "Mohammedans are burning temples, so I have to burn because I am a Mohammedan." Each individual should become a light unto himself, and he should decide – not as a Mohammedan, not as a Christian, not as an Indian, not as a Pakistani; he should decide according to his own consciousness, not according to anything else. This is what Buddha calls the discipline that is beyond discipline.

This is the definition of a religious person: he thinks the thought that is unthinkable; he practices the deed that is not doing; he speaks that which is inexpressible, ineffable; and he practices the discipline that is beyond discipline.

> *Those who understand this are near, those who are confused are far.*

If these four things are understood, you are close to truth. If you don't understand then you are far away from the truth.

> *The way is beyond words and expressions, is bound by nothing earthly. Lose sight of it to an inch or miss it for a moment, and we are away from it forever more.*

Those who understand it are close. Now let this be a criterion for you, you can judge. Let this be a touchstone for your growth. If you feel these four things are happening in your life – however, in whatsoever quantity, maybe a very small quantity, but if they are happening, then you are on the right track. If you are going away from these four things, you are going away from the way, the *dhamma*, the Tao.

The way is beyond words and expressions, is bound by nothing earthly. The ultimate truth is not bound by anything that you can see, that you can touch. It is not dependent on your senses. The ultimate truth is not material, it is immaterial. It is not earthly. It cannot be caused by anything. That's why it can never become part of science.

You can mix hydrogen and oxygen and you can cause water to be there. There is no way to create ecstasy that way. There is no way to cause God that way. There is no way to cause truth that way. You can destroy water by separating hydrogen and oxygen, you can create water by mixing hydrogen and oxygen, but there is no way to destroy truth or to cause it. It is uncaused.

It is not a chain of cause and effect. You cannot create it, it is already there. You cannot destroy it because you are it. It is the very life. You can only do one thing: either you can close your eyes towards it, either you can forget about it, you can become absolutely oblivious of it, or you can remember, see, realize.

If you are lost in too much doing, ambition, riches, money, prestige, power, then you will lose track of the truth which is always by the side of you – just by the corner, just within reach – but you are keeping your back towards it.

Or you can allow it. If you become a little more meditative and less ambitious, if you become a little more religious and less political, if you become a little more unworldly than worldly, if you start moving more withinwards than without, if you start becoming a little more alert than sleepy, if you come out of your drunk state, if you bring a little light into your being – then, then you will be close, close to home. You have never been away. Then your whole life will be transformed, transfigured. Then you will live in a totally different way; a new quality will be there in your life which has nothing to do with your doing, which is a gift, a benediction.

Lose sight of it to an inch... says Buddha, *or miss it for a moment, and we are away from it forever more.* Look into it for a single moment, come close to it even a single inch, and it is yours, and it has always been yours.

This is the paradox of a *siddhanta.* This is not a doctrine, this is Buddha's realization. He is simply trying to share his realization with you. He is not propounding a philosophy or a system of thought. He is simply pointing towards the moon, the reality.

Don't look at his pointing fingers, otherwise you will miss; you will become a Buddhist. Look at the moon the finger is pointing to. Forget the finger completely and look at the moon and you will become a buddha.

This is the problem that humanity has to settle. It is very much easier to become a Christian than to become a christ, very much easier to become a Buddhist than to become a buddha, but the reality is known only by becoming a christ or a buddha. By becoming a Christian or a Buddhist you are again becoming carbon copies. Don't insult yourself that way. Have a little respect for yourself. Never be a Christian and never be a Buddhist and never be a Hindu. Just be consciousness undefined, unbound, unmotivated. If you can do that much, all else will follow on its own accord.

Enough for today.

10

A HOLLOW BAMBOO

Osho,
Can one live and function in the world in a state of enlightenment or no-mind? Is an enlightened person self-sufficient in the world?

The state of enlightenment is not the state of individuality. There is no person in it. One who is enlightened is enlightened only because he is not, there is nobody to function. Activity continues, but there is nobody to do it. Functioning continues, but there is nobody to function it. Then it continues on its own just as stars go on moving and the seasons move, and the sun rises, and the moon comes, and the tide, and the seas, and the rivers.

An enlightened person is one with the whole; the whole functions through him. His activity is perfect because he is not there to distort it. He is just like a hollow bamboo – whatsoever song the whole chooses to sing through him, it is sung. There is nobody to hinder, there is nobody to obstruct.

An enlightened person is an enlightened emptiness – luminous emptiness. He has disappeared. If you believe in the concept of God, if you use that term, then you can say God functions through him. If you don't like that term, then you can say the whole functions through him. But he is not to function there.

When you function you create anxiety. All your functioning is in some way a sort of conflict with the whole. It is a struggle; there is motive, there is desire, there is ambition. When you are there, all illnesses are there. When you are there, neurosis is there. The ego is neurotic: it tries to impose its own goals on the whole, which is impossible. It tries to do that which cannot be done, hence gets more and more frustrated, enters deeper and deeper into hell and misery.

An enlightened person simply allows; whatsoever happens is a happening. It is very difficult to conceive it because it is not of the mind. It is very difficult to understand it because there is no experience. You can understand it only when you have dissolved, when you have become that.

There is no way to understand a buddha unless you become a buddha because it is such a totally different dimension of existence. We have never tasted of it. It is simply impossible for the mind to conceive because the mind functions through motive: there has to be a desire, there has to be a goal, there has to be the doer. The mind says if you don't do, how is it going to happen?

But millions of things are happening without anybody doing them. Who is doing the movement of the stars? Is not their functioning absolutely perfect? What is missing? What is lacking? Who is rushing these rivers to the ocean? Who goes on controlling the tide and the ebb? Who goes on maintaining this infinity, this immenseness? There is nobody. Because there is nobody that's why it is so beautiful. Because there is nobody that's why it is so absolutely perfect. If somebody is there, there is a possibility of error. If somebody is there then there is a possibility of mistakes. There is nobody, it is out of emptiness.

The seed goes on sprouting. Each moment is a miracle because each moment existence comes out of nothingness. Each moment the flower happens out of the blue. Nobody is forcing it, nobody is pulling it up. There is nobody to open the bud, it opens on its own accord. This is what Buddha calls the *dhamma*, the law, the ultimate law of life.

The enlightened person is no longer in any conflict with the ultimate law. He has surrendered, he floats, he flows with the river. He has almost become a wave in the river, he does not exist separately.

"Can one live and function in the world in a state of enlightenment or no-mind?" Yes, one can function. One has functioned. Buddha lived forty-two years after he became enlightened. Mahavira lived forty years after he became enlightened. They functioned perfectly well. And yet, the beauty is, the grandeur is that there was nobody doing it.

It is a moment to moment miracle. It is absolutely unbelievable, it is incredible to function out of nothingness, to function out of no-motive, to function out of no-mind. Just to function without having a center, without having a self.

An enlightened person is natural, spontaneous. He has no explanation why he is functioning. He will shrug his shoulders if you ask the question "Why?" He cannot explain it, he can at the most say, "It is how it is. It is how it is happening." He will say, "I don't know because there is nobody to know it." It is a mysterious functioning.

Of course the functioning is going to be totally different to your functioning. Out of your activity anxiety arises, tension. Out of your activity, fear arises – fear, are you going to succeed or not? Tension because there is competition, conflict, others are also rushing towards the same goal. Will you be able to become rich? Will you be able to become that which you want? It doesn't seem to be easy.

Mulla Nasruddin was saying to me one day, "When I was fourteen I decided that I was going to become the richest man in the world, whatsoever the cost."

Then I asked him, "Then what happened? You never became the richest man in the world. You may be the poorest. What happened then?"

Everybody wants to become the richest man in the world. Everybody wants to be the most powerful man in the world. Everybody wants to be the most strong, beautiful, intelligent, famous in the world. Of course much anxiety is created. In that anxiety you are in a sort of continuous illness, dis-ease, restlessness, a fever, in which you go on continuously trembling. And every moment there is frustration waiting for you.

Hence people say, "Man proposes and God disposes." God has never disposed anything. In your very proposition you are disposing God, hence you get in trouble because nature has its own way, the Tao has its own way; it has its own destiny. It is as if a part is trying to go on its own journey, leaving the whole behind. It is not possible, the part has to go with the whole. The tail has to go with the elephant. If the tail starts going on its own way against the elephant, separate from the elephant, then there is going to be trouble – the tail will go mad. And actually it will have to drag along with the elephant, there is no other way.

So there are only two types of people in the world. One, who have private goals – they feel they are being dragged; they feel man proposes, God disposes. Then there is another type of people in the world – very few, rare, far, far and few between, very few – who have dropped all their propositions. They don't drag, they dance. They dance because whatsoever God proposes they accept. And they have no private propositions, they don't have any desire of their own.

That's what Jesus says on the cross, that is his last message to the world, "Thy kingdom come, Thy will be done." Just a moment before he had hesitated a little, just a moment before he shouted and said, "Why have you forsaken me? Why? Why are you showing me all this?"

You cannot criticize Jesus, what he said is natural and human. He was only thirty-three, he was not yet old, he was just young, he had not seen the whole life yet, he had not tasted, he had not lived yet and suddenly he finds himself on the cross, ridiculed, insulted, rejected by his own people. And it is natural that he shouts at God, "Why have you forsaken me? Why are you showing me all this?" – human, very human.

But immediately he became aware of it. It must have escaped – this shouting against God – in a moment of unawareness. The pain may have been too much, the misery was too much. Death was just close by, he was shocked. But he regained balance. He was going to propose something. He simply said, "Thy kingdom come, thy will be done." He surrendered. He died as Christ.

In a single moment he was no longer Jesus, he was Christ. In a single moment he was no longer human, he was superhuman. The gap is very small. That's why Buddha says, "Miss it by a single inch, or by a single moment and you are thrown millions of miles away." Just a single inch was the difference between these two sentences, there was not much gap, maybe a single breath. But he was just ordinary when he shouted against God – human, weak. Just a moment later on he was reconciled, there was no problem then. If this is the way God wants it to happen, then this is the way it has to happen. He accepted.

A smile must have come to his face, and not only to his face but to his heart also. In that moment he must have expanded. Now there was nothing to shrink, to remain closed; even death was accepted. When you accept death, you have accepted God. Everybody desires for life, when you accept life you don't accept much. When you accept death you have accepted all.

An enlightened person is one who has not only accepted death. He is one who has really died, he is no longer there, the house is absolutely empty. Or, he is that emptiness. That emptiness is luminous, full of light. Now he moves hand and hand with God. Now wherever God takes him, to whatsoever land – uncharted, unmapped – he runs along, dancing. He is not dragged.

If you are dragged by life then you must be fighting with it. If you are bored by life then you must be fighting with it. If you are frustrated by life you must be fighting with it. These are indications that you are not reconciled to life, that you have not yet become mature enough to surrender; you are childish, you are in a childish tantrum.

A man who is really mature has no will of his own. He says,

"Thy will be done." It is only immature minds who go on carrying their own will, and of course they suffer. Will brings suffering, will is the way to hell. You bring suffering, you are the way to hell. You create suffering.

Of course, an enlightened person functions totally differently. He himself does not know where he is going, and he is not worried about it either. He does not think about it, where he is going. He trusts, wherever he is going, it is good. His trust is total and infinite.

He trusts life, you trust yourself. He trusts the whole, you trust a tiny part. He trusts the immense, the infinite, you trust the mediocre human mind. His trust makes him wise, your trust makes you stupid. You doubt the whole and you trust yourself. He has dropped himself and he trusts the whole. He is never frustrated, he has no regrets. He never looks back because whatsoever was, was – and whatsoever was, was good.

It is not only a mind thing. He feels it, his whole existence is radiated with "yes!" He says "yes" to life, you go on saying "no." No-saying creates ego, yea-saying drops the ego, helps the ego to drop and disappear.

The enlightened person is an absolute unconditional yes. It is very difficult to understand it unless you have tasted something of it. That is the only way to know about it.

"Is an enlightened person self-sufficient in the world?" That's why I say you can understand it only if you have known it, if you have become it. Otherwise you will go on asking questions which are irrelevant. For example: "Is an enlightened person self-sufficient in the world?" He has no self, so how can he be self-sufficient? He has no self, so how can he be in any way self-sufficient? I am not saying that he is discontented. I am not saying that he is unsatisfied, and I am not saying that he is not sufficient. I am simply saying that he cannot be self-sufficient because he has no self.

An enlightened person comes to know that independence is impossible, dependence also impossible. The reality is neither dependent nor independent; the reality is interdependent. We exist together. And when I say "we," the trees are included, the mountains are included, the skies are included. When I say "we," everything is included, nothing is excluded. We exist together. We are together. Our very being is togetherness. Nobody is self-sufficient.

That's what ordinarily we are trying to become – self-sufficient. That is our whole struggle so that we are no longer dependent on anybody. But just think: is it possible to be self-sufficient? And if it is possible for a man to become self-sufficient, will he be alive? He will be dead. Only when you are in your grave are you self-sufficient. Otherwise you will have to breathe, and you cannot be self-sufficient about it. You will have to take in the breath, the vitality, the *prana*. You will have to wait for the sun to make you warm. You will have to eat the fruit of the trees so their juice becomes your blood. You will need millions of things. How can you be self-sufficient? The very idea is foolish.

But there are people, the so-called saints, who go on teaching you "become self-sufficient." That is an ego trip. It is not possible in the nature of things to be self-sufficient because self is a falsity. Self is just an idea, it has no reality, so how can you create sufficiency around a false idea? Self in itself is nonexistential, so how can you create sufficiency around something which does not exist?

The enlightened person is one who looks into life and comes to know that "I am not, only God is, truth is. Truth is self-sufficient, the whole is self-sufficient. How can I be self-sufficient?" We are linked with everything else, and this linking is really complex. I am not only linked to you, you are not only linked to these trees, you are not only linked to the sun today – you are linked to all the people who have ever lived on the earth. If your parents were not there you would not have been here. If your grandparents were not there you would not have been here. Just go back, go back – if Adam and Eve were not there you would not have been here.

So not only are we linked with the contemporary existence, we are linked with the whole past – not only of humanity, but of the whole universe. This is easy to understand, that we are linked with the whole past, otherwise how can we be? We are part of a procession, part of a river, an ongoing river. You are also linked with the future. It is a little more difficult because we think that maybe it is right, we are linked with the past, but how are we linked with the future?

A river has two banks. It cannot flow with only one bank, otherwise it will never reach the ocean. The other bank may be hidden in deep mist, you may not be able to see it, it may be very far away.

You cannot see it, it is beyond the horizon, but still you can think that it has to be there. The past is one bank of the river of time, the future is another bank. Without the future the past cannot exist; and without the past and the future the present cannot exist. The present is the river, the past is one bank, the future is another bank.

We are not only linked with the past, we are linked with the future also. You are not only linked with your parents, you are linked with your children also – children who are not born yet. You are not only one with the past that has been here, but with the future that is going to be here. You are linked with the yesterday and the tomorrow, otherwise the today cannot exist. It has to exist between yesterday and the tomorrow – yesterdays and tomorrows. The today is just a middle turn.

If you look at it that way, then in space we are linked with everything. If the sun dies today we all will die. It is so far, the light takes ten minutes to reach to us. Ten minutes doesn't look such a big time, but for light to travel that much it is really big because the light travels so fast – one hundred and eighty-six thousand miles per second.

The sun is ten minutes away. But if it dies, suddenly you will see these trees dying, suddenly you will see yourself shrinking and dying. Suddenly you will see the whole beauty disappears from the earth because the whole warmth disappears from the earth. Warmth is life. The very throb of the heart is connected with the sun. But the scientists say the sun itself is connected to some source of light not yet discovered. Somewhere at the very center of the whole existence there must be a source the sun is connected with.

Everything is connected. Have you watched a spider's web? Just touch it anywhere and the whole web trembles. Exactly that way is life. Touch it anywhere – touch a leaf of grass and you have touched all the stars because everything is so interconnected. There are no boundaries, we are not islands, we are a continent. Nothing defines you. All definitions are man-made. All definitions are just like the fence around your house, it does not divide the earth. All boundaries are like lines on the map: it does not divide the earth, it does not divide the ocean, it does not divide the sky; it is only on the map.

An enlightened person is one who has dropped all demarcations: who is not a Christian, who is not a Hindu, who is not a Mohammedan, who is not a Buddhist, who is not a communist, who is not a fascist, who is not man, who is not woman, who is not young, who is not old; who has dropped all lines of demarcation, who lives without definition. To live without definition is to live infinitely because all definition is a finitude. To define means to make finite. An enlightened person is indefinable, infinite. He has no lines.

Somebody asked Bokuju, a Zen master, "Master, you say everything is one, then is a dog also a buddha?" That is a Zen way of asking, "Is a dog also God?" Bokuju did not answer verbally, he jumped on his fours and started barking. He was a buddha, an enlightened being. He simply showed that, "Yes! Look, here is a dog barking, and here is a buddha too." A dog is nothing but God in reverse. Just read it backwards, that is the only difference.

Everything is divine and everything is one.

The enlightened person is not self-sufficient. He is sufficient, certainly, but not self-sufficient. Sufficient because there is no problem for him, the whole is there available for him. The whole goes on supplying him even without asking. The whole takes care. He has dissolved into the whole, now the whole is responsible. The whole takes care of him. He is protected by the whole, he is sheltered by the whole. He is at home in the whole. Whatsoever happens is welcome because it is happening through the whole. How can it be wrong? "Thy will be done, thy kingdom come." He is just a zero.

So I cannot say he is self-sufficient. He is tremendously sufficient, but not self-sufficient. His sufficiency comes not from his self, his sufficiency comes because he has dropped his self. He is sufficient because he is with the whole; now how can he lack anything? It is impossible to lack anything: the sun is with him, the moon is with him, the trees, the rivers, the oceans – he is no longer poor.

An enlightened person is the richest person possible, but his richness comes from surrender, not from fight. He does not have any conflict with the whole. He has fallen in harmony, he is in a *harmonia*.

Osho,
Listening to you today I became a child. I wanted to call out, "but I am only three," as I had once done years ago at a dancing class. What to do?

This too is a dance. Listening to me you are in a subtle dance. Being with me you are in a dance with me. It can happen. If you are really in a dance your age can disappear. You can again become a child, you can regain that perceptivity that was yours when you were a child. You can regain that clarity that was yours when you were a child. You can come again close to God.

A child is very close to God because he is very close to nature. A child is still uncivilized, he is still a primitive. A child is more close to animals than the so-called human beings. A child still lives through innocence and not through knowledge.

That is my whole effort. That is what I am trying to do: to destroy all that has become a blockage in you and in your childhood. Yes, that's what I am doing. I would like you to have another childhood. I would like you to enter into your innocence again, to gain that primal innocence, to be reborn.

Nicodemus asked Jesus, "What should I do master, to know the truth?"

Jesus looked at him and said, "You will have to be reborn. As you are you cannot make any contact. You carry too many obstacles, you carry too many blocks. You will have to become a child again."

Once Jesus was standing in a market place, a crowd had gathered and somebody asked, "Master, you continuously talk about the kingdom of God, but you never say to us who will be capable to enter into that kingdom. Who will be the worthy ones?"

Jesus looked around. A small child was also there in the crowd. He took him up onto his shoulders and said, "Whosoever is like this child. Only those who are like children will be able to enter into the kingdom of God."

There was one childhood which you have lost – nothing to be

worried about, it is natural. It had to be lost. It is just in the natural course of things. That childhood was too unconscious, you cannot carry it forever. It had to collapse and disappear. It was like the first teeth, they are too soft. They will not be able to help for your whole life. They have to drop and give way for stronger teeth.

The first childhood is just like first teeth. They have disappeared, they are no longer there, and you are living without teeth, without your childhood, hence the misery. You will have to regain your childhood again, you will have to grow your childhood again. And this childhood will be very strong, tremendously strong because now it will be something conscious, it will be something that you have grown to.

The first childhood was simply a gift of heaven, the second childhood will be more yours. It will be more deep-rooted. The first childhood was lost because it was unconscious, and the more you became conscious it disappeared. The second childhood has to be conscious, then there will be no problem. Then it can be with you for eternity.

Again and again you come sometimes to a moment when you can hear the birds more clearly – again as you used to hear in your childhood, when you can see the flowers more clearly, they become psychedelic, more colorful. You can see the trees and their green. It is so strong it hurts. It goes penetrating into the heart.

Everything becomes very intense when you are a child. It was intense one day: remember yourself running on the beach, collecting seashells, or running after butterflies in a garden. Remember again how things were totally different, how life was more colorful, how everything was a miracle and a surprise. How everything was simply amazing, how everything was just unbelievably beautiful. How everything used to catch your attention, how everything used to create a romance in you and how you were full of energy, radiant, bubbling, joyous. How life was a totally different dimension. How you were delighted in small things, in meaningless things. How you were playful, how everything was a question mark, a mystery.

The same can happen again, should happen again. That's what all religion is about, to give you a second childhood. In India we call that man who attains to the second childhood, *dwij*, twice-born. He is born again, not physically, but psychologically. The first birth is out of your parents, the second birth is out of your master. The first birth is only of the body, the second birth is of the soul.

The questioner says, "Listening to you today I became a child..." You are blessed – now don't lose it. In the beginning it will be very fragile. It will come like a breeze and will be gone. It will be there dancing around you for a moment, and the next moment it is not there. It will be there like a window opening and closing. It will be there very fragile, very vulnerable. Allow it more and more, enjoy it more and more. Cooperate with it more and more. Wait for it more and more, pray for it more and more – and it will be coming more and more. Soon it will be like a strong wind. Soon it will not be just a glimpse, it will become more real, more solid.

In fact, when your second childhood becomes real, it has such a solidity that no matter can have that solidity. It is the most solid thing in existence. When it becomes solid, when it is always there – asleep it is there, awake it is there, eating, talking, sitting in silence it is there, walking in the market place it is there – when you are surrounded by it, even when you are very active, it is always there in the background.

Whenever you are inactive it comes to the fore, whenever you are too much active it goes into the background, but it goes on murmuring. Sometimes it is a distant murmur of a waterfall, sometimes it is a very wild uproar, but it remains always.

The first glimpse has happened, the first ray has entered. Now follow it, now catch hold of this ray. It will be your first connection with innocence. Don't be frightened by it, because to get frightened is very easy. To think oneself a child again, one becomes frightened. What is happening? Because in our so-called world, so-called society and culture, all over the world, the child is not respected.

The child is not thought to be real, the child is thought to be just a growing state. The child is thought to be just as a passage towards real life. The real life is when the childhood has disappeared, that's what we have been taught. The childhood is nothing but a preparation. Go to school, to the college, to the university; get prepared, get ready – then the real life begins. So childhood is just like a preface, it is not the real book. That's what we have been taught.

So again when you feel childhood raising its head, one can become scared. What is happening? Am I losing my memory? Am I losing my learning? Am I losing my adulthood? Am I losing all that I have learned at such cost, with such difficulty, with such hard work? Am I relapsing back, regressing?

If you ask a Freudian analyst, he will say, "You are regressing. Beware, don't allow this, otherwise all you have gained with such effort will be lost." But I will tell you, you are not regressing. This is not the same childhood that you have lost; this is something absolutely new. It resembles the childhood, but it is something absolutely new. It is a new childhood, a second childhood, it is a rebirth. So don't get scared, don't start feeling that something is wrong.

It happened to another woman – and it can happen to women more easily than to men because women are still a little more uncivilized than men. They are closer to nature still because this whole society is man-oriented; women have been left behind. In a way this is very fortunate. Women are still wilder. That's why they can scream and get angry and cry and weep and tears can flow from their eyes. Man has become very frozen; women are still more fluid, liquid. So it is easier for women to enter the second childhood than for men. Men will have to make a little more arduous effort.

It happened to another woman. She was very old, almost seventy. She became very much afraid. She came to me and she said, "What is happening? I feel like a child. Not only that – I feel like behaving like a child, laughing like a child, talking like a child. Not only that – I would like to tease people." A seventy-year-old woman wants to tease people like a small child.

She was afraid, naturally so. I said, "Don't be worried. Start playing with children."

She said, "What? Start playing with children? You really mean it?" I said, "Yes."

And she was really a good woman, a rare woman. She started playing with children: Siddhartha and Purva and small sannyasins became her friends. And even others were puzzled and surprised. And even others felt something tremendously beautiful happening.

She used to play in the ashram with small children; she also became friends with the small children of the laborers who were working on the Buddha Hall. It was a rare phenomenon. She accepted it and something started growing in her.

When she left, she came again and said, "Now, I am going to be in trouble, Osho, you have put me in trouble. I have enjoyed it so much, for the first time in my life there has been something significant. But how am I going to protect it in the West? People will simply put me in a madhouse. Here it is okay. Here you are, and here sannyasins are accepting, and they think that when Osho has said, then everything is okay. But who will protect me there? I don't want to lose this dimension that has opened, I don't want to close this door. My whole life has been a wastage. These few days I have again become a child, I have loved to be, I have become so grateful to be – a benediction has happened."

The same is possible for the questioner. She has a very soft heart. Let this first ray become more and more strong. Move with it, dance with it. Start singing again, start playing again. Even if people think it is mad, don't be bothered about those people because they have always been thinking that way. They thought St. Francis was mad because he had become like a child. They thought Jesus was mad, they thought Buddha was mad. They have always been thinking in those terms.

In fact, they have lost all contact with nature. They are dead people. Whenever they see somewhere some radiance, some life arising, they start feeling humiliated. They cannot believe it, that it is possible because it has not happened to them, how can it happen to somebody else? "How do you dare? It has not happened to me, how can it happen to you? Impossible! You must be imagining, or you must be in some psychological trouble."

Don't be bothered with these people. This society is mad. In this society every sane person is thought to be mad. He looks mad. It is a society of blind people. Suddenly your eyes open and you start talking about light, and all the blind people gather together and they say, "What nonsense. This man has gone mad. Light does not exist. It is written in our scriptures that light does not exist. Our prophets have proved it, our philosophers have argued about it – light does not exist. There is no God, there is no possibility of a second childhood." They will deny.

In fact, while they are denying, they are simply protecting themselves. They are afraid. If this is true then it will create a restlessness in them, a discontent – a divine discontent. And they are afraid of that discontent because that will change their whole life, their whole style. It will destroy their past. For that they don't have courage enough. For that they are not brave enough. For that they will have to lose many conveniences, much comfort, a settled life, security – no, they don't want to go that far.

It is better to say "God is dead." It is better to say "God never existed." It is better to say that people who talk about God are just poets, dreamers, day-dreamers; people who talk about *samadhi*, ecstasy, meditation, are just navel-gazers, escapists. It is better to condemn these people. That is very protective. Then you can avoid the venture of the unknown.

People are cowards, don't be worried about them. Go on your way, go on your way dancing. Remember only one thing: whatsoever feels good is good, whatsoever feels beautiful is beautiful, and whatsoever makes you joyful, gay, delighted, is truth. Let that be your only criterion. Don't be bothered by others' opinions. Let this be your only touchstone: whatsoever makes you happy is bound to be true. *Ananda*, bliss, is the only criterion of truth. So if you feel good and happy, then don't be worried.

"Listening to you today, I became a child. I wanted to call out, 'but I am only three.'" Shout it to the trees, shout it to the world, shout it to the stars, that "I am only three" – and be. Three is exactly the age when a child dies, nearabout three. The child loses all contact with nature and becomes part of the society. It is the time, the boundary line which he crosses, loses all contact with his own being, becomes a member of the society. Up to then he was just like animals and trees and rocks. Then he is a citizen, then he starts learning manners, language, etiquette. Then, by and by, he is growing out of childhood, going farther and farther away from God.

So if it has happened and you remember that "I am three," be that age, and soon you will start going even deeper. You will be two, you will be one. One day you will suddenly see you are being born, passing through the birth canal, and one day you will see you are in the womb, surrounded by your mother's warmth.

And at that moment, the first satori happens, first glimpse of *samadhi*. Because when you are in the womb there is no worry, no responsibility. You don't even breathe, the mother does that for you. When you are in a womb you are tremendously in surrender. In the womb there is no doubt, all is trust. In the womb the child knows no mind, he is simply there without any self.

The first glimpse of enlightenment comes when one has entered again into the womb, one has come to recognize that one is again in the womb – this whole universe becomes a womb. It is a womb. The whole universe becomes your mother. The whole universe suddenly becomes warm, it is not cold. It is loving. You are not in a strange world, you are at home. You are not an outsider, you are an insider. The first satori happens when you are again back in the womb of your mother.

So, go backwards. And this going backwards is not really going backwards, it is going forwards. Because you don't have any other language, that's why *childhood*, *birth*, *womb*, have to be used.

Freud had a very uncanny, intuitive sense of recognizing a few things about which he was not even convinced. Sometimes he was against them because he was not a religious person. But he had a very intuitive sense of recognizing things, howsoever vaguely, but he recognized many things.

One of his great insights was this: that religion is a search for the womb, and a religious person is one who wants again to be a child in the mother's womb. Exactly it is so. He was talking about it in a negative way, he was condemning it. But it is exactly so. Then the circle is complete. You have come to the womb again, now the womb is the whole universe. Now your whole life has become circular, complete – empty and complete, nothing and all.

Osho,
You have spoken of sex, love and compassion. I know what sex without love is, and I have known romantic love based on unfulfilled desires. But what is real love without sex? What is compassion?

Man has three layers: the body, the mind and the soul. So

whatsoever you do, you can do in three ways. Either it can be just from the body, or it can be from the mind, or it can be from the soul. Whatsoever you do, any act of yours, can have three qualities. Sex is love through the body; romantic love is sex through the mind; compassion is through the soul. But the energy is the same. Moving in a deeper way its quality changes, but the energy is the same.

If you live your love life only through the body, you live a very poor love life because you live very superficially. Sex, just of the body, is not even sex – it becomes sexuality. It becomes pornographic, it becomes a little obscene, it becomes a little brutal, ugly because it has no depth in it. Then it is just a physical release of the energy. Maybe it helps you to become a little less tense, but just to become a little more relaxed you are losing tremendous energy, tremendously valuable energy.

If it can become love you will not be losing it. In the same act you will be gaining also. On the physical level there is only loss – sex is simply a loss of energy. Sex is a safety valve in the body: when the energy is too much and you don't know what to do with it, you throw it out. You feel relaxed because you are emptied of energy. A sort of rest comes because the restless energy is thrown out, but you are poorer than before, you are emptier than before.

And again and again this will happen. Then your whole life will become just a routine of collecting energy by food, by breathing, by exercise, and then throwing it away. This looks absurd. First eat, breathe, exercise, create energy, and then you are worried what to do with it – then throw it. This is meaningless, absurd.

So sex becomes very soon meaningless. And a person who has known only sex of the body, and has not known the deeper dimension of love becomes mechanical. His sex is just a repetition of the same act again and again and again.

I have received a beautiful joke...

There was this farmer and he was having a lot of trouble with his hens. He read an advertisement in a newspaper for a Supercock: "Five hundred dollars: we guarantee to double the fertility of your chickens."

Five hundred dollars is five hundred dollars, and so it took the farmer a couple of weeks to reckon that it was worth it. Finally, a week after he sent his check off, a truck arrived, the back doors were swung open, and the driver pulled out a large case with "Super-cock" written all over it in red, white and blue. No sooner had the farmer opened the case than out sprang Super-cock.

"Where is the hen house?" cried Super-cock. Amazed, the farmer pointed up some steps. Super-cock immediately ran over and up the steps and disappeared into the hen-house. Fifteen minutes later Super-cock emerged, victorious.

The farmer said, "That was fantastic, I have never seen anything like it before in my life. You just sit down here and eat your fill of this grain."

"No, no. Do you have any ducks? I love ducks also," said the Super-cock. The farmer tried to get Super-cock to rest, as he knew how easily these new strains of cock became exhausted, and he had, after all, cost him five hundred dollars. Ten minutes later Super-cock returned from the stream where the farmer had reluctantly told him that the ducks were.

Now the farmer was really angry at Super-cock and told him that he really had to rest or he would kill himself. "You must have some turkeys? Which way is it to the turkeys?" cried the Super-cock. The farmer was so exasperated that he threw his arms in the air and walked off. Out of the corner of his eye he saw Super-cock strutting off in the direction of the turkey-house.

An hour later he happened to look up in the sky and saw buzzards wheeling over his nearby field. Cursing and swearing under his breath, he walked over to where he could now see, sure enough, his five hundred dollar Super-cock dead in the field – on his back with his feet raised in the air. Just as he was about to pick Super-cock up by the legs, Super-cock opened one eye and said, whispering, "Go away, go away. They are getting nearer."

A man who lives a life of physical sex is nothing but a Super-cock. He lives and dies just doing one thing, and all else is centered on that one thing. And it is futile, and it is not nourishing. Sex is not nourishing, it is destructive. Unless it becomes love it has no creative energy in it.

"You have spoken of sex, love and compassion. I know what

sex without love is..." It is good that you recognize that you know what sex without love is. There are many people, millions of them, who will not recognize that, who will not even accept this – they go on thinking and believing that they love. This is good, this awareness is good; then possibilities open because once you recognize that you have touched only one layer of your being, then the second layer can be opened, penetrated.

If you say that no, you know whatsoever there is to love, then it is very difficult to help you. So, good, the questioner is aware, "I know what sex without love is..." It is miserable. It simply gives you a mechanical release. You can become addicted to it: you don't enjoy it then, but you will miss it. If you don't go into it you will feel restless, if you go into it there is nothing in it.

That is what is happening in the West. People are going beyond sex – not towards love, not towards compassion because that beyond is within; people are going beyond sex in a negative way, sex is becoming absurd. They are finished with it. They are searching something else. That's why drugs have become so important. Sex is finished, that was the oldest drug, the natural LSD. Now it is finished and people don't know what to do now. The natural drug is no longer appealing, they have had enough of it. So chemicals, LSD, marijuana, psilocybin and other things are becoming more important.

In the West it is impossible now to prevent people from drugs. Unless sex starts becoming deeper and is transformed into love, there is no way – people will have to go towards drugs, helplessly. Even if they are reluctant they will have to go because the old drug of sex is finished. It is not finished because it was futile, it is finished because people lived only on the superficial level. They never penetrated into the mystery of it.

At the most people know something about what they call romantic love – that too is not love, that is repressed sex. When you don't have the possibility of making a sexual contact, that repressed energy becomes romance. Then that repressed energy starts becoming cerebral, it starts moving into the head. When sex moves from the genital organs towards the head, it becomes romance. Romantic love is not really love, it is pseudo, it is a false coin. It is again the same sex but the opportunity was not there.

In the past ages people lived very much in the romantic love because sex was not so easy. It was very difficult, the society created so many obstacles. Sex was so difficult that people had to repress it. That repressed energy would start moving into their heads, would become poetry, painting and romance, and they would have dreams, beautiful dreams.

Now that has disappeared, particularly in the West. In the East it is still there. In the West it has disappeared because sex has become available. Thanks to Freud there has been a great revolution in the West. The revolution has dropped all those barriers and inhibitions and repression about sex energy. Now sex is easily available, there is no problem about it.

It is so much available, more than you need – that has created a problem. Romantic love has disappeared. Now in the West no romantic poetry is being written. Who will write romantic poetry? Sex is so easily available in the market, who will think about it? There is no need to think about it.

Romantic love is the other side of physical sex, the repressed side. It is not love. Both are ill. What you call sex, sexuality and romantic love, both are ill states of affairs. When body and mind meet, there is love. Love is healthy. In sexuality only body is there, in romantic love only head is there. Both are partial.

In love, body and mind meet, you become a unity, more of a unity. You love the person and sex comes just as a shadow to it. It is not vice versa. You love the person so much, your energies meet with the person so deeply, you feel so good by the other's presence, the other's presence is so fulfilling it completes you. Love comes as a shadow to it.

Sex is not the center, love is the center; sex becomes the periphery. Yes, sometimes you would like to meet on the physical plane also, but there is no hankering for it. It is not an obsession, it is just a sharing of energy. The basic thing is deep. The periphery is good. With the center, the periphery is good; without the center it becomes sexuality. Without the periphery, if it is only in the center it becomes romantic love. When the periphery and the center are both together there is a togetherness of body and mind. It is not only that you desire the other's body, but you desire the other's being, then there is love. Love is healthy.

Sexuality and romantic love are ill, unhealthy. They are a sort of neurosis because they create a split in you. Love is a harmony. It is not only the body of the other, but his very being, his very presence that is loved. You don't use the other person as a means for release. You love the person. He is not, or she is not a means, but an end unto herself or unto himself. Love is healthy.

And there is another depth still left which I call compassion. When body, mind and soul meet, then you have become a great unity. You have become a trinity. You have become trimurti. Then all that is in you, from the most superficial to the deepest depth, is in a meeting. Your soul also is part of your love. Of course, compassion is possible only through deep meditation.

Sexuality is possible without any understanding, without any meditation. Love is possible only with understanding. Compassion is possible only with understanding and meditation, understanding and awareness. Not only do you understand and respect the other person, but you have come to your deepest core of being. Seeing your own deepest core, you have become capable of seeing the deepest core in the other also. Now the other does not exist as a body or a mind; the other exists as a soul. And souls are not separate. Your soul and my soul are one.

When two bodies meet,. they are separate. When two body-minds meet, their boundaries are overlapping. When two souls meet, they are one. Compassion is the highest form of love. It is possible only for a Buddha, or a Christ, or a Krishna to have compassion.

But love is possible for many. A little more understanding of life, a little more watchfulness about life, will help many to become lovers. But if you are completely unconscious then you have to live the rotten life of sex. In compassion, the energy is purest; love has completely become of the depth. In fact in compassion love is no longer a relationship, it has become a state.

When you are in sexuality you don't bother much to whom you are making love, any body will do. You just need a woman or a man, any body will do. You just need the other's body. In love, any body won't do, anybody's body won't do. You need a person who is in deep love with you, who has a certain affinity and harmony with you, in whose presence your heart starts singing, a deep bell starts ringing, in whose presence you feel a blessing. Then only is it possible for you to make love to the other person. To make love is possible only if the meeting, the inner meeting, has happened. Otherwise it is simply impossible to think, even to imagine that you are making love to a person you don't love.

In the state of compassion, sex completely disappears. In the state of love, sex remains but becomes secondary. In the state of sexuality, sex is the only thing and the primary thing. In the second state, of love, sex is secondary, follows like a shadow. The flame is there and sex follows like smoke. In the first stage of sex, there is only smoke, there is no flame; the fuel is too wet for flame. There is only smoke and smoke and smoke. In the second state there is flame but still smoke is there, surrounding the flame. The flame is clouded by the smoke. In the third state of compassion there is only flame, no smoke – it is a smokeless flame. Purity has attained absolutely.

You can make sex to as many people as you want because there is no discrimination. It is animalistic. In the state of love you discriminate. Love is very individualistic, it is very choosy. In the state of compassion all individuality has disappeared; there is universality. You are simply compassion, you are simply love. Love goes on falling, overflowing. Whosoever comes close to you is fulfilled. Whosoever dares to come close to you is inflamed, carries a new glow.

In compassion it is not a question between you and the other. You are not there, neither is the other – only one energy, one tremendous energy of existence, dancing. It is Nataraj, the dancing Shiva. The energy is in love with itself. It is tremendously ecstatic and happy. It is elated for no reason at all, it is extravagant. It has so much that it goes on pouring. It is a play.

Sex is like work, you are too much worried about it. You want to do it, you want to finish it somehow. It is like a burden on you. Love is not like a burden, it is enjoyment. You cherish it, you taste it – as a connoisseur tastes the wine. There is no hurry. There is no hurry to finish it, you would like to linger in it. You are slow, unhurried, patient.

Sex is momentary, love has a longer period for it – it lingers slowly. Compassion is eternal, it is timeless. Whether somebody is there or not is not the question then. A man of compassion has compassion. Buddha sitting under his *bodhi* tree is as loving as when he is surrounded by his sannyasins. When he is moving in the crowd he is as loving as when he is alone. Now love is a state.

If you want to change from sex towards love, try to understand your sexuality. Watch it, watch the mechanicalness of it. See the futility, see the whole absurdity of it; it is not leading you anywhere. Become a little more refined, become a little more subtle. Look not for the body, but for somebody's being. Watch, explore. Sooner or later you will find somebody who fits with you.

It can happen at first sight even because when energies fit, they fit. If they don't fit, they don't fit. You can struggle your whole life, they will not fit. If they fit, they fit immediately. Marriage has made love disappear badly, marriage has made love disappear from the earth – because marriage is arranged for other considerations: money, finance, family, prestige, astrology; all absurd. They have nothing to do with the heart of the two persons who are going to be married.

So marriage is almost always a failure; only in rare accidents it is not so – but they are accidents, exceptions. They cannot be counted. Marriage is always on the rocks because it is for wrong reasons. Only love can become the foundation of a real marriage. There is no other way because there is no other way to find that your wavelength is exactly the same as the other's, that you vibrate in the same way as the other. There is no other way to find it out.

Astrology is not helpful, neither is somebody's prestige, family. No, nothing is important. Only one thing is important – that two persons together vibrate in such a way that their vibrations become a pattern, a harmonious pattern. Only vibe can decide.

In a better world people will be allowed to move and mingle and meet as many people as possible so they can really find somebody who gets into them and they get into him, or into her – somebody who has the same quality which fits and makes you complete and fulfills you.

Love is possible. If the society is a little healthier and less perverted, love is possible. In a good healthy society, love should be natural. In a perverted society – the society in which we live and the whole world lives – love has become impossible; only sex has remained possible. But compassion will become possible only if you make all efforts to become meditative, otherwise not.

The last stage – of compassion – I call holy. The first stage I call unhealthy, ill; the second stage I call healthy, normal – society can attain to the second stage. Only when society hinders with the individual life and tries to manipulate the individual and dominate it, the first stage happens.

The third stage I call holy because it consists of the whole. That is possible only if you make individual efforts. Meditation will lead you to compassion. Buddha has said: "If you meditate, compassion will arise automatically."

Osho,
I hear what you are saying, but everything in me is saying no, no, no. I want to leave. I want to go home.

You are a fool. You have come home. Where else do you want to go?

It happened...

Once a drunkard came back to his home in the deep mid-night.

He was so drunk that he could not recognize his home. He knocked on the door. His old mother opened the door and said, "Come in."

But he said, "Old woman, I have knocked only just to ask – where is my home? Just tell me. I remember faintly, my home exists somewhere in this neighborhood. The road seems to be familiar."

The woman said, "What are you saying? You fool, Come in! This is your home!"

The same is my answer to you. You have come home. To whom are you saying no, no, no? Say yes and enter.

Enough for today.

11

A NEW LIGHT

The Buddha said:
Look up to heaven and down on earth and they will remind you of their impermanency. Look about the world and it will remind you of its impermanency. But when you gain spiritual enlightenment you shall then find wisdom. The knowledge thus attained leads you anon to the way.
The Buddha said:
You should think of the four elements of which the body is composed. Each of them has its own name and there is no such thing there known as ego. As there is really no ego, it is like unto a mirage.

I am reminded of the fateful day of twenty-first March, 1953. For many lives I had been working – working upon myself, struggling, doing whatsoever can be done – and nothing was happening.

Now I understand why nothing was happening. The very effort was the barrier, the very ladder was preventing, the very urge to seek was the obstacle. Not that one can reach without seeking; seeking is needed, but there comes a point when seeking has to be dropped. The boat is needed to cross the river but then comes a moment when you have to get out of the boat and forget all about it and leave it behind. Effort is needed; without effort nothing is possible. And also with only effort, nothing is possible.

Just before twenty-first March, 1953, seven days before, I stopped working on myself. A moment comes when you see the whole futility of effort. You have done all that you can do and nothing is happening. You have done all that is humanly possible. Then what else can you do? In sheer helplessness one drops all search.

The day the search stopped, the day I was not seeking for something, the day I was not expecting something to happen, it started happening. A new energy arose out of nowhere. It was not coming from any source. It was coming from nowhere and everywhere. It was in the trees and in the rocks and the sky and the sun and the air, it was everywhere. I was seeking so hard, and I was thinking it is very far away, and it was so near and so close.

Just because I was seeking, I had become incapable of seeing the near. Seeking is always for the far, seeking is always for the distant, and it was not distant. I had become far-sighted, I had lost the near-sightedness. The eyes had become focused on the far away, the horizon, and they had lost the quality to see that which is just close, surrounding you.

The day effort ceased, I also ceased. Because you cannot exist without effort, and you cannot exist without desire, and you cannot exist without striving.

The phenomenon of the ego, of the self, is not a thing, it is a process. It is not a substance sitting there inside you, you have to create it each moment. It is like pedaling a bicycle. If you pedal it goes on and on, if you don't pedal it stops. It may go a little because of the past momentum, but the moment you stop pedaling, in fact the bicycle starts stopping. It has no more energy, no more power to go anywhere. It is going to fall and collapse.

The ego exists because we go on pedaling desire, because we go on striving to get something, because we go on jumping ahead of ourselves. That is the very phenomenon of the ego: the jump ahead of yourself, the jump in the future, the jump in the tomorrow. The jump in the nonexistential creates the ego because it comes out of the nonexistential. It is like a mirage: it consists only of desire and nothing else. It consists only of thirst and nothing else. It consists only of future and nothing else.

The ego is not in the present, it is in the future. If you are in the future, then ego seems to be very substantial. If you are in the present the ego is a mirage, it starts disappearing.

The day I stopped seeking – and it is not right to say that I stopped seeking, better will be to say the day seeking stopped. Let me repeat it: the better way to say it is the day the seeking stopped because if I stop it then I am there again. Now stopping becomes my effort, now stopping becomes my desire, and desire goes on existing in a very subtle way.

You cannot stop desire; you can only understand it. In the very understanding is the stopping of it. Remember, nobody can stop desiring, and the reality happens only when desire stops.

So this is the dilemma. What to do? Desire is there and buddhas go on saying desire has to be stopped, and they go on saying in the next breath that you cannot stop desire. So what to do? You put people in a dilemma. They are in desire, certainly. You say it has to be stopped – okay. And then you say it cannot be stopped. Then what is to be done?

The desire has to be understood. You can understand it, you can just see the futility of it. A direct perception is needed, an immediate penetration is needed. Look into desire, just see what it is, and you will see the falsity of it, and you will see it is nonexistential. And desire drops and something drops simultaneously within you.

Desire and the ego exist in cooperation, they coordinate. The ego cannot exist without desire, the desire cannot exist without the ego. Desire is projected ego, ego is interjected desire. They are together, two aspects of one phenomenon.

The day desiring stopped, I felt very hopeless and helpless. No hope because no future. Nothing to hope because all hoping has proved futile, it leads nowhere. You go in rounds. It goes on dangling in front of you, it goes on creating new mirages, it goes on calling you, "Come on, run fast, you will reach." But howsoever fast you run you never reach.

That's why Buddha calls it a mirage. It is like the horizon that you see around the earth. It appears but it is not there. If you go, it goes on running from you. The faster you run, the faster it moves away. The slower you go, the slower it moves away. But one thing is certain, the distance between you and the horizon remains absolutely the same. Not even a single inch can you reduce the distance between you and the horizon.

You cannot reduce the distance between you and your hope. Hope is horizon. You try to bridge yourself with the horizon, with the hope, with a projected desire. The desire is a bridge, a dream bridge because the horizon exists not, so you cannot make a bridge towards it, you can only dream about the bridge. You cannot be joined with the nonexistential.

The day the desire stopped, the day I looked into it and realized it simply was futile, I was helpless and hopeless. But that very moment something started happening. The same started happening for which, for many lives I was working and it was not happening.

In your hopelessness is the only hope, and in your desirelessness is your only fulfillment, and in your tremendous helplessness suddenly the whole existence starts helping you. It is waiting. When it sees that you are working on your own, it does not interfere. It waits. It can wait infinitely because there is no hurry for it. It is eternity. The moment you are not on your own, the moment you drop, the moment you disappear, the whole existence rushes towards you, enters you. And for the first time things start happening.

Seven days I lived in a very hopeless and helpless state, but at the same time something was arising. When I say hopeless I don't mean what you mean by the word hopeless. I simply mean there was no hope in me. Hope was absent. I am not saying that I was hopeless and sad. I was happy in fact, I was very tranquil, calm and collected and centered. Hopeless, but with a totally new meaning. There was no hope, so how could there be hopelessness. Both had disappeared.

The hopelessness was absolute and total. Hope had disappeared and with it, its counterpart hopelessness, had also disappeared. It was a totally new experience of being without hope. It was not a negative state. I have to use words, but it was not a negative state. It was absolutely positive. It was not just absence, a presence was felt. Something was overflowing in me, flooding over me.

And when I say I was helpless, I don't mean the word in the dictionary sense. I simply say I was selfless. That's what I mean when I say helpless. I have recognized the fact that I am not, so I cannot depend on myself, so I cannot stand on my own ground – there was no ground underneath. I was in an abyss, bottomless abyss. But there was no fear because there was nothing to protect. There was no fear because there was nobody to be afraid.

Those seven days were of tremendous transformation, total transformation. And the last day the presence of a totally new energy, a new light and new delight became so intense that it was almost unbearable – as if I was exploding, as if I was going mad with blissfulness. The new generation in the West has the right word for it: I was blissed out, stoned.

It was impossible to make any sense out of it, what was happening. It was a very nonsense world: difficult to figure it out, difficult to manage in categories, difficult to use words, languages, explanations. All scriptures appeared dead and all the words that have been used for this experience looked very pale, anemic. This was so alive. It was like a tidal wave of bliss.

The whole day was strange, stunning, and it was a shattering experience. The past was disappearing, as if it had never belonged to me, as if I had read about it somewhere, as if I had dreamed about it, as if it was somebody else's story I had heard and somebody told it to me. I was becoming loose from my past, I was being uprooted from my history, I was losing my autobiography. I was becoming a nonbeing, what Buddha calls *anatta*. Boundaries were disappearing, distinctions were disappearing.

Mind was disappearing, it was millions of miles away. It was difficult to catch hold of it, it was rushing farther and farther away, and there was no urge to keep it close. I was simply indifferent about it all. It was okay. There was no urge to remain continuous with the past.

By the evening it became so difficult to bear it, it was hurting, it was painful. It was like when a woman goes into labor when a child is to be born, and the woman suffers tremendous pain – the birth pangs.

I used to go to sleep in those days near about twelve or one in the night, but that day it was impossible to remain awake. My eyes were closing, it was difficult to keep them open. Something was very imminent, something was going to happen. It was difficult to say what it was, maybe it is going to be my death, but there was no fear. I was ready for it. Those seven days had been so beautiful that I was ready to die; nothing more was needed. They had been so tremendously blissful, I was so contented, that if death was coming, it was welcome.

But something was going to happen: something like death, something very drastic, something which will be either a death or a new birth, a crucifixion or a resurrection, but something of tremendous import was just around the corner. It was impossible to keep my eyes open, I was drugged.

I went to sleep near about eight. It was not like sleep. Now I can understand what Patanjali means when he says that sleep and *samadhi* are similar, only with one difference: that in *samadhi* you are fully awake and asleep also. Asleep and awake together, the whole body relaxed, every cell of the body totally relaxed, all functioning relaxed, and yet a light of awareness burns within you – clear, smokeless. You remain alert and yet relaxed, loose but fully awake. The body is in the deepest sleep possible and your consciousness is at its peak. The peak of consciousness and the valley of the body meet.

I went to sleep. It was a very strange sleep: the body was asleep, I was awake. It was so strange, as if one was torn apart into two directions, two dimensions; as if the polarity has become completely focused, as if I was both the polarities together – the positive and negative were meeting, sleep and awareness were meeting, death and life were meeting. That is the moment when you can say the creator and the creation meet.

It was weird. For the first time it shocks you to the very roots, it shakes your foundations. You can never be the same after that experience; it brings a new vision to your life, a new quality.

Near about twelve my eyes suddenly opened – I had not opened them. The sleep was broken by something else. I felt a great presence around me in the room. It was a very small room. I felt a throbbing life all around me, a great vibration – almost like a hurricane, a great storm of light, joy, ecstasy. I was drowning in it.

It was so tremendously real that everything became unreal. The walls of the room became unreal, the house became unreal, my own body became unreal. Everything was unreal because now there was for the first time reality.

That's why when Buddha and Shankara say the world is maya, a mirage, it is difficult for us to understand because we know only this world, we don't have any comparison. This is the only reality we know. What are these people talking about – this is maya, illusion? This is the only reality. Unless you come to know the really real, their words cannot be understood, their words remain theoretical. They look like hypotheses. Maybe this man is propounding a philosophy: "The world is unreal."

When Berkeley in the West said that the world is unreal, he was walking with one of his friends, a very logical man; the friend was almost a skeptic. He took a stone from the road and hit Berkeley's feet hard. Berkeley screamed, blood rushed out, and the skeptic said, "Now, the world is unreal? You say the world is unreal, then why did you scream? This stone is unreal, then why did you scream? Then why are you holding your leg and why are you showing so much pain and anguish on your face. Stop this? It is all unreal."

Now this type of man cannot understand what Buddha means when he says the world is a mirage. He does not mean that you can pass through the wall. He is not saying this – that you can eat stones and it will make no difference whether you eat bread or stones. He is not saying that. He is saying that there is a reality. Once you come to know it, this so-called reality simply pales, simply becomes unreal. With a higher reality in vision the comparison arises, not otherwise.

In the dream, the dream is real. You dream every night. Dream is one of the greatest activities that you go on doing. If you live sixty years, twenty years you will sleep and almost ten years you will dream. Ten years in a life – nothing else do you do so much. Ten years of continuous dreaming, just think about it, and every night. And every morning you say it was unreal, and again in the night when you dream, dream becomes real.

In a dream it is so difficult to remember that this is a dream. But in the morning it is so easy. What happens? You are the same person. In the dream there is only one reality. How to compare? How to say it is unreal? Compared to what? It is the only reality. Everything is as unreal as everything else so there is no comparison. In the morning when you open your eyes another reality is there. Now you can say it was all unreal. Compared to this reality, dream becomes unreal. There is an awakening: compared to that reality of that awakening, this whole reality becomes unreal.

That night for the first time I understood the meaning of the word maya. Not that I had not known the word before, not that I was not aware of the meaning of the word. As you are aware, I was also aware of the meaning, but I had never understood it before. How can you understand without experience?

That night another reality opened its door, another dimension became available. Suddenly it was there, the other reality, the separate reality, the really real, or whatsoever you want to call it: call it God, call it truth, call it *dhamma*, call it Tao, or whatsoever you will. It was nameless. But it was there, so opaque, so transparent, and yet so solid one could have touched it. It was almost suffocating me in that room. It was too much and I was not yet capable of absorbing it.

A deep urge arose in me to rush out of the room, to go under the sky – it was suffocating me. It was too much, it will kill me! If I had remained a few moments more, it would have suffocated me – it looked like that.

I rushed out of the room, came out in the street. A great urge was there just to be under the sky with the stars, with the trees, with the earth, to be with nature. And immediately as I came out, the feeling of being suffocated disappeared. It was too small a place for such a big phenomenon. Even the sky is a small place for that big phenomenon. It is bigger than the sky. Even the sky is not the limit for it. But then I felt more at ease.

I walked towards the nearest garden. It was a totally new walk, as if gravitation had disappeared. I was walking, or I was running, or I was simply flying; it was difficult to decide. There was no gravitation, I was feeling weightless as if some energy was taking me. I was in the hands of some other energy.

For the first time I was not alone, for the first time I was no longer an individual, for the first time the drop had come and fallen into the ocean. Now the whole ocean was mine, I was the ocean. There was no limitation. A tremendous power arose as if I could do anything whatsoever. I was not there, only the power was there.

I reached to the garden where I used to go every day. The garden was closed, closed for the night. It was too late, it was almost one o'clock in the night. The gardeners were fast asleep. I had to enter the garden like a thief, I had to climb the gate. But something was pulling me towards the garden. It was not within my capacity to prevent myself. I was just floating.

That's what I mean when I say again and again "float with the river, don't push the river." I was relaxed, I was in a let-go. I was not there. *It* was there, call it God – God was there.

I would like to call it *It* because God is too human a word, and has become too dirty by too much use, has become too polluted by so many people. Christians, Hindus, Mohammedans, priests and politicians – they have all corrupted the beauty of the word. So let me call it *It*. *It* was there and I was just carried away, carried by a tidal wave.

The moment I entered the garden everything became luminous, it was all over the place: the benediction, the blessedness. I could see the trees for the first time – their green, their life, their very sap running. The whole garden was asleep, the trees were asleep, but I could see the whole garden alive; even the small grass leaves were so beautiful.

I looked around. One tree was tremendously luminous – the maulshree tree. It attracted me, it pulled me towards itself. I had not chosen it, God himself had chosen it. I went to the tree, I sat under the tree. As I sat there things started settling. The whole universe became a benediction.

It is difficult to say how long I was in that state. When I went back home it was four o'clock in the morning, so I must have been there by clock time at least three hours, but it was infinity. It had nothing to do with clock time. It was timeless.

Those three hours became the whole eternity, endless eternity. There was no time, there was no passage of time; it was the virgin reality: uncorrupted, untouchable, immeasurable.

And that day something happened that has continued, not as a continuity, but it has still continued as an undercurrent. Not as a permanency – each moment it has been happening again and again. It has been a miracle each moment. That night, and since that night, I have never been in the body. I am hovering around it. I became tremendously powerful and at the same time very fragile. I became very strong, but that strength is not the strength of a Mohammed Ali. That strength is not the strength of a rock, that strength is the strength of a roseflower – so fragile in his strength, so fragile, so sensitive, so delicate.

The rock will be there, the flower can go any moment, but still the flower is stronger than the rock because it is more alive. Or, the strength of a dewdrop on a leaf of grass just shining in the morning sun – so beautiful, so precious, and yet can slip any moment. So incomparable in its grace, but a small breeze can come and the dewdrop can slip and be lost forever.

Buddhas have a strength which is not of this world. Their strength is totally of love, like a roseflower or a dewdrop. Their strength is very fragile, vulnerable. Their strength is the strength of life, not of death. Their power is not of that which kills, their power is of that which creates. Their power is not of violence, aggression; their power is that of compassion.

But I have never been in the body again, I am just hovering around the body. And that's why I say it has been a tremendous miracle. Each moment I am surprised I am still here, I should not be. I should have left any moment, still I am here. Every morning I open my eyes and I say, "So, again I am still here?" Because it seems almost impossible. The miracle has been a continuity.

Just the other day somebody asked a question: "Osho, you are getting so fragile and delicate and so sensitive to the smells of hair oils and shampoos that it seems we will not be able to see you unless we all go bald." By the way, nothing is wrong with being bald, bald is beautiful; just as black is beautiful, so bald is beautiful. But that is true and you have to be careful about it.

I am fragile, delicate and sensitive. That is my strength. If you throw a rock at a flower nothing will happen to the rock, the flower will be gone. But still you cannot say that the rock is more powerful than the flower. The flower will be gone because the flower was alive. And the rock – nothing will happen to it because it is dead. The flower will be gone because the flower has no strength to destroy. The flower will simply disappear and give way to the rock. The rock has a power to destroy because the rock is dead.

Remember, since that day I have never been in the body really; just a delicate thread joins me with the body. And I am continuously surprised that somehow the whole must be willing me to be here because I am no longer here with my own strength, I am no longer here on my own. It must be the will of the whole to keep me here, to allow me to linger a little more on this shore. Maybe the whole wants to share something with you through me.

Since that day the world is unreal. Another world has been revealed. When I say the world is unreal I don't mean that these trees are unreal; these trees are absolutely real, but the way you see these trees is unreal. These trees are not unreal in themselves – they exist in God, they exist in absolute reality – but the way you see them you never see them; you are seeing something else, a mirage.

You create your own dream around you and unless you become awake you will continue to dream. The world is unreal because the world that you know is the world of your dreams. When dreams drop and you simply encounter the world that is there, then the real world...

There are not two things, God and the world. God is the world if you have eyes, clear eyes, without any dreams, without any dust of the dreams, without any haze of sleep. If you have clear eyes, clarity, perceptiveness, there is only God. Then somewhere God is a green tree, and somewhere else God is a shining star, and somewhere else God is a cuckoo, and somewhere else God is a flower, and somewhere else a child and somewhere else a river

– then only God is. The moment you start seeing, only God is.

But right now whatsoever you see is not the truth, it is a projected lie. That is the meaning of a mirage. And once you see, even for a single split moment, if you can see, if you can allow yourself to see, you will find immense benediction present all over, everywhere: in the clouds, in the sun, on the earth.

This is a beautiful world. But I am not talking about your world, I am talking about my world. Your world is very ugly, your world is your world created by a self, your world is a projected world. You are using the real world as a screen and projecting your own ideas on it. When I say the world is real, the world is tremendously beautiful, the world is luminous with infinity, the world is light and delight, it is a celebration, I mean my world – or your world if you drop your dreams.

When you drop your dreams you see the same world as any Buddha has ever seen. When you dream, you dream privately. Have you watched it, that dreams are private? You cannot share them even with your beloved. You cannot invite your wife to your dream, or your husband, or your friend. You cannot say, "Now, please come tonight in my dream. I would like to see the dream together." It is not possible. Dream is a private thing, hence it is illusory, it has no objective reality.

God is a universal thing. Once you come out of your private dreams, it is there. It has always been there. Once your eyes are clear, a sudden illumination – suddenly you are overflowing with beauty, grandeur and grace. That is the goal, that is the destiny.

Let me repeat: without effort you will never reach it, with effort nobody has ever reached it. You will need great effort, and only then there comes a moment when effort becomes futile. But it becomes futile only when you have come to the very peak of it, never before it. When you have come to the very pinnacle of your effort – all that you can do you have done – then suddenly there is no need to do anything any more. You drop the effort.

But nobody can drop it in the middle, it can be dropped only at the extreme end. So go to the extreme end if you want to drop it. Hence I go on insisting – make as much effort as you can, put your whole energy and total heart in it so that one day you can see now effort is not going to lead me anywhere. And that day it will not be you who will drop the effort, it drops on its own accord. And when it drops on its own accord, meditation happens.

Meditation is not a result of your efforts; meditation is a happening. When your efforts drop, suddenly meditation is there: the benediction of it, the blessedness of it, the glory of it. It is there like a presence, luminous, surrounding you and surrounding everything. It fills the whole earth and the whole sky.

That meditation cannot be created by human effort. Human effort is too limited, that blessedness is so infinite, you cannot manipulate it. It can happen only when you are in a tremendous surrender. When you are not there, only then it can happen. When you are a no-self: no desire, not going anywhere; when you are just herenow, not doing anything in particular, just being – it happens. And it comes in waves and the waves become tidal. It comes like a storm, and takes you away into a totally new reality.

But first you have to do all that you can do, and then you have to learn non-doing. The doing of the non-doing is the greatest doing, and the effort of effortlessness is the greatest effort.

Your meditation that you create by chanting a mantra or by sitting quiet and still and forcing yourself, is a very mediocre meditation. It is created by you, it cannot be bigger than you. It is homemade, and the maker is always bigger than the made. You have made it by sitting, forcing in a yoga posture, chanting "Rama, Rama, Rama" or anything – "blah, blah, blah," anything. You have forced the mind to become still. It is a forced stillness. It is not that quietness that comes when you are not there. It is not that silence which comes when you are almost nonexistential. It is not that beatitude which descends on you like a dove.

It is said when Jesus was baptized by John the Baptist in the River Jordan, God descended in him, or the holy ghost descended in him like a dove. Yes, that is exactly so. When you are not there peace descends in you, fluttering like a dove, reaches in your heart and abides there and abides there forever.

You are your undoing, you are the barrier. Meditation is when the meditator is not. When the mind ceases with all its activities – seeing that they are futile – then the unknown penetrates you, overwhelms you. The mind must cease for God to be. Knowledge must cease for knowing to be. You must disappear, you must give way. You must become empty, then only you can be full.

That night I became empty and became full, I became non-existential and became existence. That night I died and was reborn. But the one that was reborn has nothing to do with that which died, it is a discontinuous thing. On the surface it looks continuous but it is discontinuous. The one who died, died totally; nothing of him has remained.

Believe me, nothing of him has remained, not even a shadow. It died totally, utterly. It is not that I am just a modified *rup* – transformed, modified form, transformed form of the old. No, there has been no continuity. That day of March twenty-first, the person who had lived for many, many lives, for millennia, simply died. Another being, absolutely new, not connected at all with the old, started to exist.

Religion just gives you a total death. Maybe that's why the whole day previous to that happening I was feeling some urgency like death, as if I was going to die – and I really died. I have known many other deaths but they were nothing compared to it, they were partial deaths. Sometimes the body died, sometimes a part of the mind died, sometimes a part of the ego died, but as far as the person was concerned, it remained. Renovated many times, decorated many times, changed a little bit here and there, but it remained, the continuity remained. That night the death was total. It was a date with death and God simultaneously.

Now this sutra.

> *The Buddha said:*
> *Look up to heaven and down on earth and they will remind you of their impermanency. Look about the world and it will remind you of its impermanency. But when you gain spiritual enlightenment you shall then find wisdom. The knowledge thus attained leads you anon to the way.*

Look up to heaven and down on earth and they will remind you of their impermanency. Look. You don't look, you never look. Before you look you have an idea. You never look in purity, you never look unprejudiced. You always carry some prejudice, you always carry some opinion, ideology, scripture, your own experience or others' experiences, but you always carry something in the mind. You are never naked with reality.

And when Buddha says, *Look up to heaven and down on earth*... he means look with a naked eye, with no coatings of opinions, ideas, experiences, borrowed or otherwise.

Have you seen a naked eye? As far as humanity is concerned it is very rare to come across a naked eye. All eyes are so dressed up: somebody has a Christian eye, somebody has a Hindu eye, somebody has a Mohammedan eye; they look differently.

When a Mohammedan reads the Gita he never reads the same thing that a Hindu reads in it. When a Jaina reads the Gita he reads something else again. A Hindu can read the Bible but he will never read that which a Christian reads. The Bible is the same. From where does this difference come? The difference must be coming from the eye, the difference must be coming from the mind.

Have you ever read a single page of a book without bringing your mind in it, without corrupting it by your mind, by your past, without interpreting it? Have you ever looked at anything in life? If not, then you have not looked at all, then you don't have real eyes. You have just holes, not eyes.

The eye has to be receptive, not aggressive. When you have a certain idea in the eye, in your mind, it is aggressive. It immediately imposes itself on things. When you have an empty eye, naked, undressed, not Christian, not Hindu, not Communist – just pure seeing, innocent, primal innocence – innocent as an animal's eye or a child's, a newborn child... A new-born child looks around, he has no idea of what is what – what is beautiful and what is ugly, he has no idea. That primal innocence has to be. Only then you will be able to see what Buddha says.

You have been looking in life but you have not come to see that all is impermanence. Everything is dying, everything is decaying, everything is on a death procession. People are standing in a death queue. Look around, everything rushing towards death. Everything is fleeting, momentary, flux-like; nothing seems to be of eternal value, nothing seems to abide, nothing seems to hold, nothing seems to remain. Everything just goes on and on and on, and goes on changing. What else is a dream?

Buddha says this life, this world that you live in, that you are surrounded with, that you have created around yourself, is but a dream – impermanent, temporary. Don't make your abode there, otherwise you will suffer because nobody can be contented with the temporary. By the time you think it is in your hands it is gone. By the time you think you have possessed it, it is no longer there. You struggle for it; by the time you achieve it, it has disappeared.

Beauty is fleeting, love is fleeting, everything in this life is fleeting. You are running to catch shadows. They look real, but by the time you have arrived they prove mirages.

Look up to heaven and down on earth and they will remind you of their impermanency. Look about the world and it will remind you of its impermanency. It is one of the most fundamental principles of Gautama the Buddha: that one should become aware of the impermanent world we are surrounded with. Then immediately you will be able to understand why Buddha calls it a dream, a maya, illusion.

In the East our definition of truth is that which abides forever; and of untruth, that which is there this moment and next moment is not there. Untruth is that which is temporary, momentary, impermanent. And truth is that which is, always is, has been, will be. Behind these fleeting shadows find the eternal, penetrate to the eternal because there can be bliss only with the eternal; misery only with the momentary.

But when you gain spiritual enlightenment... That's why I was reminded of my own experience and I talked about it to you.

But when you gain spiritual enlightenment you shall then find wisdom. Wisdom cannot be found through scriptures, it is an experience. It is not knowledge, wisdom is not knowledge. You cannot gather it from others, you cannot borrow it. It is not information. You cannot learn it from the scriptures. There is only one way to become wise and that is to enter into a live experience of life.

Something is said by Buddha – you hear it. Something I say – you hear it but you don't become wise by hearing it. It will become knowledge. You can repeat it, you can repeat it even in a better way. You can become very skillful, efficient, in repeating it. You can say it in better language, but you don't have the experience.

You have never tasted the wine yourself. You have simply seen some drunkard moving, wobbling on the road, fallen in a gutter.

You have simply watched a drunkard, how he moves, how he stumbles, but you don't know what the experience is. You will have to become a drunkard, there is no other way.

You can watch a thousand and one drunkards and you can collect all information about them, but that will be from the outside and the experience is inner. That will be from without, and you will collect it as a spectator. And the experience cannot be attained by seeing, it can be attained only by being.

Now the modern world has become very obsessed by seeing; the modern world is the spectator's world. People are sitting for hours in the movie houses, just watching, doing nothing. In the West people are glued to their chairs for hours, six hours, eight hours even, just sitting before their TVs. You listen to somebody singing and you see somebody dancing and you see somebody making love – that's why people are so much interested in pornography – but you are a spectator.

The modern man is the falsest man that has ever existed on the earth, and his falsity consists in that he thinks he can know by just seeing, just by being a spectator. People are sitting for hours seeing hockey matches, volley ball matches, cricket matches – for hours. When are you going to play yourself? When are you going to love somebody? When are you going to dance and sing and be?

This is a very borrowed life. Somebody dances for you; maybe you can enjoy it, but how can you know the beauty of dance unless you dance? It is something inner. What happens when a person is dancing? What happens to his innermost core?

Nijinsky, one of the greatest dancers, used to say that there came moments when he disappears, only the dance remains. Those are the peak moments when the dancer is not there and only the dance is. That's what Buddha is saying – when the self is not there.

Now Nijinsky is moving into an ecstasy, and you are just sitting there watching the movement. Of course those movements are beautiful. Nijinsky's movements have a grace, a tremendous beauty, but it is nothing compared to what he is feeling inside. His dance is a beauty, even when you are just a spectator, but nothing compared to what is happening inside him.

He used to say that there are moments when gravitation disappears. I can understand because I have come across the feeling myself when gravitation disappears. And it was not only for moments that gravitation disappeared for me. Now I have lived for years without gravitation. I know what he means.

Even scientists were very much puzzled, because there were moments in Nijinsky's dance when he would leap and jump – and those leaps were tremendous, almost impossible leaps. A man cannot leap that way; the gravitation does not allow. And the most beautiful and amazing part was that when Nijinsky would be coming back from the leap he would come so slowly that it is impossible. He would come so slowly as if a leaf is falling from a tree – very slowly, very slowly, very slowly.

It is not possible, it is against physical laws, it is against physics. Gravitation does not make any exceptions, not even for a Nijinsky. And he was asked again and again, "What happens? How do you fall so slowly? – because it is not within your power to control, the gravitation pulls you." He said, "It does not happen always, only rarely, when the dancer disappears. Then sometimes I am also puzzled, surprised, not only you. I see myself coming so slowly, so gracefully, and I know that the gravitation does not exist in that moment."

He must be functioning in another dimension where the physical law does not exist, where another law starts working that spiritualists call the law of levitation.

And it seems absolutely rational and logical to have both the laws, because each law has to be counterbalanced by another law in the opposite direction. If there is light there is darkness, if there is life there is death, if there is gravitation there must be levitation that pulls you up. There must be ways where a person is pulled up.

There are stories, especially the story about Mohammed – that he went to heaven with his physical body; not only with his physical body, with his horse. Sitting on a horse, he simply went to heaven, upwards. It looks absurd, Mohammedans have not been able to prove it, but the meaning is clear. The story may have not exactly happened, but the meaning is clear.

The meaning is to be understood, it is very symbolic. It simply says that there is a law of levitation and if Mohammed cannot be pulled by levitation, then who will be pulled? He is the right person, a person who exists not. The ego is under gravitation, the no-ego is not under gravitation – a weightlessness arises.

Nijinsky went mad because he was simply a dancer and he never knew anything about meditation, ecstasy, enlightenment. That became a trouble for him.

If you don't understand and if you don't move with awareness, and suddenly you stumble upon something which cannot be explained by ordinary laws, you will go mad because you will be disturbed by it. It is so weird, it is so eerie. You cannot explain it. You start getting disturbed by it. He himself started getting disturbed by the phenomenon. Finally it was so staggering it disturbed his whole mind.

God is very destructive. If you don't go rightly, you will be destroyed because God is fire. Many people go mad if they don't move rightly. If they don't move under right guidance they can go mad. It is not a child's play; one has to understand.

And God, if it happens like an accident, you will not be able to absorb. Your old world will be shattered and you will not be able to create a new order, a new understanding, because for the new understanding you will need new concepts, a new framework, a new gestalt. That is the whole meaning of finding a master.

It is not just from gullibility that people become attached to masters, it has a scientific base to it. Moving into the unknown is a tremendous risk. One should move with somebody who has already moved into it. One should move hand in hand with somebody who knows the territory. Otherwise the thing can happen so shatteringly that you will be at a loss.

Many people go mad if they don't know that somebody's help is needed. Somebody is needed like a midwife. You will be born, but somebody will be needed to watch over it. His very presence will be helpful, you can relax. The midwife is there, the doctor is there – you can relax.

They don't do much, you can ask an obstetrician, they don't do much; what can they do? But their very presence relaxes the woman who is going under labor. She knows the doctor is there, the nurse is there, the midwife is there. Everything is okay, she goes, she relaxes, she is no longer fighting. She knows if something goes wrong people are around who will put it right. She can relax, she can trust.

The same happens to a disciple. It is a process of rebirth. A master is needed, but from the master don't go on collecting knowledge; from the master take hints and move into experience.

I talk about meditation. You can do two things. You can collect whatsoever I say about meditation, you can compile it. You can become a great knowledgeable person about meditation because every day I go on talking about meditation from different dimensions in different ways. You can collect all that, you can get a PhD from any university. But that is not going to make you wise, unless you meditate.

So whatsoever I am saying, try it in life. While I am here don't waste time in collecting knowledge – that you can do without me, that you can do in a library. While I am here take a jump, a quantum leap into wisdom. Experience these things I am saying to you.

But when you gain spiritual enlightenment you shall then find wisdom. Wisdom is only through one's own experience. It is never from anybody else. Wisdom always happens as a flower opens, just like that. When your heart opens, you have a fragrance – that fragrance is wisdom. You can bring a plastic flower from the market, you can deceive neighbors...

I used to live near Mulla Nasruddin once. I used to see him every day pouring water into a pot which was hanging in his window, with beautiful flowers. I watched him many times. Whenever he would be pouring water, there was no water, the pot was empty. I could see that there was no water and the pot was empty, but he would pour twice every day, religiously.

I asked Nasruddin, "What are you doing? You don't have any water and you go on pouring it, that which is not there! And I have been watching you for many days."

He said, "Don't get disturbed. These flowers are plastic flowers. They don't need water."

Plastic flowers don't need water, they are not alive. They don't need soil, they are not alive. They don't need fertilizers, they are not alive. They don't need any manure, they are not alive.

Real flowers are like wisdom. Wisdom is like real flowers, knowledge is plastic. That's why it is cheap. It is very cheap, you can get it for nothing because it is borrowed. Experience is a radical change in your life; you cannot be the same.

If you want to become wise you will have to go through transformations, a million and one transformations. You will have to pass through fire. Only then whatsoever is there which is ugly and useless will be burnt, and you will come out as pure gold.

The knowledge thus attained leads you anon to the way. And only the wisdom, the knowledge thus attained through one's own experience, through one's own enlightening experience, through one's own satori, *samadhi*, makes you capable of falling in tune with the way.

Buddha calls it *dhamma*, Tao. Then you are in harmony, what Pythagoras calls *harmonia*. Then you are suddenly not there, only the law is there, the *dhamma* is there, the way is there – or call it God – is there. Then you are simply with the whole. You go with it wherever it goes. Then you don't have any goal of your own. Then the whole's destiny is your destiny. Then there is no anxiety, no tension. Then one is immensely relaxed.

In fact, one is so relaxed that one is not. The ego is nothing but accumulated tensions through lives. When you are totally relaxed and you look within, there is nobody. It is simple purity, emptiness, vastness.

> *The Buddha said:*
> *You should think of the four elements of which the body is composed. Each of them has its own name and there is no such thing there known as ego. As there really is no ego, it is like unto a mirage.*

Buddha says ego is just a concept, an idea, it does not exist in reality. When a child is born he is born without any "I." By and by he learns it, by and by he learns that there are other people and he is separate from them. Have you watched small children when they start speaking? They don't say, "I am thirsty." They say, "Bobby is thirsty." They don't say, "I am thirsty." They don't have any "I."

By and by they learn the "I" because they start feeling "thou." Thou comes first, then comes "I", as a reaction to "thou." They started feeling that there are other people who are separate from Bobby, and they are called "thou, you." Then by and by they start learning the "I."

But it is just a utility. Useful, perfectly useful – use it. I'm not saying stop using "I" because that will create troubles. But know well that there is no "I" within you; it is just a linguistic convenience. Just as a name is a convenience so is the "I."

When a child is born he has no name. Then we call him Ram or Krishna, and he becomes a Ram. Later on if you insult the name Ram he will start fighting, and he had come in the world without a name. And he has no name, it is just a label – utilitarian, needed, but nothing true in it. He can as well be called Krishna or Mohammed or Mansoor or anything. Any name will do because he is nameless.

That's why I change your names when I initiate you into sannyas, just to give you a feeling that the name can be changed, it does not belong to you. It can easily be changed. It has a utility in the world, but it has no reality.

The child learns that his name is Ram. The name is for others to call him. He cannot call himself Ram because that too will be confusing. Others call him Ram, he has to call himself something else, otherwise it will be confusing.

Ram Teerth used to call himself Ram, in the third person. It was very confusing. He was a beautiful man, and just not to use "I" because the "I" has created so much trouble – just as a gesture, he used to call himself Ram. When he went to America he would say suddenly, "Ram is thirsty," and people would not understand. What does he mean Ram is thirsty? They would look around, who is Ram? And he would say, "This Ram is thirsty." But this is confusing. You say, "I am thirsty," and things are settled because when you use the name it seems that somebody else is thirsty.

So there is a need for a name others can call you, and there is a need for something, a symbol, that you can call yourself. It is a need of the society, it has nothing to do with existence or reality.

You should think of the four elements of which the body is composed. Buddha says the body is composed of fire, earth, water, air. These four things are there, they are real things, and there is nothing else. Behind these four things there is just pure space inside you. That pure space is what you really are – that zero space.

Buddha does not want to call it even a self because the self carries again some distant reflection of the ego. So he calls it no-self, *anatta*. He does not call it *atma*, self, he calls it *anatma*, no-self. And he is right, he is absolutely right. One should not call it any name.

I have come across it. It has no name, and it has no form. It has no substance, and it has no center. It is just immense, pure, empty, full. It is pure bliss: *Sat-chit-anand*, it is truth, it is consciousness, it is bliss, but it has no "I" sense in it. It is not confined by anything, it has no boundaries. It is pure space. To attain to that purity is what Buddha says is nirvana.

The word *nirvana* is beautiful. It means blowing out a flame. There is a lamp, you go and blow the flame of the lamp. Then Buddha says, "Do you ask where the flame has gone now? Can anybody answer where the flame has gone now?" Buddha says it has simply disappeared into infinity. It has not gone anywhere, it has gone everywhere. It has not gone to any particular address, it has become universal.

Blowing out a flame is the meaning of the word *nirvana*. And Buddha says when you blow out your ego, the flame of the ego, only pure space is left. Then you are nobody in particular, you are everybody. Then you are universal. Then you are this vast benediction, this bliss, this beatitude. Then you are it.

Enough for today.

OSHO INTERNATIONAL MEDITATION RESORT

Each year the Meditation Resort welcomes thousands of people from more than 100 countries. The unique campus provides an opportunity for a direct personal experience of a new way of living – with more awareness, relaxation, celebration and creativity. A great variety of around-the-clock and around-the-year program options are available. Doing nothing and just relaxing is one of them!

All of the programs are based on Osho's vision of "Zorba the Buddha" – a qualitatively new kind of human being who is able *both* to participate creatively in everyday life *and* to relax into silence and meditation.

Location

Located 100 miles southeast of Mumbai in the thriving modern city of Pune, India, the OSHO International Meditation Resort is a holiday destination with a difference. The Meditation Resort is spread over 28 acres of spectacular gardens in a beautiful tree-lined residential area.

OSHO Meditations

A full daily schedule of meditations for every type of person includes both traditional and revolutionary methods, and particularly the OSHO Active Meditations™. The meditations take place in what may be the world's largest meditation hall, the OSHO Auditorium.

OSHO Multiversity

Individual sessions, courses and workshops cover everything from creative arts to holistic health, personal transformation, relationship and life transition, transforming meditation into a lifestyle for life and work, esoteric sciences, and the "Zen" approach to sports and recreation. The secret of the OSHO Multiversity's success lies in the fact that all its programs are combined with meditation, supporting the understanding that as human beings we are far more than the sum of our parts.

OSHO Basho Spa

The luxurious Basho Spa provides for leisurely open-air swimming surrounded by trees and tropical green. The uniquely styled, spacious Jacuzzi, the saunas, gym, tennis courts…all these are enhanced by their stunningly beautiful setting.

Cuisine

A variety of different eating areas serve delicious Western, Asian and Indian vegetarian food – most of it organically grown especially for the Meditation Resort. Breads and cakes are baked in the resort's own bakery.

Night life

There are many evening events to choose from – dancing being at the top of the list! Other activities include full-moon meditations beneath the stars, variety shows, music performances and meditations for daily life.

Or you can just enjoy meeting people at the Plaza Café, or walking in the nighttime serenity of the gardens of this fairytale environment.

Facilities

You can buy all of your basic necessities and toiletries in the Galleria. The OSHO Multimedia Gallery sells a large range of OSHO media products. There is also a bank, a travel agency and a Cyber Café on-campus. For those who enjoy shopping, Pune provides all the options, ranging from traditional and ethnic Indian products to all of the global brand-name stores.

Accommodation

You can choose to stay in the elegant rooms of the OSHO Guesthouse, or for longer stays on campus you can select one of the OSHO Living-In program packages. Additionally there is a plentiful variety of nearby hotels and serviced apartments.

www.osho.com/meditationresort
www.osho.com/guesthouse
www.osho.com/livingin

FOR MORE INFORMATION

For any information about OSHO books, please contact:

OSHO Media International

17 Koregaon Park, Pune - 411001, MS, India

Phone: +91-20-66019999 Fax: +91-20-66019990

E-mail: distribution@osho.net

Website: http://www.osho.com

For More Information

For a full selection of OSHO multilingual online destinations, see

www.OSHO.com/AllAboutOsho

The official comprehensive website of OSHO International is

www.OSHO.com